THEOLOGY OF LAW AND AUTHORITY IN THE ENGLISH REFORMATION

EMORY UNIVERSITY STUDIES IN LAW AND RELIGION

John Witte Jr., General Editor

BOOKS IN THE SERIES

Faith and Order: The Reconciliation of Law and Religion
Harold J. Berman

*The Ten Commandments in History:
Mosaic Paradigms for a Well-Ordered Society*
Paul Grimley Kuntz

Theology of Law and Authority in the English Reformation
Joan Lockwood O'Donovan

Political Order and the Plural Structure of Society
James W. Skillen and Rockne M. McCarthy

*The Idea of Natural Rights:
Studies on Natural Rights, Natural Law, and Church Law, 1150-1625*
Brian Tierney

The Fabric of Hope: An Essay
Glenn Tinder

Religious Human Rights in Global Perspective: Legal Perspectives
Johan D. van der Vyver and John D. Witte

Early New England: A Covenanted Society
David A. Weir

Religious Human Rights in Global Perspective: Religious Perspectives
John D. Witte and Johan D. van der Vyver

THEOLOGY OF LAW AND AUTHORITY IN THE ENGLISH REFORMATION

Joan Lockwood O'Donovan

William B. Eerdmans Publishing Company
Grand Rapids, Michigan / Cambridge, U.K.

© 1991 Emory University

First published 1991 by Scholars Press for Emory University

This edition published 2004 by Wm. B. Eerdmans Publishing Co.
255 Jefferson Ave. S.E., Grand Rapids, Michigan 49503 /
PO Box 163, Cambridge CB3 9PU U.K
All rights reserved

Printed in the United States of America

09 08 07 06 05 04   7 6 5 4 3 2 1

Library of Congress Cataloging-in-Publication Data

ISBN 0-8028-4850-8

www.eerdmans.com

The Emory University Studies in Law and Religion is an occasional series of monographs, anthologies, textbooks, and translations of classic texts in the field of law and religion. The series has been established by the Law and Religion Program at Emory University to foster further exploration of the religious dimensions of law, the legal dimensions of religion, and the interaction of legal and religious ideas, institutions, and methods. The volumes published in this series will help meet the growing demand for literature in the burgeoning interdisciplinary field of law and religion.

Send inquiries to:
Emory University Studies in Law and Religion
Gambrell Hall
Emory School of Law
Atlanta, Georgia 30322

CONTENTS

PREFACE
  Curran Tiffany, Christian Legal Society vii

INTRODUCTION 1

CHAPTER I
  Theological Precursors of the English Reformation 11

CHAPTER II
  John Wyclif and the Franciscan-Augustinian Antinomies 29

CHAPTER III
  Sir John Fortescue and the Law of Nature 43

CHAPTER IV
  William Tyndale and the Lutheran Dialectic 55

CHAPTER V
  St. Germain and Henry VIII's Church Take-Over 67

CHAPTER VI
  Thomas Cranmer and the Dilemma of the Erastian Reformer 81

CHAPTER VII
  The Marian Exiles and the Puritan Option 91

CHAPTER VIII
  The Elizabethan Settlement and Its Detractors 109

CHAPTER IX
  Hooker's Theological Consolidation of the English Church 129

CONCLUSION 155

BIBLIOGRAPHY 163

PREFACE

During the 1980s a new ingredient boiled up in the caldron of American politics—an outspoken religious involvement from a new quarter. The so-called religious right vigorously joined the chorus of voices on the right and left in public debate. The Center for Law and Religious Freedom of the Christian Legal Society joined the voices advocating religious liberty. It championed in the courts and (on occasion) in the legislature the liberty of high school students to meet for prayer and Bible study when other students were meeting in interest groups of their own choosing; the right of religious schools to govern their own personnel and curriculum; the right of pastors to counsel without governmental review; the right of the Unification Church to organize its finances as do other churches. In these contests, the Christian Legal Society met with some judicial and legislative successes, some so unexpected as to awe us with a sense of the sovereign hand of God. There were some reverses too, and the battle goes on.

Contests with government have faced not only public school students but religious families and religious institutions as well—churches, synagogues, the Salvation Army, schools, camps, hospitals, youth homes, and day care centers. Whether the government action is administrative, legislative, or judicial, it is too often over-intrusive and suppressive of religious practice. We speak not of disagreements over building or safety or health laws, but of intrusions into the manner of religious community life. In these conflicts between religious theology and government ideology, which shall prevail? Is authoritative interpretation of the Constitution the last word, or is there another standard by which even the Constitution may be judged? If the people are sometimes to judge the Constitution in a public amendment process, what higher law or principles might they look to for guidance?

Religious communities are scrambling for resources to keep up with these public contests for the defense of their faiths. Yet their antagonists are often funded by large and ideologically liberal organizations as well as by government itself. Too often the courtroom advocacy and legislative lobbying of the contending religious group is poorly presented. Even when professionally handled, the arguments may reflect the expediency of the immediate contest without consistent presentation of principle. Pleas for justice may be framed on the assumption that some current sociological doctrine governs, when tradition might suggest a different perspective, and theology might invoke still another.

After seeing many court briefs, and many legislative arguments, some of us in the Christian Legal Society have reached a conviction that the landmarks have been obscured. Not only our foes but also many of our friends are in disagreement on ruling principles; they are (to put it modestly) in philosophical disarray. These modern debates over civil liberties, and over religious liberty—the mother of all civil liberties—have become poor indeed in contrast to our rich heritage from Luther and Calvin, or Witherspoon and Wilberforce.

The Christian Legal Society has thus begun to gather a few of those who even today have chosen to become learned in both theology and law. These scholars unfolded to us wisdom from a time when theology was the ground of law, and scholars were frequently well-grounded and active in both. We learned that in the history of the West the principal branches of the Christian community have each presented a distinctive perspective on divine and human law and authority. These perspectives arose in the historical struggles the different communities faced and were worked out according to their somewhat different understandings of applicable Scriptural teaching. The differences were affected by varying views of the different traditions on such basic questions as the depravity of man, the completeness of regeneration, and the breadth of the mandate of the church—as well as views on such overarching questions as the place of the Old Testament canon in the New Testament economy. We have continued seeking to learn more of these historical perspectives. This, then, is the inspiration for the book you hold and others that we are having prepared.

It was not our thought that we might in our collective wisdom choose something from among these different traditions, classify it as truly Biblical and launch a campaign to apply it to present problems. Rather, contemporary protagonists of religious liberty, and others of Biblical orientation simply interested in underlying principles of law and government, might gain insights from their own and sister traditions which would challenge their thinking. They might find root concepts to compare with their own and their opponents' arguments. They might trace a path of changes in their own tradition. Observers not directly involved in public law or policy contests might find interesting benchmarks with which to gauge contestants.

One can see today, in debates over public issues within the variegated American Christian community, fascinating parallels to some of these historic traditional views forged in the Reformation period. Yet some of today's protagonists have switched positions, and the concepts are no longer ordered in the coherent and systematic theological perspectives of earlier days. In recent years for example, we have seen Jerry Falwell, from a strong Baptist tradition, advocating policy which has a Calvinist ring to it. We have seen Mennonite successors to the separatist Anabaptist tradition find fellowship with Roman Catholics in actively urging upon government the adoption of their world peace policies. Might we all profit from looking more closely at our cultural pasts, to see from whence we have come?

There is today a confusion not only of differing theological voices among the religious communities, but of still other conflicting philosophical voices, some in a position to influence government and the course of religious liberty. There is beneath the cacophony of voices a confusion in America as to the very nature of law, leading to confusion as to what can and cannot be accomplished through adoption of laws. With the attempted scope of law pushed beyond its reasonable capacity, we have a state of affairs in which laws are multiplying conflicts instead of resolving them.

The Center for Law and Religious Freedom, as a servant of the church and others concerned for religious freedom, now seeks with this small book *Theology of Law and Authority in the English Reformation* and others, to make a scholarly and historically-based contribution in the growing debate on the nature of law, and the role of government as the minister of law. It is pertinent in our selection that the English church, the British Government for which it provided the theological and philosophical foundation, and the common law and common law courts which shared with the church (and steadily increased its share of) the ministry of law, are the primary seedbed out of which grew our American institutions of law and government. Our focus will be instructive also for readers in the other nations which inherited those traditions, and certainly for British readers.

Our audience might well be not only lawyers and judges, who formulate, judge, and practice law but also theologians and philosophers, who articulate perspectives from which goals, forms, and limits of the law draw meaning and purpose. We hope our offerings will be accessible to all who have a taste for history, have some understanding of law and of theology, and are open to

Biblical perspectives. We commend this book to lawyers, pastors and others interested in the growing controversy over how religion and government are to understand themselves, when they meet at the crossroads and in the courts.

The focus is not just the proper relation of church and state. Nor do we seek to define anew what is "the state" and its God-ordained role. Rather we plan in each book to look to the perspective on law and government historically presented by one of the major branches of the Christian community in the West. We will not propose a legal or political ideology for today, but we hope our readers will be stimulated to recover and use some time-tested and enduring principles, illuminated in the hard fought battles of the past.

In this first book the author, Dr. Joan Lockwood O'Donovan, who lives and works in Oxford, England, begins with early stirrings of Reformation ideas. She shows us men of the church and men of the law profoundly wrestling with Biblical and natural law concepts—on the nature of authority and law for the civil and spiritual realms. We see Continental antecedents and English applications. She examines the different streams of reformation in the turbulent reigns of Henry VIII and Mary; Puritans in and out of the Establishment; the Elizabethan Settlement; and the consolidation of the English Church and Anglican theology under Thomas Hooker. Most importantly, we see drawn together from diverse perspectives, certain pervasive threads as to the place of law in God's order, the derivation of authority from law, and the Scripture as the locus of these understandings.

Dr. O'Donovan portrays luminaries of the faith who were not only discerners of social applications of Biblical truth, but whose teachings became elements of the governing fabric of a great nation. Some were of academic leaning, yet found themselves in the thick of dangerous public confrontations. Some suffered the loss of lands and properties. Some were imprisoned. Some were forced to wandering as fugitives, or into exile, or martyrdom. Some were counsellors to lords and kings, holders of high office. Some went to early graves from the fatigue of their labors. The book deals primarily with the struggle for the ascendancy of ruling doctrines, but gives us impressions also of these fascinating lives.

The witness of these lives may be exemplary for us, quite apart from the instruction in the doctrines of law and government. These are men of powerful intellect, faithful to the Lord, entrusting not only their gifts and their careers, but their lives to the uncertain outcomes of dangerous contest—for the truth as they saw it. They were not revolutionaries, nor even rebels; they did not view contest as arising under some Hegelian necessity; yet they did not shrink from contest or rest in academic seclusion or privilege. May their like come forth in our time and nation.

In the Reformation era there was acute consciousness of the battle for prevailing belief systems. In the Modern American era of "separation of church and state" consciousness, there is a prevalent and misleading assumption that theological contests may be removed from the public arena—official neutrality will supposedly put aside "divisive" religious contests. This quaint notion, lulled by some peaceful years of social consensus, is more persistent in America than elsewhere. Yet in America opinions of religious intensity continue to line up on both sides in battle over the death penalty, abortion, curbing obscenity, and other issues of moral conviction.

The reality is that there is no neutrality of ideology. People will worship the true God or idols (or as we see in the Old Testament, sometimes both). The Chaldeans worshipped their military might (Hab. 1:16). The New Testament points a finger at covetousness as idolatry (Col. 3:5), and at some "whose god is their belly" (Phil. 3:19). Jesus spoke of the worship of Mammon (Matt. 6:24).

We in the Christian Legal Society believe that no one ideology or religion ought to be coercively "established," which is the historical pattern on every continent. Most Western nations have disestablished the church, and eastern European nations are now lifting the constitutional primacy of the Communist party and its ideology, though the contrary pattern still reigns in Moslem and the third world nations. Yet, despite much agreement on "disestablishment," we know that many beliefs and practices, both good and evil, may be encouraged or censured under social governance without being legally required or prohibited. Moreover, some activities the majority concludes are destructive may, on the basis of a common morality, be civilly or criminally dis-established by law: gambling, prostitution, sodomy, obscenity, child pornography, torture of animals, harmful drugs, etc. Marriage can be established and favored in the law; child neglect can be disfavored.

The common morality which prevails in legislatures and pervades in courts and government agencies has a mix of competing religious and ideological roots. Conscientious persons and associations must and will insist that civil and criminal laws reflect their deepest moral convictions, regardless of talk of government neutrality. The government may be neutral enough to allow and even to referee the contest, but when it accepts one set of arguments in establishing law—legislative or judicial— it has taken sides in the necessary choice of a moral framework.

In the art of government, are religiously inspired voices in public debate to be considered a separable category? All contenders for public policy, when not advocating some admittedly self-interested measure, are proposing to infuse into governmental law or practice some philosophically-rooted moral concepts, or to apply moral concepts claimed to be already established. We have shown that the "separation of church and state" does not avoid the contest among citizens, of whatever religious or philosophical persuasion, in choosing moral values for making and administering civil and criminal law. Dr. O'Donovan, in her opening words, sharpens the focus on the nature of the contest and the concepts. "From a theological perspective," she writes, "it is arguable that all public disagreement is fundamentally about authority and law, divine and human, whatever may be the ostensible issues."

Indeed it may be said that in every age and nation the moral framework which achieves the sanction of law and public authority is religious in character. The institution of law, clothed with compulsory sanctions, reflects the fundamental values, the ultimate concerns for directing human conduct—in effect the "god" prevailing in that society. Professor Harold Berman, at Emory University and for many years professor of law at Harvard University and a leading expert on Soviet law, reflects this view in speaking of Marxism-Leninism: "It is not only a theory of society and history but also a militant faith . . . something not only believed but also believed in, something to be committed to and practised in one's daily life."

Faith in Marxism-Leninism as a basis for society has been shattered in recent upheavals. But the stability of Judeo-Christian culture, the matrix of our own law and government, is also in great disarray. Not just the fibre of arguments in religious liberty contests, not just the philosophical understanding of the institution of law, but the entire culture is in turmoil. Whether or not we share the moral indignation of the religious right when we see the blights in our culture, we must not close our eyes to the reality that the foundations of law are eroding along with the culture—at the very time that so many social institutions have been literally encrusted with laws and regulations, whether in education, medicine, commerce, labor, communications, or charity.

The majesty of the law was once considered to be rooted in the creation order, guided by explicit moral precepts, and founded on historic Biblical faith. Now, lacking such faith, law is increasingly viewed and applied as the instrument of politics, rather than the charter under which government is servant. The law's roots, and the wisdom nurtured through generations, are faded from view. Recall the ancient cry of Habakkuk: "So the law is slacked and justice never goes forth. For the wicked surround the righteous, so justice goes forth perverted" (Hab. 1:4, RSV).

Are Christians and others who share common perspectives of their sacred books, called to realms of political and legal contest to seek a restoration of good stewardship in these realms? Can a restoration of tranquillity be sought by Christians as a favorable factor for the spread of the gospel, as Paul seems to say in his first letter to Timothy? (I Tim. 2:2-4) Perspectives vary with religious tradition, but the teaching in the holy books of Christians, of Jews and of Moslems also, is that God does hold societies, and His people within them, accountable for justice and righteousness. It seems implicit that some with a zeal to fulfil this responsibility are called to be in the public arena, political or legal.

In recent years we have seen some reawakening on the part of evangelical believers, and many traditional Roman Catholics and Orthodox believers as well, to an awareness that the contest to shape the moral role of government and law will go on irrespective of our consciously religious participation or lack of it. We now hear calls to non-contestants, if they are morally concerned, to add action to their prayers and to reenter the "public square." The response is still small, in the face of our adversaries, but it is growing.

However these traditionally believing communities, particularly evangelicals, are lacking some useful equipment for the contest. They are short in institutional memory of the Biblical and theological understandings by which the church, the body of believers over the centuries, crucially participated in forging the cherished institutions of limited government we enjoy in the nations of the West.

As the religious public increases its occupation with public disputes, we have heard calls for renewed attention to Biblical principles bearing on public issues. It is indeed healthy and humbling to dig afresh in the Word for principles of human governance. This should and will be done. Yet the Bible is not a manual that tells the reader how to run a machine, or the governor how to run his office. Its lessons are learned not in the reading only, but with perseverance in submitting and prayerful application. The governance principles in Scripture are interwoven with other more dominant lessons. In the Scripture itself we also see learners, pointed for instruction to the historical experience of their forefathers.

Thus we are presenting a study which is historical in nature, and in the Jewish-Christian understanding that God reveals Himself in history, and this would include the history of the church's participation in forging the fabric of law and governance within a nation.

Curran Tiffany
Christian Legal Society

INTRODUCTION

From a theological perspective, it is arguable that all public disagreement is fundamentally about authority and law, divine and human, whatever may be the ostensible issues. In our age of political debate about rights and freedoms, benefits and utility, such an argument carries little conviction. Precisely for this reason it is salutary for us to immerse ourselves in the public theological preoccupations characteristic of sixteenth-century European societies.

Among such societies, the English Tudor public especially claims our attention for its unsurpassed theoretical devotion to law and authority. This devotion may both explain and be explained by the singularly prominent role of statutory law and governmental initiative in the reformation of the English church. During the reigns of Henry VIII, Edward VI, and Elizabeth I, the monarch "in Parliament" legislated the financial, juridical, and doctrinal reconstruction of the church, reinforcing its legislative moves at every stage with intensive propaganda. The resulting Church of England was supremely a political-legal edifice resting on the authority of the temporal sovereign and the general assembly of the realm. Moreover, the political and legal domination of the English Reformation was not merely formal but material as well: the commanding practical and tactical issue in the war with Rome being that of the jurisdiction exercised by and over the clergy. It is not, therefore, surprising that public theological discussion and conflict in Tudor England should center on issues of law and authority.

These issues had a long history in the English setting, being the legacy of several centuries of discussion, conflict, and compromise. The seedbed of much sixteenth-century political thought lay in the scholastic flowering of the thirteenth and early fourteenth centuries: in the mature political theories of Thomas Aquinas (1225-1274), William of Ockham (c.1285-1347), and Marsilius of Padua (c.1275-1342). The combinations, interpretations, and modifications of Aristotelian and Augustinian political concepts developed by these thinkers defined the issues and options for succeeding generations of English and continental theologians, lawyers, and statesmen. Without them the subsequent formulation of legal-constitutional doctrines in the civil and ecclesiastical spheres, of antipapal and anticlerical positions, and of programs for political and ecclesiastical reform would be unimaginable.

The late fourteenth and early fifteenth centuries witnessed the blossoming of Ockham's cautious revisions of accepted medieval political doctrine in the more venturous and systematic political conceptions of Jean Gerson (1363-1429) and John Wyclif (1330-1384). While Gerson developed Ockham's constitutional limitations of papal rule into full-blown conciliarist theory, Wyclif developed his Franciscan criticism of Rome's excessive temporal possessions and jurisdiction into a large-scale assault on the church's worldly goods and powers. Wyclif's timely and uncannily prophetic program for ecclesiastical reformation also bore the fragrance of Marsilius' secularist and antipapal radicalism. Under the banner of Scriptural authority, he launched a theological campaign against the vast wealth, prestige, and power of the church's "caesarian" hierarchy, aimed at dispossessing it. While pressing to its ecclesiastical limits Ockham's Franciscan ideal of evangelical poverty, he also radicalized Ockham's spiritual conception of ecclesiastical jurisdiction into a denial of all jurisdiction to the visible church, after the manner of Marsilius. Correspondingly, he converted Ockham's defence of autonomous civil authority into a defence of royal absolutism, transferring to the pontifical king the papal "plenitude of power." Finally, he forged Ockham's Augustinian opposition of God's righteousness and man's depravity, Christ's command and human law into a piece of artillery to level the pretensions of papal tradition and canon law, while leaving intact the authority of secular rule.

It is unquestionably the case that Wyclif's reforming vision anticipated for good and for ill the practical agenda, legal machinery, and theological justification of King Henry VIII's ecclesiastical policies, even though the precise influence of Wycliffite ideas in early Tudor society is uncertain. At the same time, it is arguable that the theologically, morally, and politically problematic aspects of Henry VIII's church take-over are attributable more to the less adulterated Marsilian views of Henrician lawyers and politicians such as Thomas Cromwell (1495-1540) than to Wyclif's Marsilian face. In Wyclif's vision the glorification of civil rule and its absolutist claims is balanced by confidence in the public authority and power of God's revealed truth in the Scriptures, by the conviction that God's Word will always have its faithful and capable expositors, who will be listened to by ruler and subjects alike. Unlike Marsilius, Wyclif avoids, even if by a hair's breadth at points, the pitfall of enthralling Christ's saving truth to political officialdom and expediency. The supremacy of divine truth and commandment over political authority, to which all the great, early English reformers dedicated themselves, is the legacy of the Ockhamist-Wycliffite tradition, refracted in the spread of Lutheranism, standing up to the pressures of secularist, absolutist, and pragmatic political orientations.

An equally forceful combatant against political absolutism and pragmatism in the Tudor Reformation was the Thomist natural-law tradition of English constitutionalism, authoritatively laid out by the leading English jurist of the fifteenth century, Sir John Fortescue (c.1394-c.1476). Fortescue's celebrated extolling of "royal and political rule" placed the English monarchy within a legal-constitutional framework that recognized simultaneously the self-sufficiency of secular law and its obligation to conform to the dictates of natural equity. While endorsing a plurality of types of law and legal authorities in the Thomist fashion, Fortescue displayed a fateful tendency to resolve all political issues by an appeal to the law of nature, reducing the political significance of God's revealed Word to a confirmation of the principles of universal equity, and thereby removing from political relevance the supernatural demands of the divine law. In the sixteenth century Fortescue's disciple Christopher St. Germain (1460-1540), expressing the consensus of Henrician common lawyers, sought to extend the competence of secular statute and common law over ecclesiastical property and jurisdiction, arguing that the canon law was improperly regulating strictly political matters. Thus, the natural-law tradition of English jurisprudence supplied ammunition for the Tudor lay revolt against an oppressive and corrupt system of church law and church courts. Unfortunately, the accomplishment of this lay rebellion in curbing the coercive and mercenary arm of the clergy fell short of assisting the establishment and maintenance of sound ecclesiastical discipline. The laity were more desirous of seeing the yoke of the church broken than desirous of seeing it lightened in the spirit of Christ's promise in Matthew 11:29-30, and were overly sanguine about the role of the civil power in their emancipation. Consequently, natural-law theory became handmaid to a secularizing enterprise of which St. Thomas would scarcely have approved.

The formidable challenge confronting Protestant-leaning clergy and divines in Henry VIII's reign was to place the church's authority and discipline solidly on an evangelical footing. This challenge was more theologically and ecclesiastically arduous than the challenge of cleanup and repair confronting their Roman-leaning reforming colleagues. Luther's revolutionary doctrine of the sinner's justification by faith in the grace of Christ alone was theologically fundamental to evangelical reform but not theologically sufficient. It entailed the startling reinterpretation of the church's essence and authority as proclamatory: as resting on its apostolic commission to *proclaim* the Law's condemnation of sinful man and Christ's overcoming of the Law by his death and resurrection. While effective in freeing the church from the works-righteousness of the pope's juridical system, Lutheran ecclesiology was less effective in evolving adequate institutional forms for Christ's discipline of grace. Above all, it failed to give adequate expression to the degree of organizational freedom from secular interference and control required by the church's divine mission.

It is fair to say that the English church did not emerge from the Lutheran phase of its reconstruction with a strong, resourceful, and evangelical polity and discipline. The fault, however, can hardly be laid exclusively at Luther's door. Inevitably, the early English reformers deployed their energies in initiating and consolidating major doctrinal shifts and carrying through their liturgical implications. The monumental doctrinal and liturgical innovations of Archbishop Thomas Cranmer (1489-1556) and his associates show the vital importance of this groundwork. Their progress was necessarily slow, impeded by constant shifts of royal policy and by conservative resistance from clerical and lay quarters. Moreover, while they did not succeed in overhauling the church's legal machinery for regulating ministerial and disciplinary matters, they accomplished a feat without which such overhauling could not proceed with authority and confidence, namely, the production of English Bibles. All the early Henrician reformers of lasting repute—Tyndale, Barnes, Garret, Frith, Bilney, Cranmer, Coverdale and Rogers—were involved in one or more phases of English Bible production: in developing the linguistic tools, preparing the texts, arranging the publication, and assisting the distribution of English New Testaments and complete Scriptures. Increased access to, familiarity with, and use of the Scriptures, on the part of clergy and laity alike, constituted an indispensable basis for ecclesiastical criticism, reorganization, and renewal. Nevertheless, that structural reform of church offices and discipline did not engage the thought and energy of leading Henrician Protestants to any noticeable degree no doubt reflected the prevailing Lutheran ecclesiology.

It was not until the second half of Edward VI's reign that a vital concern with the external form of the church and its ground of authority began to emerge. This emergence is largely attributable to the presence in England from 1549 to 1553 of continental theologians and pastors indebted more to Zwingli, Calvin, and Bullinger than to Luther and Melanchthon. Such distinguished immigrant divines as Martin Bucer (1491-1551), Peter Martyr (1500-1562), Bernardino Ochino (1487-1564), John à Lasco (1499-1560), and John Knox (1513-1572) brought with them experiences of Christian congregational life and understandings of the institutional church that were radically foreign to English soil. From Strassburg, Zürich, and Geneva they imported parochial and Presbyterian forms of church government and discipline combining strong ministerial leadership with responsible lay involvement. An eloquent demonstration of the Reformed model was offered by à Lasco's London church, which united German-, French-, and Italian-speaking congregations under a single Genevan-style constitution. The latter, to the permanent discomfiture of the English Protestant bishops, provided for extensive Biblical and theological instruction of the laity, discipline by elders, and congregational nomination and ratification of church officers appointed by the governing council. Not only was à Lasco's model to be appropriated by the exiled English Protestants (who included a good number of Edward VI's bishops) during Queen Mary's persecution, but it was also to become, with minor alterations, the platform of mainstream Elizabethan Puritanism.

While the immediate impact of this influx of continental Protestantism on English sentiments about church order and discipline is difficult to gauge, two probable signs of it were the controversy over ecclesiastical vestments and Archbishop Cranmer's abortive attempt to reform the canon law. The vestiarian controversy of the early 1550s was principally over the issue of whether "papistical" vestments should be abandoned by the English clergy on account of their idolatrous associations, but it also touched on the right of the secular authorities to legislate controversial church policy. Bishop John Hooper (d.1555), the most outspoken clerical opponent of the traditional and legally prescribed ceremonial garb, argued against the enforcement of official dress requirements on the various grounds of Scriptural command, the right of the individual conscience, and the jurisdiction of the church over such divisive matters of ceremony and discipline. Anticipating the range of Elizabethan objections to parliamentarily legislated clerical vestments, Hooper at one time placed the matter outside the sovereign's jurisdiction, while at another, conceded the sovereign's right to institute ecclesiastical ceremonies "not derived from Catholicism."[1]

Less radical, but potentially more consequential, was Archbishop Cranmer's undertaking to revise the unwieldy, confusing, and at points unedifying corpus of church law, unencumbering it from its weight of "irrational and sub-Christian principles."[2] While "deriving all ecclesiastical jurisdiction from the Crown," Cranmer's *Reformation of Ecclesiastical Laws* nevertheless aimed at reinforcing the traditional legal authority of the church courts, against the destructive tactics of the civil law and common law lawyers backed by lay hostility.[3] Moreover, it strengthened the church's polity by introducing annual diocesan conferences of lay as well as clerical delegates, thereby enhancing the bishops' consultation with their flocks. The untimely political demise of Cranmer's reform program left the English Church with such organizational and disciplinary deficiencies as would before long invite the Puritan project of total demolition and reconstruction.

The importance of Mary's Protestant persecution for the development of English political and ecclesiological thought is hard to exaggerate. The significance was twofold. Firstly, it occasioned the continental exile of English Protestants that brought them into contact with more radical Lutheran and Calvinist ideas. Secondly, it confronted Protestant dissenters with, from their perspective, the antithesis of the godly king in the person of an unregenerate idolatress who systematically flouted God's ordinances. The response of the exiles to these novel provocations was to articulate concepts of the church's autonomous and prophetic authority and of the divinely prescribed purpose and limitations of political rule. In both conceptual realms the émigrés drew on indigenous English traditions, amalgamating them with European influences. Not surprisingly, this exilic theology gave precedence to civil over ecclesiological concerns, given that the indispensable condition of all further advancement of reformation in the English Church was the termination, by divine or human device, of Queen Mary's reign.

Elements of both the Ockhamist-Wycliffite and the natural-law, constitutional traditions were present in the political formulations of such prominent English Protestant thinkers as Bishop John Ponet (c.1516-1556), formerly of Winchester, Bishop John Aylmer (1521-1594), formerly of London, Christopher Goodman (c.1520-1603), and Laurence Humphrey (c.1527-1590) and in the inflammatory clarion calls of the notorious Scot John Knox

---

1. M. Knappen, *Tudor Puritanism* (Gloucester, MA, 1963), 88.
2. A.G. Dickens, *The English Reformation* (London, 1964), 250.
3. Of particular concern was the authority "over marriage, tithes, testaments, perjury, slander, . . . benefices, [and] heresy." Ibid.

(1505-1572), in whose wake appeared the writings of all the English exiles except Ponet. Those of Ponet and Knox most powerfully embody the principles of a new revolutionary politics, but their principles are not everywhere identical, as they rely on different strands of English political tradition. Whereas Ponet formulated his principles of public sovereignty and the people's right of resistance in heavy dependence on the natural-law tradition of English constitutionalism, Knox's principles of universal political responsibility and prophetic criticism appeal more to the Ockhamist-Wycliffite polarities. Ponet subjects political right and authority to the rule of law in conformity with natural equity, and hedges the political expression of sovereignty by the constitutional structures of a "mixed state." Knox, by contrast, places no constitutional restraints on the universal civil duty to resist idolatry, grounding it on divine command alone, and he seldom relates corporate responsibility to the civil dictates of natural justice. The systemic opposition between divine and human law supporting his revolutionary posture is inimical to Ponet's revolutionary interpretation of the English legal-constitutional framework. Nevertheless, both theologians drew impetus for their radicalism from two controlling theo-political premises: that political rule is chiefly ordered to the promotion of God's glory and the fulfillment of the "First Table" of the Decalogue; and that the individual conscience is the ultimate judge of political right and responsibility, measuring men's laws (whether civil or ecclesiastical) against God's ordinances.

Influential as these political formulations proved to be on future generations, their immediate impact on Elizabeth's polity was slight. Naturally, the queen loathed them, and the politically powerful among her subjects were disposed to side with her. The combined threat of the pope and the Spanish king was alone sufficient to sustain their allegiance to their monarch's full sovereignty and royal prerogatives. Neither were Puritan-minded churchmen any more inclined to weaken their chief bulwark against the Catholic menace. And so there emerged among reformers of every stripe a tacit agreement to deflect criticism away from the queen and onto her bishops. Under Elizabeth, rebellion was largely an ecclesiastical phenomenon, directed against the church authorities.

The leading theological spokesmen for the Puritan rebellion, Thomas Cartwright (1535-1603) and Walter Travers (1548-1635), were not untouched by the political radicalism of the exile period. They imbibed its principles and arguments, but recast them in an ecclesiological mould. Typical of Elizabethan Puritanism as a whole, their reforming zeal was channelled by a vision of the Godly Church rather than of the Godly Commonwealth, closer in spirit to the clerical legalism of the French master,

Calvin himself, than to the prophetic theocratism of his unruly Scottish disciple.

In the presbyterian system, the earthly body of Christ's faithful people is the supremely sovereign community, divided into territorial hierarchies of jurisdiction. Sovereignty attaches to each jurisdictional level, from the national church to the local congregation: indeed, the parochial church body remains the fundamental self-governing unit. The parochial consistory (or council of elders) derives its governing authority from the sovereign congregation, ruling it representatively. Congregational sovereignty is embodied in institutions of election and consent, notably, in the congregational nomination and ratification of consistoral church appointments. Although restricted in its scope, the principle of consent articulates the equality of all confessing church members in their faith and in their communal responsibility. However, in view of the practical limitations of this principle, its theological proponents preferred to speak of "delegated," as opposed to "popular," sovereignty. The church of Cartwright and Travers was, then, a legally constructed polity of an essentially "mixed" constitution: under the sovereign kingship of Christ, the divine law-giver; under an aristocracy of governing elders; and under the democratic principle of consent.

Unlike secular political forms which were considered by the Presbyterians to be variable and mutable, the outward form of the church was regarded as invariable and immutable, fixed eternally by divine decree. The Scriptures reveal to them the eternal necessity and perfection of the Presbyterian constitution, commanded by Christ to be established by His apostles and their helpers, the evangelists. God's law for His Church leaves little to sinful human discretion: man is not free to introduce superfluous (and probably pernicious) ecclesiastical offices, ranks, privileges, ceremonies, and disciplines. In fact, God's law for human conduct in every sphere leaves little room for rational deliberation and compromise. His command is excellent, precisely as it is explicit, particular, and exact. Civil as well as religious duties are defined by a plethora of particular divine commands, as is apparent in the ongoing validity of much of the Mosaic judicial (as distinct from moral) law. Human law not perceptibly derived from express divine command is, for the most part, the wayward invention of man's blind and self-seeking nature. His devising of political constitutions or regimes is a striking exception, owing to the latitude divinely granted to human rational construction and choice in this matter. Even here, the political options are limited to those approved as equally "good" or "acceptable" by God's revealed Word.

Unquestionably, Cartwright's and Travers' model of Presbyterian discipline incorporated principles common to the English natural-law, constitutional tradition, despite their repudiation of natural law as a theological stance. In all probability, these principles entered the Puritans' orbit through Ockhamist-influenced and continental sources. However that may be, the Presbyterian model elicited a powerful theoretical endeavor at the end of the sixteenth century to reinstate natural-law theology in the ecclesiological sphere. This endeavor was Hooker's *Laws of Ecclesiastical Polity*.

Richard Hooker (1554-1600) devoted the better part of his intellectual and literary energies to vindicating the English church establishment against hostile Presbyterian ecclesiological premises. He astutely perceived that these dangerous premises concerned the source, form, and knowledge of the laws regulating the church's external organization and action in the ministerial, ceremonial, and disciplinary spheres. Cartwright and Travers found these laws exclusively in the divine commandments promulgated by the Biblical law-givers, chiefly by Moses and Christ; and on this basis condemned numerous traditional and prominent features of the Anglican polity, such as episcopacy, royal oversight, patronage, the operation of church courts, and parliamentary law-making in ecclesiastical affairs. Spurning occasionalist and piecemeal defences of Anglican structures and practices, Hooker responded with a systematic and comprehensive exposition of their underlying principles. These he developed from the Thomist natural-law tradition, which placed public political order under the laws of right reason in its unassisted working. After setting out the rational foundations of secular polity, Hooker argued for an extension of its constitutional laws to ecclesiastical polity. Armed with the natural political principles of the people's sovereignty, of public deliberation, resolve, and consent, he proceeded to demonstrate the justice and fitness of English church government.

Obviously, Hooker's whole elaborate apology rested on his generous circumscription of the competence of the individual's unassisted reason. He largely brought within its province the bulk of contentious ecclesiastical issues over which the Anglicans and Presbyterians were locking horns. In so doing, he never disregarded the frequent overlapping of the jurisdictions of reason and revelation, natural and supernatural law, or their subtle intermeshing. Nevertheless, his monumental synthesis of divine and human law and authority, which would endow Elizabeth's national church order with a lasting theoretical confirmation, leaves us with the impression of reason's aspiring ascendancy on all theological fronts, not least on that of interpreting and validating Scriptural truth. In practical ecclesiastical matters, Hooker is deservedly revered for his "judicious" wisdom, but his ecclesiology is wanting at one point: at the point of the intersection of divine and human law. He accords to natural reason such latitude in the devising of ecclesiastical polity that the implications of Christ's law for the church's external form are not developed with sufficient rigor. The Presbyterians' rigor in this regard is admirable, however regrettable their confusions of divine and human law.

It is, perhaps, lamentable that the theological tension between God's law and man's law, divine and human authority, so strenuously asserted by Wyclif at the dawn of the English Reformation, should have slackened in the course of reform under the weight of English Erastianism, including Wyclif's own.[1] From Wyclif to Hooker this tension is undercut by the pervasive determination to build a national church that would both reflect and secure the glories of English society. What is remarkable is the degree to which, within this unwavering determination, the pursuit, dissemination, and practice of the evangelic law took place.

---

1. Throughout our study we have employed the term "Erastianism" to designate a deeply-rooted English perspective on church-commonwealth relations that endorses control of ecclesiastical matters by the secular authorities. Although the term derives from the views of the Swiss theologian Thomas Erastus, which were influential among English established-church supporters only after 1589, (and so is properly attached to an Anglican divine such as Richard Hooker), it is conveniently applied to the stances of a broad historical spectrum of English thinkers.

One

THEOLOGICAL PRECURSORS OF THE ENGLISH REFORMATION

While John Wyclif is the preeminent forerunner of the English Reformation, anticipating with astonishing accuracy its intellectual and practical machinery, William of Ockham (c.1285-1347) and Marsilius of Padua (c.1275-1342) are background influences of certain, if incalculable, significance. They stood together, figuratively and literally, in their theological opposition to Pope John XXII and in their subsequent refuge from papal condemnation in the imperial court of Ludwig of Bavaria. Staunch defenders of the Emperor's dignities as the chief guardian of world political order and peace, they pledged their allegiance to Ludwig despite his flagrant defiance of and assault on papal power.[1] Excommunicated themselves, in company with their imperial patron, they not only theologically disowned the Pope as a heretic, but took sanctuary with the secular ruler who had undertaken (albeit unsuccessfully) his deposition.

---

1. When Pope John XXII refused to approve the election of Ludwig as Emperor, excommunicating him for claiming the Imperial Crown without papal consent, Ludwig, backed by the Imperial forces, had himself crowned in Italy and John XXII deposed as a heretic, elevating a more co-operative friar to the Apostolic Chair as Nicholas V. Speedily John XXII regained the papacy, and he and his successors resisted all Ludwig's pleas for reconciliation with Rome.

The two exiles were united in their repudiation of papal absolutism in favour of a more communal and spiritual understanding of ecclesiastical authority. In their common persuasion they are both accurately depicted as revolutionaries against the Hildebrandine triumphalist and papalist church. Yet their revolts were dissimilar, not merely in degree but in fundamental direction. Whereas Ockham's revolt was principally theological, intending modest adjustments of authority relations within the church and between ecclesiastical and civil rulers, Marsilius' revolt was principally political, intending major power redistributions between ecclesiastical and civil rulers in the first place, and only secondarily within the church. Both revolts held the promise of a stronger and emancipated secular order, but only Marsilius' portended a thorough-going secular domination of ecclesiastical affairs.

It is in keeping with the more pronounced radicalism of Marsilius' political program that its impact on English Reformation thought and practice reached its zenith during the revolution in church-commonwealth relations under Henry VIII. It appealed to and abetted the anticlerical, secular-minded, and self-interested outlook of powerful Henrician laymen and the rationalist and statist aims of Henry's chief administrator, Thomas Cromwell (1485-1540). With the completion of Henry's legal reconstruction of the English church, Marsilius' antipapal radicalism had served its national purpose, and its lingering influence worked primarily through the offence it occasioned. Not so with Ockham's political ideas, which reverberated throughout all phases of the English Reformation, resonating with both Lutheran and Calvinist influxes, largely through the widespread influence of his celebrated students, Jean Gerson (1363-1429), Gabriel Biel (1410-1495), and John Mair (1467-1550)[1] Equally as remarkable as the scope of Ockham's theological-political legacy is its complexity, which provides us with a key to understanding both predictable and unpredictable links among Wycliffite-Lutheran, Calvinist Puritan, and establishment Anglican perspectives. Both Wycliffite and Puritan concepts of the epistemological primacy of Scriptural revelation and the ecclesiological primacy of the evangelical law draw on the Ockhamist tradition, as do extreme Reformed views on the civil duty of resistance to idolatrous magistrates, and the moderate Puritan (and to some extent Anglican) principles of popular sovereignty and political consent. It is hardly an exaggeration to claim that out of the different strands of Ockham's epistemological and political thought is woven the peculiar texture of English Reformation doctrines of law and authority.

---

1. These lines of Ockhamist influence are discussed briefly by Q. Skinner, *The Foundations of Modern Political Thought* (Cambridge, 1978), 2: 23-4.

A. WILLIAM OF OCKHAM ON SPIRITUAL AND TEMPORAL LAW AND AUTHORITY

The relevant political concepts in Ockham's voluminous corpus naturally group themselves into two theoretical complexes, concerning: (1) the basis, purpose, and limitations of authority and government in the church; and (2) the basis, purpose, and limitations of civil authority and government. Within the first complex, the controlling themes are the rule of the evangelical law of liberty and poverty, the epistemological authority of Scripture and of individual judgment, the spiritual headship of the pope and its twofold foundation in divine and human election. Corresponding to and contrasting with these are the controlling themes of the second complex, which include the divine origin and purpose of civil rule, the role of natural equity and popular consent, and the juridical rights of the temporal ruler over the church.[1]

1. Authority and Government in the Church

Ockham's complex and protracted consideration of the subject of authority in the church has its origin in a struggle which altered and overshadowed the course of his career, namely, the struggle between Pope John XXII and the Franciscan Order over the issue of evangelical poverty. During his detainment at Avignon for suspected heresy on unrelated grounds, Ockham was recruited by the Franciscan Minister General and fellow sojourner, Michael of Cesena (d.1342), to the public defence of the Franciscan cause against repeated papal assaults.[2] In 1322 Pope John XXII had issued a bull repudiating the Franciscan status of "complete legal poverty" and renouncing "papal ownership of goods used by the Franciscans."[3] He declared the Franciscan principle of separating the rightful use (*usus iuris*) of goods consumed by use from their legal ownership or possession (*a proprietate rei seu dominio*) to be opposed to law and reason (*repugnat iuri et obviat rationi*).[4] Further, he had anathematized the Franciscan attribution of total poverty to Christ and his apostles on the twofold ground that it rendered their use of consumable things unlawful and contradicted the clear testimony of Scripture to their (individual and commu-

---

1. For this thematic organization I am greatly indebted to the comprehensive, insightful, and well-documented study A. S. McGrade, *The Political Thought of William of Ockham* (Cambridge, 1974).

2. In 1324 Ockham was summoned from his teaching at Oxford to answer charges of eucharistic heresy before a papal examining commission at Avignon.

3. McGrade, *Political Thought*, 10-11.

4. From the bull *Quia vir reprobus*, quoted by Ockham in *Opus Nonaginta Dierum*, which is reprinted in *Guillelmi De Ockham Opera Politica* (Manchester, 1940-1963), 1: 299.

nal) rightful possession of temporal necessities.[1] Against this undermining of the Franciscans' position, Ockham was induced to compose the lengthy tract *Work of Ninety Days* (1332-3), vindicating evangelical poverty as a Scripturally and rationally sound principle.

In heavy dependence on contemporary Minorite literature, Ockham sets forth the argument that the mere use of things (whether consumed by use) without legal ownership or recourse conforms to the perfect law and example of Christ followed by the Apostles and the primitive church; and, moreover, it accords with original natural equity. The command of Christ to would-be disciples, as to his chosen company, is to "go, sell what you possess and give to the poor" (Matt. 19:21), to relinquish everything—"houses or brothers or sisters or father or mother or children or lands" (Matt. 19:29)—for the sake of a heavenly perfection that "proceeds out of the magnitude of divine love."[2] Far from being unjust and unlawful, the self-denying abdication of possessions issues in the form of using things ordained by the law of nature, the *ius poli* (literally, the law of the heavens), defined by Ockham as "natural equity which, apart from all human ordinance, and even divine ordinance in so far as it is purely positive, is consonant with right reason, or is consonant with purely natural right reason, or is consonant with right reason derived from those things that are divinely revealed to us."[3] According to the ius poli, the rightful use of temporal goods is ordered to the relief of the pressing physical needs of those who hold them. Beyond the immediate relief of their subsistence needs, individuals and communities rightly hold temporal goods only for the purpose of relieving the dire necessities of others.[4] In addition, the rightful "possessors" of temporal goods must hold and use them with inward rectitude (*ex conscientia recta*), innocent of avarice or evil intention.[5] Thus, to use things lawfully (*iure poli*) is to use them morally well (*bene moraliter*).

Over against the evangelical and natural law of holding and using things Ockham sets the *ius fori* (literally, the law of the forum), which he defines as "justice established by human pact or ordinance or by explicit divine ordinance."[6] About this political law of possession, Ockham makes two notable and contrasting points. On the one hand, he firmly upholds its authority over those communally subject to it, including its executors, so that it should not

---

1. See Ockham's quotations from *Quia vir reprobus* heading Chapters I-IV and VI of *Opus Nonaginta Dierum*, in Ockham, *Opera Politica*, 1: 294, 299, 313-314, 332, 361.
2. *Opus Nonaginta Dierum*, chap. ll, in Ockham, *Opera Politica*, 2: 413.
3. *Opus Nonaginta Dierum*, chap. 65, in Ockham, *Opera Politica*, 2: 574.
4. Ibid., 2: 576.
5. Ibid.
6. Ibid., 2: 573-4.

be violated at will without "the authority of a superior," such as the prince.[1] For conventional or customary law is authoritative "after natural law" in securing the unity of communal life. On the other hand, Ockham presents it as habitually running counter to the ius poli, in granting possessions to evil and avaricious men who are unworthy of them; so that "many things are possessed by the ius fori that are not possessed well, and many things are possessed well that are not possessed by the ius fori."[2] In view of this habitual opposition, the *Fratres Minores* do well to live in exclusive obedience to the law of Christ and nature.

Pope John XXII's unrelenting condemnation of Franciscan obedience as heretical drove Ockham irresistibly to conclude that the Pope was himself a heretic, and thus forced him to grapple with the ensuing epistemological and political dilemma of authority in the church. His foremost contribution to the resolution of this dilemma was his separation of epistemological or cognitive authority from political (in this case, prelatical) authority in his treatise *The Dialogue*, the first part of which was completed before the death of John XXII in 1334.[3]

In discussing the correction of "erring" believers in Book 4, Ockham argues that "legitimate correction" involves necessarily a clear demonstration to the *errans* of his reputed errors, bare condemnation by a superior ecclesiastical authority being insufficient.[4] It follows that those are best qualified to correct errors who are most capable of demonstrating them; and in this regard, the theologians (*doctores*) rank higher than the prelates. For their exposition of "divine Scripture"—the pre-eminent (but not exclusive) standard of doctrinal orthodoxy—the theologians are to be preferred even to the supreme pontiff.[5] Thus, the theologians especially are not required to surrender their opinions under papal correction without their errors being clearly shown to them, although the same right belongs to simple Christians (*simplices*) as well. Moreover, theologians exercise epistemological authority

---

1. Ibid., 2: 574.
2. Ibid., 2: 579.
3. *Dialogus de Imperio et Pontifica Potestate*, reprinted in Guillelmus de Occam O.F.M., *Opera Plurima* (London, 1962), 1: i.
4. *Dialogus*, pt. 1, bk. 4, chap. 13, in Ockham, *Opera Plurima*, 1: xxvi.
5. *Dialogus*, pt. 1, bk. 4, chap. 14, in Ockham, *Opera Plurima*, 1: xxvii. While Scripture is the pre-eminent locus of divine truths necessary to be believed for salvation, it is not the sole locus. Apart from Scripture, Ockham recognizes an independent Apostolic tradition transmitted orally or in the writings of the faithful, "historical chronicles" composed by the faithful, and "revelation or inspiration manifestly given [to the faithful] in a divine manner." Ibid.

among believers, not as an official class, but as worthy individuals trusted for their Scriptural erudition and moral rectitude.[1]

As the erring believer is not obliged to surrender his opinion in the absence of rational persuasion, so he is obliged to surrender it in the presence of such persuasion, regardless of who undertakes it—whether superior prelate, friend, or even inferior subject.[2] In this manner Ockham separates the authority of correction from institutional or official jurisdiction, thereby supplanting "the traditional distinction between authoritative and fraternal correction" by "the concept of a cognitively legitimate correction."[3] In a corresponding move he universalizes the privilege and duty of correcting within the church, extending it to all parts and grades, clerical and lay. No believer is exempt from the responsibility of interrogating, correcting and, if necessary, bringing to punishment holders and propagators of heretical doctrine, even if they should include the presiding pope and his supporters. Albeit in the case of the pope and his supporters Ockham envisages an institutional order of precedence for initiating public action against the offenders, the prerogative descending from the "bishops" and "prelates" to the "doctors" and "masters," to the "religious" (monastic heads), secular rulers, and "public potentates," and ultimately to the "laity" and "simple Christians."[4] Nevertheless, no one is excluded by the lowliness of his office from the corporate struggle to suppress heresy. In view of this universal obligation, the Franciscan theologians are unquestionably justified in publicly opposing John XXII's heretical constitutions.

Ockham's elevation of epistemological over political authority and his diffusion of the former throughout the visible church necessarily imply an antipapalist and nonhierarchical conception of the community of Christ. In Book 5 of *The Dialogue*, he explicitly repudiates any attempt to identify one or another part or office of the church with "the whole church," ascribing to it the inerrancy promised by Christ to "the whole."[5] The "whole church," which is Christ's spiritual body of true believers, resides on earth in the faithful scattered throughout the institutional church. It is this spiritual body that mediates Christ's divine authority, and not an isolated structural part.

1. Ibid.
2. *Dialogus*, pt.1, bk. 4, chap. 21, in Ockham, *Opera Plurima*, 1: xxix.
3. McGrade, *Political Thought*, 57.
4. Ockham's discussion of the responsibility of the above classes to take action against papal heresy appears in *Dialogus*, pt. 1, bk. 7, chaps. 35-56. See McGrade, *Political Thought*, 48, n. 9.
5. Ibid., 73. See also John Ryan's discussion of the epistemological authority of "the totality of believers" in *The Nature, Structure and Function of the Church in William of Ockham* (Chico, CA, 1979), 29-31.

Undeniably, the earthly church has a divinely appointed head: the pope as successor to St. Peter (whose apostolic primacy Ockham never disputes) is Christ's chosen "vicar" of his flock.[1] But the pope's headship is divinely established and conferred for the sake of the spiritual welfare of the universal church, and is bounded by the exigencies of the corporate good.[2] This communal *telos* and limitation of papal rule is expressed in the procedure of papal election: the pope receives his supremacy directly from God (*immediate a Deo*), but not without human agency (*ministerio*), the electors being the ministers of God's ordination.[3] While Ockham refrains from explicitly making the election the vehicle of communal consent, he implicitly endorses this principle, in positing the "natural right" to elect the pope with the people over whom his jurisdiction extends.[4]

As the evangelical law with respect to poverty prompted Ockham's consideration of papal authority, so the evangelical law with respect to freedom advances it. He never tires of pitting against the triumphalist definition of the pope's "plenitude of power" (*plenitudo potestatis*) the liberty inherent in Christ's rule for his church. Papal "plenitude" conferred by Christ cannot mean the unilateral power regularly to do or impose anything in both spiritual and temporal affairs not expressly against divine or natural law, even in violation of the "*ius gentium*," whether civil or canon.[5] For such "plenitude" would render the evangelical law one of intolerable slavery, much more tyrannical than the Mosaic law.[6] But Christ's law does not impose many and onerous external observances, ceremonies, and duties; it does not make punishing exactions of men's corporal possessions, or infringe their civil rights

---

1. See Ockham's *Octo Quaestiones de Potestate Papae*, q. 2, chap. 3, in Ockham, *Opera Politica*, 1: 74; *De Imperatorum et Pontificum Potestate* (Oxford, 1927), 4-5; and *Breviloquium* (Paris, 1937), bk. 2, chap. 16, pp. 48-51.

2. See, e.g., *Octo Quaestiones*, q. 3, chap. 4, in Ockham, *Opera Politica*, 1: 106 (". . . beatus Petrus nullam potestatem recepit a Christo, nisi propter bonum sibi subiectorum ad obtinendum regnum caelorum. . . .") and *De Imperatorum*, chap. 6, p. 12 ("Ex his concluditer quod principatus papalis est propter utilitatem et commodum subditorum institutus, et non propter honorem aut gloriam vel utilitatem seu temporale commodum principantis. . . ."). John Ryan rightly points out that Ockham qualifies or relativises the authority of all ecclesiastical offices by means of the "generalised principle" of the church's "common good." See Ryan, *The Nature*, 17-19.

3. Ockham offers the analogy of baptism, wherein "gratiam recipit a solo Deo, non tamen sine ministerio baptizantis." *Octo Quaestiones*, q. 2, chap. 3, in Ockham, *Opera Politica*, 1: 74.

4. *Dialogus*, pt. 3, bk. 2, chap. 3, vi, cited in McGrade, *Political Thought*, 130.

5. *Octo Quaestiones*, q. 1, chap. 2, in Ockham, *Opera Politica*, 1: 15. See also *De Imperatorum*, chap. 1, p. 5; *Breviloquium*, bk. 2, chap. 1, pp. 16-17.

6. *Octo Quaestiones*, q. 1, chap. 6, in Ockham, *Opera Politica*, 1: 29. See also *De Imperatorum* chap. 1, p. 6; *Breviloquium*, bk. 2, chap. 3, pp. 18-20.

and liberties. Rather, Christ's law shuns all burdens not conducive to men's spiritual welfare. Thus the pope, in exercising his plenitude, should avoid burdensome and excessive, arbitrary and frivolous demands on his subjects, whether legislating conduct or punishment. He should content himself with the discipline proper to his pastoral and ministering care of Christ's body.[1] The pope, though diligent in procuring obedience to the laws of God and nature, and ready to command in matters of public utility and necessity, should, nevertheless, seek wherever possible to rule with the knowledge and consent of the church, and to confine his government to those things requisite to "the salvation of souls" and the heavenly "regiment . . . of the faithful."[2] Only so does he conform to the servanthood of Christ as against the lordly dominion of the Gentile rulers (Matt. 20:25-28; Luke 22:25-27). It shall now become apparent that some aspects of Gentile lordship denied to the pope are permitted to the temporal potentates up to a point.

2. Political Rationality and Temporal Autonomy

Ockham's discussion of temporal rule, as found in his treatises *A Brief Account of the Power of the Pope* (1341-2), *Eight Questions on the Power of the Pope* (1342), and *The Power of Emperors and Popes* (1346-7), proceeds by analogy and contrast with his discussion of spiritual rule. The two rules are analogous, in that both originate in divine ordination, are directed to the common good, and are structured by the principle of freedom. These analogies, however, harbor contrasts.

Firstly, temporal authority is not conferred directly by God alone (*a solo Deo*) with or without mere human instrumentality (outside of Scripturally revealed exceptions). Rather, it is conferred by the people (*ex donatione populi*) with divine authorization. The Book of Genesis tells us that God in creation bestowed temporal possession of earthly goods on the "human race in common," ordaining that appropriation of these benefits should be made with the consent and will of the human community. The power of directing the distribution of temporal goods, or the "supreme lay power," originally resided, therefore, with the human community, which has freely invested it in a single ruler— the emperor—such that it cannot be withdrawn arbitrarily by popular will.[3] In establishing imperial rule, the human community has acted on consideration of the public good, following natural equity, and not on

---

1. A concise list of impositions to be avoided by the pope is given in *De Imperatorum*, chap. 5, pp. 10-12.
2. Ibid., ch. 7, p. 14. See also *Breviloquium*, bk. 2, chap. 5, pp. 22-25.
3. *Octo Quaestiones*, q. 2, chap. 6, in Ockham, *Opera Politica*, 1: 78-9. See also *Breviloquium*, bk. 4, chaps. 12-13.

"some special [divine] mandate miraculously revealed."[1] Nevertheless, the imperial ruler, once invested by human positive law, holds his office "*a solo Deo*," having no "regular" superior but God.[2]

By so arguing, Ockham counters the papalist doctrine deriving the *imperium* (and all secular authority) from the pope's "plenitude," substituting popular for papal mediation of temporal power. Accordingly, he transfers the "regular" responsibility for deposing "damnably" criminal, destructive, and tyrannical emperors from the papal office to the Roman people, or their delegated representatives, confining the pope's interference to cases where it is solicited by an impotent or unwilling laity, or rendered necessary by the incorrigible negligence or corrupt loyalty of those primarily responsible.[3] At the same time, however, he concedes the pope's spiritual superiority over the emperor, including his authority to judge the supreme temporal ruler for spiritual crimes. Indeed, he refuses to deprive the pope of coercive authority in spiritual matters in order to satisfy the secularist demand for a unitary jurisdiction.[4] Rather, he prefers to reduce the area of potential spiritual-temporal conflict by carefully discriminating the spheres of jurisdiction. In circumscribing the temporal sphere, he subscribes to the traditional Fransciscan-Augustinian view of secular rule as instituted chiefly for the correction and punishment of wrongdoers.

In that the emperor is sovereign possessor of temporal goods, supreme judge, and executor of human law, his rule is necessarily commanding (*dominativus*) rather than ministering (*ministrativus*). It requires both preponderant coercive power and abundant wealth. His jurisdiction, while formally antithetical to the pope's, extends over the church in two respects. Firstly, the clergy, or "spirituality," are subject to imperial law (or some subordinate territorial law) for secular crimes—a fairly bold rejection on Ockham's part of well-established, if resented, clerical privilege. Secondly, the spirituality hold their temporal goods from the emperor (or subordinate secular ruler) according to imperial (or other territorial) law and are obliged to make grants to the secular authority upon urgent public necessity. In his treatise *Whether the Prince for His Own Support, in Waging War, is Able to Accept the Goods of the Church Against the Pope's Will*, Ockham affirms the obligation of the English clergy to assist financially, without papal consent, King Edward III's prosecution of his rights to the French throne. He argues that English clerical possessions (especially "superabundant" possessions)

---

1. *Octo Quaestiones*, q. 2, chap. 6, in Ockham, *Opera Politica*, 1: 80.
2. Ibid.
3. Ibid., q. 2, chaps. 9-10, in Ockham, *Opera Politica*, 1: 87-91.
4. Ibid., q. 3, chap. 3, in Ockham, *Opera Politica*, 1: 104-5.

were originally granted by the king and laity for service in "pious causes" that advance common utility, foremost among which is defence of one's country and its monarch's rights.[1] Finally, he proposes that the emperor, as "faithful defender of the church," has the "occasional" (as opposed to "regular") responsibility of deposing a manifestly heretical pope whom the church has proclaimed as such.[2]

Thus, in his treatment of church-empire relations, as in his treatment of the internal structures of each, Ockham strives to differentiate and separate authorities, and to effect subtle shifts of loci without disruptively undermining existing institutional balances. His theoretical achievement for posterity must be measured against the near impossibility of his intended undertaking.

B. MARSILIUS OF PADUA: DEFENDER OF THE PEACE

Born between 1275 and 1280, rector of the University of Paris in 1313, Marsilius of Padua completed his treatise *Defender of the Peace* in 1324, and fled to the court of Ludwig of Bavaria in Nuremberg two years later, upon Pope John XXII's condemnation of his work.[3] Thus, unlike Ockham who wrote most of his political treatises after his excommunication and exile, Marsilius wrote his daring manifesto before his condemnation and flight. Nevertheless, it must be said that the *Defender of the Peace* is more blatantly and truculently antipapal in its polemic than any of Ockham's writings. Marsilius was far too devoted to a rigorously consistent and unambiguous theological-political project to have any use for Ockham's subtle dialectics of moderation. The architectonic boldness of the *Defender of the Peace* partly accounts for its serving the Roman Church as a measure of heretical deflection with which each generation of heretics was associated in papal accusations. Thus, Wyclif, Hus, and Luther were all charged with borrowing from

---

1. *An Princeps Pro Suo Succursu*, chaps. 7-8, in Ockham, *Opera Politica*, 1: 255-260.
2. *Dialogus*, pt. 1, bk. 6, in *Opera Plurima*, 1: c. Ockham undoubtedly regarded his patron, the Emperor Ludwig, as having the rightful authority to depose John XXII, given the pope's "manifest heresy" in regard to evangelical poverty, although Ludwig was never powerful enough to exercise it after his initial unsuccessful assault. However, it may be asked whether the church had met Ockham's condition for imperial deposition of the pope: namely, her proclamation of papal heresy. No "general council" had condemned the pope, but chiefly a group of outspoken Franciscan theologians, including Ockham. Nevertheless, as Ockham was convinced of the truth of this condemnation, we must assume that it carried for him the authority of the "whole church."
3. These scant details of Marsilius' life, about which little is known, are provided by Alan Gewirth's introduction to his translation of *Defensor pacis* in *Marsilius of Padua, the Defender of Peace* (Toronto, 1980), ixx [hereinafter Gewirth, *Defensor pacis*].

the "accursed Marsilius."[1] As we shall see, Rome's outrage at his formulations was not unjustified, for they contain radical departures from the prevailing medieval perspectives on society and the church. They represent an inversion of the Hildebrandine model much more thoroughgoing than that subsequently accomplished by Wyclif.[2] Controlling Marsilius' standpoint is his concept of the state: its origin and purpose, its form, its parts, and its perfection. From this concept proceeds his understanding of law and authority, temporal and spiritual.

1. The Sovereign and Omnicompetent State

At the outset Marsilius accepts Aristotle's definition of the state as "the perfect community having the full limit of self-sufficiency, which came into existence for the sake of living, but exists for the sake of living well."[3] The state enables the preservation and enhancement of human life through the development of the "diverse genera and species" of arts and sciences. But even more critical for its form, it establishes and enforces a standard of justice by which disputes and quarrels are regulated.[4] The regulation of "matters of justice and benefit" by "reasonable ordinance" or the natural law of equity is the constitutive feature of civil community that distinguishes it from the more primitive community of the household.

The state that is self-sufficient in its provision of the conditions of "living" and "living well" is functionally complete, having the "parts" or "offices" necessary to self-sufficiency.[5] Marsilius arranges these offices under the two generic categories of serving life in "this world" and serving life in "the other or future world." These categories express two fundamental sets of human needs, both of which are natural, in that men desire to live well both in this world and in the future world.[6] While the second set of needs is neither demonstrable nor self-evident, Marsilius points out that "most laws or religions promise that in the future world God will distribute rewards to those who do good and punishment to doers of evil." The "final end" or "office" of

---

1. Preface to *Defensor pacis*.
2. The "Hildebrandine model" of the church, enshrined in the decrees of Pope Gregory VII (Hildebrand: 1021-85), is an hierarchical and triumphalist one, in which the Pope is the repository or mediator of all divinely granted earthly authority, and the spirituality exercises superior power over the temporality.
3. Aristotle, *Politics*, bk. 1, chap. 2. 1252b 29.
4. Gewirth, *Defensor pacis*, 13.
5. These parts or offices are of six kinds, according to Aristotle *Politics*, bk. 7, chap. 8: the agricultural, the artisan, the military, the financial, the priestly, and the judicial or deliberative.
6. Gewirth, *Defensor pacis*, 15.

the priesthood is, therefore, to teach the promises of God concerning the future life and to instruct men in the law of God by which the promises are obtained. But it has as well a secondary, this-worldly cause of vital importance to the state, namely, "the goodness of human acts both individual and civil, on which depend almost completely the quiet or tranquility of communities and finally the sufficient life in the present world."[1] Regardless of the truth or falsity of priestly instruction about "human resurrection" and "eternal reward and punishment," it "induces in men reverence and fear of God, and a desire to flee the vices and to cultivate the virtues," making them "well disposed both in themselves and toward others," with the consequence that "many disputes and injuries cease" and communal "tranquility" and "the sufficient life" is "preserved with less difficulty."[2] Such is the purely civil or political end of the priesthood.

Despite the magnitude of the priesthood's contribution to civil peace and self-sufficiency, this part is not the principal "efficient" cause of the political good. This cause is "the ruler" who secures the end of the state by establishing, determining, and conserving its other parts. The ruler is the first and foremost part of the state, whose action *alone* is continuously indispensable to its wellbeing. Only the ruler can effect the right proportioning and integrated working of the assemblage of civil spheres by means of his judicial authority. For his judgment and execution of "sentences concerning civil justice and benefit" according to a legal standard of justice is the medicine to cure injuries inflicted by one civil sphere on another, restoring "due equality or proportion" through the regimen of punishment and compensation.[3]

The primacy of the ruling part over the others is expressed as forcefully in the action of establishing as in the action of judging. Perhaps Marsilius' most radical political proposition is that "the ruler must establish and differentiate the parts and offices of the state from the appropriate matter," meaning that he not only circumscribes the offices but also appoints to them men with suitable "functional habits."[4] To ensure an ongoing supply of candidates for these diverse offices requires a stringent educational program of selection and training conducted by the government. The priestly office is not exempt from this secular regulation, even though its ground and essence is divine. Marsilius overcomes the seeming contradiction by defining the priesthood in two ways, as "a habit of the soul" and as a part of the state established for the

---

1. Ibid., 19.
2. Ibid., 19-20.
3. Ibid., 64.
4. Ibid., 65.

public benefit, and by assigning two corresponding causes to it, one divine and one human.[1]

While the ruler is the effective origin of all authority in the state, the "primary" origin is "the legislator," that is, "the people or the whole body of citizens, or the weightier part thereof."[2] Strictly speaking, the legislator is the "efficient cause" of the parts or offices of the state, and the ruler is "the instrumental or executive cause . . . through the authority granted to him for this purpose by the legislator. . . ."[3] To the legislator belongs the "efficient power" to establish, correct, and even to depose the ruler and to make the laws. Hence, that method of establishing the government is best which most fully articulates the sovereignty of the body politic, and this is election. Accordingly, it is preferable that monarchial rule be founded on election rather than hereditary succession.[4] This offensive judgment was reversed by Marsilius' English translator!

2. Law in its "Proper" Sense and "Other" Senses

The legislator establishes both the ruler and the standard by which he rules, which is law in its "proper sense." The law, properly speaking, is civil, as defined in the concluding book of Aristotle's *Ethics*: "It is an ordinance made by political prudence, concerning matters of justice and benefit and their opposites, and having 'coercive force,' that is, concerning whose observance there is given a command which one is compelled to observe, or which is made by way of such a command."[5] Although the product of "political prudence," the civil law is decisively characterized not by its conformity to a true standard of civil justice or benefit but rather by its intrinsic relation to coercive authority enforced in the present world. It is the element of this-worldly, coercive jurisdiction that is missing from the "other" senses of law, which include the science of civil law and the evangelical law.

These latter two senses come under the general meaning of law as a standard of human action, especially of "controlled" or voluntary action. The science of civil law determines the standard of human acts directed to the sufficient life in this world, in so far as they are "transient" rather than "immanent"— "crossing over" into a subject other than the agent rather than remaining within the agent, and of "benefit or harm, right or wrong" to that

---

1. Ibid., 233.
2. Ibid., 45.
3. Ibid., 62.
4. Ibid., 32.
5. Aristotle, *Ethics*, bk. 10, chap. 9. 1180a 21. Gewirth, *Defensor pacis*, 36.

other subject.[1] By contrast, the evangelical law lays down the standard of human voluntary acts, whether immanent or transient, "ordered toward glory ... in the future world." Unlike the science of civil law that aims only at discovering standards and not at enforcing them with coercive measures, the evangelical law "distributes punishments or rewards, but inflicts these in the future world, not in the present one. . . ." Thus, the civil law alone is the coercive standard of this-worldly, transient human acts.[2]

The executors of the civil law and of the evangelical law are both judges with coercive authority, the former being the civil ruler and the latter being Christ himself. However, Christ exercises judgment over men only in the future world; in the present one the evangelical law has no executor with coercive power. The priest, "according to the evangelic Scripture," is a judge only in the sense that he conveys knowledge "in this world of divine law." After Christ's example, he judges in the manner of a physician: teaching, commanding, predicting, or judging about the things that are profitably done or omitted to "attain eternal life and avoid punishment." His authority extends to exhorting, censuring, and rebuking the transgressors of divine law, but stops short of inflicting temporal punishment or dispensing temporal reward to the obedient. Indeed, the authority to punish or reward utterly defeats the work of assisting believers to the obedience that, by the grace of Christ, merits eternal salvation.[3] In the case of an offence that is simultaneously against the evangelical and the civil laws, heresy being the prime example, the sentence of acquittal or conviction must be pronounced by the ruler, while the theological judgments involved in the case are left to the priests. To Marsilius' mind, the Scripture is equally adamant in subjecting Christ's apostles and their successors to the coercive jurisdiction of the ruler in all temporal affairs as in denying them all coercive jurisdiction.

3. The "Spiritual" Church

The church, according to Marsilius, is by nature "spiritual," as opposed to "temporal," and priestly authority is likewise "spiritual." In this terminological opposition, "temporal" refers primarily to the realm of civil acts, but more broadly to acts, whether immanent or transient, ordered to the sufficiency of the present life. By contrast, "spiritual" refers primarily to the realm of evangelical acts circumscribed by the divine law, including "ecclesiastic sacraments and their effects, . . . theological virtues, and the gifts of the Holy Spirit ordering us toward eternal life." "Spiritual" also more generally denotes

1. Ibid., 158.
2. Ibid., 159.
3. Ibid., 164.

acts, whether immanent or transient, directed toward the attainment of a blessed life in the future world, including contemplation, adoration and worship of God, prayer, charity, and ascetical self-denial.[1] The church is spiritual because constituted by spiritual action; the priestly authority is spiritual because regulative of spiritual action.

This is not to imply that the word "church" fundamentally signifies "the priesthood." Far from it. Its proper signification is "the whole body of the faithful who believe in and invoke the name of Christ, and all parts of this whole body in any community, even the household."[2] Spiritual action, action in obedience to God's revealed law, is the privilege and burden of all Christians. Nevertheless, the priesthood is spiritual in two respects in which the laity is not, and which are bound up with its special authority. First and foremost, the priestly office is a divinely imprinted character of the soul bestowed only on God's appointed. This character, originally imprinted on the souls of Christ's apostles, and bestowed on their successors through the priestly laying on of hands, is the power whereby the priest administers the sacraments and binds or looses men from sins. In this character resides the "essential" or "inseparable" authority of the priesthood, possessed equally by all its members.[3] The priest's "spiritual" authority has no coercive aspect: even in the sacrament of penance his power is that of discerning and declaring the cancelling or retaining of sins which has been accomplished by Christ already and not that of cancelling or retaining sins.

The second and derivative respect in which the priest is spiritual is that he is committed by his office to embrace the state of spiritual or evangelical perfection exhibited by Christ and His apostles. He is called to the status of "supreme poverty," defined by Marsilius (and by Ockham) as the renunciation of "all acquired legal ownership, both in private and in common," entailing "the power to claim and to prohibit another from temporal things (called 'riches') before a coercive judge." This status involves the priest's voluntary self-deprivation, "both in private and in common, [of] all power, holding, handling, or use of temporal things over and above what is necessary quantitatively and qualitatively for his present subsistence."[4] Marsilius' apostolical priesthood should live "exproprietarily" (to anticipate Wyclif's term), without civil possessions and civil jurisdiction, enjoying only the right of a limited *usufruct*. The temporalities of the clergy that support their ministry should remain in the legal possession of either the legislator (being identical with the

---

1. Ibid., 104-105.
2. Ibid., 103.
3. Ibid., 235.
4. Ibid., 204.

whole company of believers) or the private donors who granted them for the sake of the apostolical ministry of preaching, performing the sacraments and almsgiving. Correspondingly, the power to appoint to all ecclesiastical benefices should belong to "the entire multitude of believers of that place through their election or express will" (unless, we may presume, such right is retained by a private patron). The multitude may, however, delegate its appointing authority to a clerical person responsible to it.[1]

Marsilius' democratic and lay-oriented approach to clerical appointments presupposes his all-important distinction between the priesthood as a divinely imprinted habit of the soul and as a humanly constructed office for the benefit of the civil community. This distinction allows him to derive the directive and regulative authority exercised by some priests over others from the human community and not from divine commission. Thus, the appointment of a bishop to oversee clerical ministry in a particular place is the prerogative of the believers "in that place," episcopal authority being "external" and "inessential."[2] In a fateful Erastian move, Marsilius allocates the power of "election, assignment, and presentation of persons to be promoted to ecclesiastical orders" not only to the local community of believers, but also to "the human legislator," or to "the ruler by its authority."[3] The ruler's licensing of ecclesiastical appointments is an inevitable practical consequence of his being "the efficient cause" of all civil offices. By this means, and on professed Scriptural authority, Marsilius subjects the spiritual authority of the priesthood to the highest civil controls.

Neither Marsilius' spiritual church nor his sovereign state can tolerate a supreme Roman Pontiff with "plenitude of power" extending beyond the boundaries of the priesthood to civil rule. Indeed, the controlling aim of both discourses comprising the *Defender of the Peace* is to show forth the papal claim to, and exercise of, such power as theologically indefensible and politically injurious. In contrast to Ockham's position, Marsilius' first discourse demonstrates the incompatibility of papal plenitude with the plenitude of coercive power belonging to the human legislator in the civil realm. His second discourse demonstrates the universal inclusiveness of civil jurisdiction to cover all the temporal powers of the priesthood. The combined argument of both discourses invalidates the papal plenitude in every existing contentious mode: in the appointment to church offices and the distribution of ecclesiastical benefices; in the coercive disciplining and deposition of priests; in the binding and loosing men from guilt and punishment, including

1. Ibid., 258.
2. Ibid., 237.
3. Ibid., 259.

excommunication, interdict, and reconciliation; in the consecration of priests; in the interpretation of Scripture and the definition of right belief and observance; in the exercise of coercive jurisdiction over civil authorities and in matters of non-ecclesiastical offices and goods. The only mode of plenitude (in a diminished sense of the term) that Marsilius allows to the Roman bishop is the plenitude of spiritual "priority or leadership" over all priests and churches, exercised "by authority of the faithful human legislator."[1] And it is apparent in this formulation that the plenitude of authority belongs to "the faithful human legislator which lacks a superior," that is, to the sovereign people—a new Messianic *defensor pacis*.[2]

1. Ibid., 316.
2. Ibid., 287.

Two

JOHN WYCLIF AND THE FRANCISCAN-AUGUSTINIAN ANTINOMIES

John Wyclif (c.1330-84) was a forerunner of the English Reformation in a way that Ockham was not, in that he championed a program of ecclesiastical reform that anticipated in striking detail the legislative agenda of King Henry VIII and his parliaments. In breaking with the papacy and abolishing the religious orders, Henry VIII "carried out to the letter the reforms which Wyclif had advocated," and with the legal machinery that he had approved.[1] This was not mere historical coincidence, even given the skepticism of some modern scholars concerning Wyclif's influence on the eve of the Tudor Reformation.[2] For Wyclif's ideas on the necessity, the theological basis, and the execution of ecclesiastical and religious reform never died out completely, despite the effective suppression over generations of his heretical progeny, the Lollards.[3] While early Tudor Lollardy was

---

1. A. Kenny, *Wyclif* (Oxford, 1985), 102-3.
2. K.B. McFarlane in *Wycliffe and English Non-Conformity* (Middlesex, 1972) appears to take quixotic pleasure in the historical futility of Wyclif's life work. His epilogue is memorable for the ironic observation: "Thanks to a Reformation he did little or nothing to inspire and in effect everything possible to delay, he has been hailed for centuries as its Morning Star, the herald of its dawn." Ibid., 169.
3. Even before Wyclif's death, followers of his doctrines who also produced literalistic Bible translations had incurred the label "Lollard"—"a Middle Dutch word meaning 'mumbler'" that had previously been applied to "the Beghards and other Netherlandish

characteristically a beleaguered underground affair of poor and uneducated people, its conventional beliefs had enough strategic currency to provide, as A.G. Dickens puts it, "a spring-board of critical dissent" for reforming action, as well as "reception-areas for Lutheranism," the most notable of which was the community of London merchants and book agents who introduced Lutheran literature into England. Not insignificant evidence for the timely resurgence of Wyclif's inspiration in the opening phase of the English Reformation is the fact that "between 1530 and the death of Henry VIII, at least nine Wycliffite treatises are known to have been set forth in print . . . ."[1] What continues to shock the unsuspecting reader is the systematic and comprehensive treatment of so many touchstones of Protestant doctrine in Wyclif's writings.

To understand Wyclif's reforming vision, we must penetrate the complexities and ambiguities of his theological conceptions of law and authority. Here we encounter doctrines that have called forth the admiration of generations of Protestant scholars, as being clear and forceful statements of Protestant principles. The first and foremost asserts the unconditional authority of Scripture as the one perfect Word of God, eternal and unchanging, in which all being, truth, and law stand revealed, and by which all earthly claims to authority are judged. The second and closely connected doctrine sets forth the church universal as the entire body of the predestined, whose head is Christ and whose essence is Christ's law of love revealed in Scripture. The third doctrine, asserts that all right of lordship over persons and things is granted immediately by God, who is bound by His eternal law to bestow it on the righteous. In this sinful world unrighteous men have civil jurisdiction and possession of property, but their lordship, being without divine title, is merely apparent and transient. Finally, Wyclif's fourth doctrine asserts the obligation of obedience to temporal powers under which all Christians are placed by the law of Christ. It accords to the Christian king, as supreme temporal lord and executor of the evangelical law, a temporal dignity and honor unlimited by any other communal authority or office.

With this theological munition Wyclif waged a protracted war on behalf of the English King and secular magnates against the corrupt worldliness of the fourteenth century church: against the secular pomp and power of its

---

pietists." Typically, the Lollards condemned the papacy, the ritualism and superstition, the temporal riches, and the jurisdiction of the Roman church, emphasizing positively the primacy of preaching over sacramental celebration for the clergy, and free access to the vernacular Scriptures for the laity. A.G. Dickens, *The English Reformation* (London, 1964), 23-4.

1. Ibid., 37.

"caesarian prelates"; the excessive wealth and complacency of its monastic establishments; the religious, moral, and occasionally criminal, indiscipline of its lower clergy. He attacked ecclesiastical endowment in its manifold forms: episcopal and monastic benefices, cathedral canonries, prebends, and archdeaconries, and the plural livings of the wealthier clergy, pressing for the complete disendowment of the clerical estate. He attacked ecclesiastical tithes and the plethora of legal exactions and penalties imposed by the clergy on the laity. Finally, he attacked the vast jurisdiction and civil possessions in land and revenue amassed by the papacy, challenging its historic claim to supremacy. His reforming assault on clerical wealth and privilege, sustained throughout his prolific corpus, stands out as a monument of Christian reflection on law and authority, welding together theological and civil traditions into an imposing instrument of change.

As Wyclif conducted much of his campaign in his capacity as theological spokesman for powerful lay patrons, we should not overlook the circumstances and progression of his career, with its striking ironies and enigmas. The first twenty years, from approximately 1354 to 1374, connect him with Oxford and the Schoolmen, with such illustrious predecessors in the university as Robert Grosseteste (c.1175-1253), Johannes Duns Scotus (1265-1308), and William of Ockham among its friars, Richard Fitzralph (c.1295-1360) and Thomas Bradwardine (1290-1349) among its more recent seculars. Wyclif financed these years of uninterrupted study, lecturing and writing by successively occupying two clerical livings simultaneously with a joint canonry and prebend. As his modest income did not, apparently, permit him to honor the obligation attached to the canonry of providing a vicar in his stead, he was both an "absentee" and a "negligent" pluralist. While we may regard his practice as preposterously inconsistent with his profession, we must keep in mind that the financial options open to a secular clerical scholar invariably involved the abuses of absenteeism and pluralism, and that Wyclif's perpetuation of these abuses was unspectacular as compared with his more favoured colleagues.

As to his intellectual labor at Oxford, Wyclif distinguished himself in his early years as a fervent and capable defender of philosophical realism (that is, of the theory that the "universals" of meaning, intercourse, and thought have objective being), against the dominant Ockhamist tradition in which he had been educated. In his treatise on universals contained in his *"Summa" On Being* (c.1365-72), Wyclif, under the sway of St. Augustine and his disciples, attributes the highest being to the transcendent, unchanging, and eternal universals contained in the mind of God. These are the "Ideas"—the "patterns and paradigms" by which God creates all creaturely being, the divine causes of the universals or determining forms of finite substances.[1] On this realist foundation Wyclif later erects his controlling epistemological principle of the supreme authority of Scripture. For the Scriptural Word is the actualization in the world of the divine mind, bearing the transcendent universals of all created being. As such, it is the repository of all truth and all law, whether logical, ethical, metaphysical, physical, historical, and so on. Above all, it is the mirror of God's eternal will, incarnate in Jesus Christ, which is the salvation of His elect. Correspondingly, Wyclif comes to view the church universal as an eternal, immutable, and perfect archetypal unity, comprehending all the predestined—past, present and future.[2] Moreover, on the basis of his Augustinian realism, he judges universals to be superior objects of human desire; such that all sin consists in man's preferring a less universal to a more universal good.[3] This superiority of universal over particular will be reflected in his understanding of the commonwealth as comprised of universal spiritual goods held in common, and not by exclusive possession. These epistemological, ecclesiological, and political doctrines only receive separate and systematic development after Wyclif has entered the turbulent public forum.

He launched his political activity at "a critical and exceptional time" in the relations between the English church and the country's secular powers.[4] The unresolved conflicts in two areas of disputed claims had become intolerably acute. The first was the taxation of the clergy, the second, the pope's right of appointment to the higher offices of the English church. Both issues had been thrust into the foreground by the English Crown's protracted wars with France, in which nationalistic sentiment had expanded as the country's finances had contracted. During the dotage of Edward III and the minority of the future Richard II, the princes and magnates were engaged in a head-on collision course with the church over these delicate matters. When in 1370 the clergy in their convocation resisted a parliamentary request for a grant to meet rising military expenses, the new government of 1371 tried to wrest a large sum from the church by direct taxation. Almost as soon as the harassed clergy had reluctantly submitted, the lay government intervened, to the great relief of the prelates, to forbid their compliance with a similar papal order for war funds. Encouraged by the success of their interdict and the pope's

---

1. See Kenny, *Wyclif*, chaps. 1-2 for a concise and accessible synopsis of Wyclif's thought on universals, being, and truth.
2. The foundation of Wyclif's central epistemological and ecclesiological doctrines in his early realist commitment is argued persuasively by William Farr in *John Wyclif as Legal Reformer* (Leiden, 1974).
3. Kenny, *Wyclif*, 10.
4. McFarlane, *Wycliffe and English Non-Conformity*, 46.

strained finances, the King's councilors decided to press their opposition to the pope's claim to appoint to English benefices in the patronage of the church. Instead of invoking the entirely adequate existing legislation against papal "provision," the councilors, preferring to negotiate directly with Pope Gregory XI, mounted a diplomatic mission in 1374 to which Wyclif was appointed.[1]

Wyclif's entry into the royal service preceded his writing of *On Civil Dominion* (1375-6), his formidable treatise on civil rule and possession, divine and human law and authority, comprising the third book of his theological *Summa*. However, his reflections in this treatise draw on a longer involvement with the issue extending back to the Parliament of 1371, at which he heard two Austin friars of his acquaintance defend the government's right to conscribe the church's wealth in wartime by means of taxation and confiscation of property. It is not unjust to view Wyclif's treatise as a comprehensive reply to the clerical argument that, on account of the spirituality's superior authority, its property must be kept inviolate from secular uses.[2] While the theological import of Wyclif's ideas goes well beyond the practical question of ecclesiastical possessions, his arguments, nevertheless, prove him an able spokesman for the convictions and ambitions of the King's councillors, whose number included his powerful patron John of Gaunt, the second surviving son of Edward III. Not surprisingly, the publication of *On Civil Dominion* was ill-received by the English bishops, who, for this and other offenses, brought charges against Wyclif in 1377. As predictably, Pope Gregory XI issued bulls late in the same year condemning eighteen propositions from his works, and addressed to Edward III, the University of Oxford, and senior English prelates. Fortunately for Wyclif, the royal council ignored the bull and retained his official services, while the bishops, out of prudential considerations, did not press their charges.

Wyclif's voluminous writings toward the end of the decade appeared in the shadow of the Great Schism. By 1378 the successor of Pope Gregory XI, the Italian Pope Urban VI of Rome, had so alienated his cardinals that they elected a rival, Pope Clement VII, to reside at Avignon. While the schism undoubtedly spared Wyclif further papal persecution, it, nevertheless, scan-

---

1. The famous fourteenth century legislation against papal provision was comprised by the Statutes of Provisors (1351, 1390), which authorized harsh penalties (including imprisonment and expulsion) for prelates and clerks accepting papal appointment to higher English ecclesiastical "dignities"; and the Statutes of Praemunire (1353, 1365, 1393), which prohibited appeals from the royal courts to the papal courts in suits relating to the patronage of English benefices.

2. McFarlane, *Wycliffe and English Non-Conformity* indirectly imputes this intention to Wyclif's treatise.

dalized him, undermining the dignity of the papal office and breeding cynicism about its occupants. Thus, toward the end of 1378, he concluded his antipapal defence of the authority and inerrancy of Scripture, *On the Truth of Sacred Scripture*, followed in the next year by the sixth, seventh, and eighth treatises of his theological *Summa*: *On the Church*, *On the Office of King*, *On the Power of the Pope*. All of these arguments sought to set ecclesiastical authority on another footing than that of the present papacy, while adjusting its relationship to civil lordship in favour of the latter.

During his assault on the hierarchy, endowment, and abuses of the church, Wyclif sustained a following in secular and even religious circles. Only when he turned his attack on the doctrine of transubstantiation did he witness the wholesale defection of his sympathizers and allies. In 1380 the University of Oxford, which had hitherto jealously protected its rebel son, condemned two eucharistic propositions taught by Wyclif, and even John of Gaunt could not prevent his departure from the university.[1] To exacerbate Wyclif's vulnerable situation, his writings were claimed as inspiration by one of the leaders of the Peasant's Revolt, an anti-poll tax protest that broke out in 1381. This embarrassment was bitter medicine to a vigorous supporter of the lay nobility, who had always passed over the obvious revolutionary implications of his theory of civil dominion for secular authority, while exhibiting them relentlessly in the ecclesiastical sphere. However, Wyclif survived the incident to spend his few remaining years bombarding the clerical establishment from the reclusion of his living at Lutterworth. His doctrines were anathematized after his death by the Council of Constance (1415), which also tried and burnt his spiritual successor John Hus (c.1372-1415), leader of the revolutionary religious movement in Bohemia.

A. EVANGELICAL AND CIVIL DOMINION

In his treatise in three books, *On Civil Dominion*,[2] Wyclif repeatedly conceives dominion or lordship as a mode of having or possessing earthly goods by a title that confers the right of use and disposal in respect to them. This title is granted by God, as sovereign Lord of His creation, to the righteous or virtuous man, made deserving by divine grace.[3] Lacking divine grace

---

1. The two condemned propositions are: "that the substance of bread and wine remain[s] after the consecration, and that the body of Christ is not corporally but figuratively present in the sacrament." Kenny, *Wyclif*, 91.
2. J. Wyclif, *Tractatus De Civili Dominio*, ed. J. Loserth, for the Wyclif Society, 4 vols. (London, 1885-1904).
3. Ibid., 1: 6ff.

and approval, the sinner has no true or evangelical possession of temporalities: his "having" is merely "natural," "creaturely," issuing in nothing but abuse.[1] Occasionally, Wyclif describes "civil possession" as a third kind of having, distinct from both "natural" and "evangelical." His distinction between "natural" and "civil," however, refers primarily to the different types of goods possessed, whether of body and mind ("natural") or of external social possession ("civil"), rather than to the manner of possessing them. Nevertheless, the theological status of civil possession is an area of considerable ambiguity in Wyclif. On the one hand, he recognizes civil possession to be possession by title or right conferred by human authority (whether by law, convention, or royal prerogative). This humanly conferred right appears as a somewhat independent sphere of legitimacy and dignity intermediate between the spheres of natural and evangelical possession. On the other hand, he argues at length that the human grant of itself confers no right to possess, but only declares an anterior right granted by God.[2] He affirms with Ockham that God's authority is sufficient: His grant to the righteous does not stand in need of the human confirmation of civil title. Moreover, civil authority does not give legitimacy to unrighteous possession, for the latter violates the divine law upon which the institution of lordship rests. Thus the possession of natural or civil goods by the unrighteous is an unlawful appropriation of them from their rightful possessors. But God permits this appropriation for a time, to carry out His manifold purposes of punishing the unrighteous, testing His saints, and manifesting His mercy to good and bad alike.

Not only does civil authority not confer right of possession, the right that it does confer is essentially incompatible with righteous possession. Here Wyclif applies to the sphere of lordship St. Augustine's doctrine of the two opposing loves entrenched in Franciscan theology—love of God and love of self. The opposition, broadly speaking, is between a divinely directed love, wherein created beings are loved in and through God as objects of His love, and an earthly directed love, wherein created beings are loved before God and instead of Him. In the light of this polarity, righteous possession of earthly goods is possession by participation in God's knowledge and love of the world. To the righteous, God chiefly gives Himself, as charity and grace; and whoever has God, has all creaturely things in their ideal being, as directly loved and known by Him, and consequently also in their actual existence. With Ockham and the whole Franciscan tradition, Wyclif believes that righteous possession is that spiritual possession of earthly goods promised by

1. Ibid., 1: 16ff.
2. Ibid., 1: 25ff.

Christ to those who have sacrificed all for His sake and the sake of the Gospel in Mark 10:25, 30. It is the possession of everything in common that characterized the apostolic and sub-apostolic communities. A more abundant mode of having, spiritual possession is inclusive, permitting an unlimited number of "lords," and inalienable, except by unrighteousness. Thus spiritual lordship is far removed from civil lordship, which is essentially divisive, exclusive, and alienable at pleasure.[1]

As contingent upon the fall of mankind from his "natural" (created) state of innocence, civil possession needs to be protected by coercive human sanctions: they alone can safeguard the separate interest of each man in his property and his liberty to dispose of it. But it is just this separate interest in property that constitutes the sin of civil possession, in that it necessarily entails an inordinate attachment to worldly goods to the detriment of the love of their Giver.[2] In civil possession, property is put in the service of its lord, or the community of titled lords; whereas, in evangelical possession temporal goods commonly held are put in the service of God and neighbor, according to the divine law of love.[3] In the world to come all possession will be evangelical: common administration of goods under the lordship of Christ.

Wyclif's polarization of evangelical and civil lordship suggests that the civil sphere is one of institutionalized sin (albeit necessary in this fallen world), with which Christ's faithful followers should have nothing to do. There would seem to be an eschatological tension between the community of Christ's disciples and civil organization that is potentially revolutionary. Indeed, the revolutionary implications of this tension were not lost on Wyclif's historical progeny, the descendents of the Hussites in Bohemia and Moravia, with their sectarian perfectionism, nor entirely on his own countrymen. Nevertheless, the destabilisation of feudalistic and hierarchical social organization was neither intended nor effected by his theology of lordship, and the explanation for this lies primarily in his doctrine of the church.

B. THE CHURCH MILITANT UNDER THE LAW OF CHRIST

The community of the predestined, past, present, and future, has a threefold being: as the "church militant" struggling on earth, as the "sleeping church" resting in purgatory, and as the church triumphant reigning eternally with Christ.[4] The unity of the predestined church is the mystical unity of the

---

1. Ibid., 1: 47ff., 125ff.
2. Ibid., 1: 127ff.; 3: 160ff.
3. Ibid., 1: 77ff., 96; 3: 178ff.
4. Ibid., 1: 381.

body of Christ: the unity of a single supernatural universal in which all the predestined participate.¹ The church militant, however, as a temporal and visible allegiance, is "a mixed body," consisting of the predestined and the reprobate together. It is coterminous with the Christian society, the political community or "realm," so that the universal church militant is an aggregate federation of discrete realms.² The structure of the church is, therefore, the hierarchical, diversified structure of the realm, composed of the three orders of clergy, temporal lords, and commons, which are the politically represented orders of late medieval society.³ In that the whole church is bound by the law of Christ, each estate embodies this rule in its distinctive activities. And yet the efficacy of each depends on the organic complementarity of them all, and this means a subjection of the lower to the higher. The clergy comprise the highest order, their office being the closest imitation of Christ's spiritual life of poverty, chastity, contemplation, and charity. To perform their office of spiritual lordship, the clergy must live "exproprietarily," without civil possessions and jurisdiction. Both possessions and jurisdiction properly belong to the temporal lords, whose office it is to defend Christ's law with coercive authority, punishing evil-doers and protecting the entire church militant. Ranking below the temporal lords in wealth and jurisdiction are the commons, whose office is to sustain the superior orders by laboring with their hands or practicing a craft or industry.

Wyclif's functional division of the church intersects his theory of lordship in a complex manner. On the one hand, his sharp distinction between the offices of the clergy and the temporal lords reinforces the polarity between civil and evangelical lordship. Only the clergy are fitted for evangelical lordship by their dispossessed state patterned directly on Christ's example. The temporal lords, by their propertied state, are fitted for an inferior lordship, encumbered by venial sins and the superfluities of the flesh. On the other hand, Wyclif's functional hierarchy constitutes a stable social and ethical order in which all the estates have a share in legitimacy. Within the church militant the temporal lords perform a divinely ordained service that is teleologically ordered to the higher evangelical virtue. Despite its necessary imperfections, civil lordship remains a form of obedience to the law of Christ, against which the civil possessor need not be guilty of more than minor abuses.

1. Ibid., 1: 360.
2. J. Wyclif, *Sermones*, ed. J. Loserth, for the Wyclif Society (London, 1886-1889), 4 vols., 4: 7, 179; J. Wyclif, *Tractatus De Ecclesia*, ed. J. Loserth, for the Wyclif Society (London, l886), 30, 424.
3. Wyclif, *Sermones*, 2: 22-26, 175-176.

Parallel to Wyclif's polarization of civil and evangelical lordship is his polarization of civil and evangelical law, the latter polarization being similarly affected by his functionally diversified ecclesiology. On the one hand, the evangelical law is the eternally perfect and sufficient rule of the predestined church, being the command of Christ, the uncreated Law.[1] By the law of charity, Christ, "our law-giver" (*legiter noster*), keeps His people in His love, procuring their salvation. Only obedience to this law is the vocation of all Christians.

The universal obligation to honor Christ's law is for Wyclif the most commanding justification of a Bible-reading laity. The Bible alone gives clear, simple, and certain knowledge of Christ's law; ecclesiastical tradition, by contrast, offers confused, difficult, and uncertain knowledge—truth alloyed with error, God's word alloyed with man's word. Moreover, in that the human tradition of the church represents an ongoing defection from the Gospel, the present teaching of prelates, theologians, and parish priests alike is bound to contradict and confute rather than confirm the teaching of Christ.[2] To halt the church's waywardness, both clergy and laity must be directly instructed by Holy Scripture, wherein they will discover the chief necessity of preaching and practicing God's Word. This chief necessity constitutes the "dignity' of the priesthood—this, and not celebration of the Eucharist.[3]

The sufficiency of the evangelical law for the church renders additional human laws (canonical or civil) unnecessary and undesirable. Either they accord with Christ's law, thereby proving "superfluous," or they run contrary to His law, thereby violating His will. In either case they are injurious, offending the completeness and sovereignty of Christ's command. To the objection that man's present sinful condition prevents the single adoption of Christ's law, Wyclif replies that this law includes adequate measures for the disciplining of evil-doers. The evangelical law is perfectly suited to govern the realm, in that it best teaches righteousness, provides just rules for the punishment of offenders, and makes clear the due rewards of the wicked and the good. Secular authorities may be assured of their full power under Christ to extirpate evil-doing, as Scripture teaches in Matthew 10:34 and Romans 13:4.[4]

In undermining the civil law, Wyclif, however, cannot escape the legal requirements of civil possession. He cannot simply dispense with the body of law evolved to secure the peaceful administration of property. His admission

---

1. Wyclif, *De Civili Dominio*, 1: 348-9; 2: 179.
2. J. Wyclif, *De Veritate Sacrae Scripturae*, ed. R. Buddensieg, for the Wyclif Society (London, 1905-1907), 3 vols., 2: 129ff.
3. Ibid., 2: 150ff.
4. Wyclif, *De Civili Dominio*, 1: 432-36.

of the temporal lords as an estate of the church commits him to viewing the civil law as distinct from but conformable to the evangelical law.[1] Indeed, he conspicuously incorporates English common and statute law into his legal machinery for the evangelical reform of the clerical estate. Restoring the evangelical law to the church militant means returning the clergy to the condition of apostolic dispossession. To accomplish this requires an appeal to English civil law for the purpose of establishing the legal right of the temporal lords to dispossess the clergy.[2] Against the Hildebrandine argument that the legal authority of the church's temporal endowment derives by hereditary right from Christ and His apostles as possessors of all earthly goods, Wyclif first asserts the poverty of Christ and His disciples, and then invokes the "charters of our realm" to prove that all ecclesiastical property had been conferred originally by the laity in the form of free alms, with the intention of freeing the clergy from worldly cares so that they might devote themselves wholly to prayer, alms-giving, and administration of the sacraments. The nature of the endowment is such that the donors may withdraw it, should they judge to be inadequately performed the services for which it was conferred.[3] In Wyclif's opinion, the clergy, by seeking worldly wealth and jurisdiction, have made fraudulent use of their endowment, frustrating the intention of the donors. Consequently, the temporal lords have the right to deprive them of their endowment. This lay prerogative is particularly applicable to the lower clergy who lack proper episcopal oversight and correction.[4] While Wyclif's appeal to English law is habitually vague and oversimplified, (in, for example, his blurring of historically distinct types of tenure), nevertheless, he is drawing on a legal principle established by a considerable body of legislation when he contends that all clerical endowment is conditional, such that intervention in the church's affairs is a legal right of the laity.[5]

---

1. Ibid., 1: 130, 185-6.
2. Wyclif's "legal artifice" of ecclesiastical reform is succinctly and comprehensively laid out in the second part of Farr, *John Wyclif as Legal Reformer*.
3. Wyclif, *De Veritate Sacrae Scripturae*, 3: 13-19. The endowment is held by feudal tenure based on a "bilateral agreement" of the form "*do ut facias.*" Farr, *John Wyclif as Legal Reformer*, 101.
4. Wyclif, *De Veritate Sacrae Scripturae*, 3: 19-26.
5. Farr, *John Wyclif as Legal Reformer* provides a detailed account of the legislation embodying the various legal aspects of this principle, including: the Second Statute of Westminster and the Statute of Carlisle, issued by Edward I in 1285 and 1306 respectively, the latter elaborated upon by Edward III in 1350-51 and 1376; the Statutes of Provisors and Praemunire issued by Edward III in 1351 and 1353 (see note 9), this legislation of Edward occurring within Wyclif's lifetime.

C. THE PONTIFICAL KING

In regard to property, the law of the land is the law of the church. As significantly, the civil law is the king's law, the king being the lord of all the temporalities of his domain, its supreme legislator and chief magistrate. In the office of the king the unity of the two laws—civil and evangelical, human and divine—comes to repose for Wyclif. For the king, as pre-eminent legislator and judge, is foremost defender of God's law and executor of His justice. Not the pope but the king alone is sovereign in the realm, holding a plenitude of jurisdiction by divine mandate. Accepting the necessity of a single, undivided, sovereign authority, Wyclif makes the king both supreme protector and supreme interpreter of the evangelical law. It is the king's duty not only to compel obedience to God's law, but to ordain righteous laws, and to annul unrighteous ones.[1] For this latter undertaking, he must, above all else, be instructed in the law of God; in the pursuit of which wisdom he will place himself under the guidance of trusted theologians. Only those who have devoted their lives to "searching the Scriptures" are worthy and able to arm the king against the "sophisticated evasions" of God's law taught and practiced by the clerical hierarchy, from the pope downward.[2] The security of the realm makes it especially imperative that the king have sound theological advice on two matters: on what constitutes heresy, and on the real scope of the royal power over against the "blasphemous excess of power" claimed by the pope.[3] While not extolling kingship as the absolutely best form of rule—that distinction belongs to the aristocracy of judges ruling by the divine law alone, as I Samuel makes clear—Wyclif nonetheless exalts the theologically informed evangelical king, ruling by means of a civil law conformed to the law of Christ, as the best regime under the conditions of human sinfulness.[4]

Just as Wyclif spiritualizes priestly authority, causing it to rest on demonstrated virtue and the fulfillment of evangelical duties, so he concentrates temporal authority in the secular offices crowned by the royal office. The office of the king surpasses all others in the "palpable honor" (*honorificencia sensibilis*) owing to it, chiefly because it is a sensible representation of divine sovereignty. Thus men's reverential fear of the king as God's vicar reflects their reverential fear of God Himself.[5] Bearing the image of Christ's Godhead, the king ministers His law with bold severity, whereas the

---

1. Wyclif, *De Civili Dominio*, 1: 188-90.
2. Ibid., 1: 403-4.
3. J. Wyclif, *Tractatus De Officio Regis*, eds. A. W. Pollard and C. Sayle, for the Wyclif Society (London, 1887), 125.
4. Wyclif, *De Civili Dominio*, 1: 185-199.
5. Wyclif, *De Officio Regis*, 5, 14.

priest, bearing the image of Christ's manhood, ministers the same law with gentle persuasion.[1] Only strict obedience to the king's law is consonant with the honor due to his office, as we are instructed by Christ Himself (Matt. 22:21) as well as by St. Peter (I Pet. 2:13-14, 17) and St. Paul (Rom. 13:1-7). Even to the unjust, sinful and tyrannical ruler, subjection is due on account of the dignity of his office, as long as the wrongs he perpetrates are injurious only to his subjects' welfare and not to the cause of God (*causa dei*).[2] In the former instance, the injured must endure their affliction with the patience of Job; in the latter, they are called to faithful resistance unto death.[3]

By contrast, the obedience owing to degenerate priests takes the form, not of patient endurance, but of considered reproof, stern argument, and forceful resistance.[4] Thus when the king's law is being violated by the clergy's immoral, fraudulent, and extortionate abuse of their temporal endowment (which habitual abuse, argues Wyclif, is both heretical and treasonous), the king and his appointed officers are entitled and obliged to correct the abuses and punish the offenders with the confiscation of their property, as the civil law provides in such criminal conduct. As the bishops derive their jurisdiction from the king, they, too, are susceptible of correction and the punishment of forfeiture, unless they prove their service to the realm by implementing its righteous laws for the edification of clergy and laity alike. Wyclif offers three such laws for restoring the church to Christ's rule: firstly, that the bishops be obliged to oversee clerical discipline in their dioceses, correcting faults and encouraging virtues; secondly, that the king through his bishops enforce the residence in all parishes of learned and zealous curates, whether native or foreign; and, thirdly, that the king undertake the extension, defence and reform of the theological faculty, by exercising his prerogative in

---

1. Ibid., 13. This theologically arresting notion of the two images of Christ's Godhead and manhood, borne by king and priest respectively, is not original to Wyclif, but has a history in earlier medieval contests between the secular and ecclesiastical powers. For example, it is developed quite elaborately in the fourth treatise of the *Tractatus Eboracenses*, a collection of controversial pamphlets that appeared during the dispute over lay investiture of bishops between Anselm of Canterbury and the kings of England (1100-1107). To demonstrate the just authority of the king over the priest, the author maintains that: "The Priest represents the human nature of Christ, in which he is inferior to the Father, while the king represents Christ's divine nature, in which he is equal to the Father; the priest represents Christ as suffering death, and offering himself as a sacrifice to God the Father, the king represents Christ as about to be crowned with glory and honor, and to reign for ever in his heavenly throne over all authorities and powers." See R. W. Carlyle and A. J. Carlyle, *Mediaeval Political Theory in the West*, 6 vols. (London, 1903-1936), 4: 274. See also ibid., 3: 135-6.
2. Wyclif, *De Officio Regis*, 5-9.
3. Ibid., 8.
4. Ibid., 21.

presenting competent theologians to benefices and in relieving the theological curriculum of its superfluous and unedifying lectures in Roman civil law.[1]

Such is Wyclif's program for converting the degraded liberty of the Hildebrandine church into true evangelical freedom. While his reforming vision harbors the specter of a new servitude—a mere revolution in the sense of the eternal return of the same—it also harbors the promise of a real emancipation for the church that will continue to exhibit its binding force to future generations.

---

1. Ibid., 152-192.

Three

Sir John Fortescue and the Law of Nature

Sir John Fortescue (c.1396-c.1486), whose major writings succeed Wyclif's by nearly a century, presents us with a natural temper, an intellectual orientation, and a public career far removed from Wyclif's. For Wyclif was a theologian, eager to press English civil law into the service of theological ends, while Fortescue is a common lawyer, devoted to the legal and judicial welfare of his country, and convinced that theological knowledge makes an indispensable, if limited, contribution to this end. Whereas Wyclif's political thought drew on an Augustinian tradition that collapsed the fundamental tensions of Augustine's dualistic vision in the direction of monarchial absolutism, Fortescue's political thought draws on a Thomistic-Aristotelian tradition of natural-law thinking oriented to steering England's limited monarchy toward increased respect for the rule of law. Consistent with their divergent theoretical and practical orientations, Wyclif endorsed a single epistemological and political authority, while Fortescue endorses a pluralistic balance of authorities in both the epistemological and political realms. Temperamentally and intellectually, Fortescue conforms much more to the "*via media*" spirit of the Anglican tradition. Indeed, the translator of his treatise on natural law recognizes an important continuity when he remarks parenthetically on the resemblance between the first part of this work and the first book of Richard Hooker's *Laws of Ecclesiastical Polity*.[1] One might wish that Fortescue's exposition and application of natural-law theory had Hooker's coherence and clarity. However, to dwell on its theoretical shortcomings would be to miss its primary significance in furthering the consolidation and development of English legal and political traditions. It must be remembered that Fortescue was not only England's most influential legal-political thinker of the fifteenth century, but also its most distinguished judicial personage. His theological formulations are deserving of our attention not least because of their practical, legal applications.

Fortescue's public career is remarkably full and eminent. Born around 1396, he was a member of Lincoln's Inn before 1420 and its governor three times. Elected to parliament seven times between 1421 and 1437, he was made a sergeant-at-law in 1430. Over 25 years he served as justice of the peace 35 times in 17 counties or boroughs and was made chief justice of the King's Bench in 1442.[2] Here, we are told, "his reputation as a great judge was soon and permanently established, and here he continued for more than eighteen years to pronounce those judgments and expositions of the laws which are still quoted with respect."[3]

Fortescue's legal career was abruptly terminated in 1461 by the dethronement of his royal master, King Henry VI, and the accession to the throne of Edward Duke of York. His fate was joined to the deposed king's, not only by virtue of his high appointment, but also on account of his constant support of the Lancastrian title to the throne against the claims of York. His estates forfeited upon his attainder by parliament, he travelled north with the royal forces, finally fleeing to Edinburgh with the defeated king and queen, where he continued to serve Henry VI as his "chief counsellor." It was probably during this exile in Scotland that he composed his treatise *On the Law of Nature*,[4] wherein he applied the law of nature to the determination of the rightful succession to the English throne. After the capture and imprisonment of Henry VI, he accompanied Queen Margaret and Prince Edward to France, remaining with them seven years. From his exile near St. Mihiel he wrote *In*

---

1. The Right Hon. Chichester Fortescue notes this resemblance in the concluding paragraph of his "Remarks" on *De Natura Legis Naturae* in *The Works of Sir John Fortescue, Knight*, collected by Thomas (Fortescue) Lord Clermont (London, 1869), 346.

2. These biographical details are supplied by E.F. Jacob's brief account of Fortescue's life in *The Fifteenth Century: 1399-1485*, in *The Oxford History of England*, ed. Sir George Clark (Oxford, 1961). Fuller biographical and chronological accounts accompany the translations of his writings.

3. *Life of Sir John Fortescue*, in *The Works of Sir John Fortescue*, 8.

4. J. Fortescue, *De Natura Legis Naturae*, reprinted in *The Works of Sir John Fortescue*, 65-184.

Praise of the Laws of England,[1] a glowing apology for the government and laws of England, to which his devotion never wavered. While in France he figured prominently in negotiations between Queen Margaret and the Earl of Warwick, issuing in a proposed alliance that carried the promise of an undertaking to restore Henry VI to power. In anticipation of such a restoration, Fortescue committed to paper certain proposals of an administrative and reforming kind, intended to "strengthen the effective power of the Crown" in England, under the title *On the Monarchy of England*.[2] A stroke of extreme misfortune deprived his proposals of any immediate influence, for on April 14, 1471, the very day of his arrival in England with Margaret and the prince, Warwick was slain and Henry VI captured at Barnet. Although taken prisoner at a subsequent battle, Fortescue was spared and his estates returned to him for his last years in retirement, but the attainder was not reversed until he had written in defence of King Edward IV's title, refuting his earlier arguments against it.

The most enduring and influential features of Fortescue's thought are his grounding of kingly rule in the law of nature, and his division of it into two types: royal, and royal and political. Neither his elaboration of the law of nature nor his analysis of kingship exhibits originality, being for the most part repetition of concepts and categories found in Aquinas, Aristotle, and Augustine. It is, perhaps, the conceptual ambiguities and shifts in Fortescue's thought that hold most interest for us, as reflecting Renaissance tendencies toward intellectual rationalism and pluralism.

A. THE AUTHORITY OF THE LAW OF NATURE

In *On the Law of Nature* Fortescue refers a weighty question concerning the right of royal succession in sovereign kingdoms to the law of nature. While recognizing that not all questions of legal right and equity require resolution by direct recourse to the law of nature, he argues the insufficiency of human law to decide this case. The pronouncements of Roman civil law, although capable of displaying "the merits of this case," lack the authority "to decide it absolutely"; whereas those of the "sacred canons," although possessing the requisite authority, do not offer a certain determination of the issue.[3] Only the law of nature gives authoritative and certain judgment in the matter: authoritative, because it is superior in excellence and dignity to all human

---

1. J. Fortescue, *De Laudibus Legum Angliae*, reprinted in ibid., 337-383.
2. Jacob, *The Fifteenth Century*, 314. The work is reprinted in *The Works of Sir John Fortescue*, 449-474.
3. J. Fortescue, *De Natura Legis Naturae*, in *The Works of Sir John Fortescue*, 66.

"customs" (*consuetudines*) and "statutes" (*statuta*), certain, because every just form of human rule is established by, and takes its right from the law of nature—"under it the power of kings took its beginning; by its authority and force also all just kings have reigned and do reign."[1]

The excellence and superior dignity of the law of nature resides in its origin and essence: for it was instituted by God "from the beginning of the rational creation, and varies not by time, but abides immutable."[2] The law of nature is an emanation of the original justice bestowed on man at his creation, being "of one quality and essence" (*unius esse qualitatis et essentiae*) with it.[3] Indeed, Fortescue defines the law of nature as "the truth of justice which is capable of being revealed by right reason" (*justitiae veritas quae recta ratione poterit revelari*).[4] As justice is coeval with man, so, too, is the law of nature. It is justice that determines the relationship of the law of nature to human rule.

Original justice, Fortescue tells us, is God's gift to man by which he is empowered to fulfil his divinely decreed "office" of "prelacy" or "primacy" (*praelatoram*). When God created the first man "to rule all living things of the earth," He equipped him with "the rule and model of governing."[5] This model is that of "uprightness," called by Anselm "rectitude of will" and by Augustine "a good will." It is "a constant and perpetual will assigning to each and every man his right," as the civil laws say of justice. It is, as St. Thomas says, the will by which those who govern guide "free men to their own good or to the common good."[6] In transgressing God's commandment by the evil-working of his own mutable will, Adam repudiated this divinely granted unchangeable will. He thereby lapsed into that purely natural state of corruption and mortality wherein his reason was no longer subject to the supernatural Good, his lower passions no longer subject to his reason. Nevertheless, justice did not desert sinful man, although deserted by him; as "God, who fills the whole world with His essence, presence, and power, is sometimes present, sometimes absent, so doth justice abide ever in man, and with man, never devoid of effect, but always ruling him and paying him, one way or the other, the wages which he hath earned."[7] Deprived of the power of super-natural

1. Ibid., 68.
2. Ibid.
3. Ibid., 99.
4. Ibid., 101.
5. Ibid., 98.
6. Ibid., 97.
7. Ibid., 103-104.

grace to make man equal with the angels, justice is still justice, the same in its essence and operation.

Thus natural law is unchanged by the changed state of man, being the continual pouring forth of the forces of justice "in diverse modes" that "obtain diverse names."[1] Concretely, the law of nature embraces a multiplicity of forms, some of which precede man's sin, others of which are necessitated by it. If these concrete forms appear contradictory, the contradiction does not reside in justice itself, but in the altered human condition. For instance, the law of nature created property and, consequently, all types of contract contingent on it. Property, however, did not belong to Adam's "state of innocence," but arose with his expulsion from the garden and sentencing to a life of toil for the necessities of existence. The law of nature rules both states of humanity with "constant and perpetual" justice, says Fortescue, "and thus the equity of natural justice, which once allotted to man in his innocence a share of all things, is no other than that equity which for his offence deprives man, corrupted by sin, of the blessing of such community."[2]

The immutable principle of natural justice that gives substance to the law of nature is definitively expressed by the commandment of Jesus: "All things whatsoever ye would that men should do to you, do ye even so to them; for this is the law and the prophets" (Matt. 7:12). The "law" to which Jesus refers, Fortescue tells us on the authority of "the Canons," is the law of nature, which, it would seem, is identical with the second of the "two greatest commandments" upon which hang "all the law and the Prophets." In other words, the law of nature embodies one half of the evangelical law, concerning what is due to our neighbor. It stands in no tension, but is one with the law of Christ's kingdom, the law of love. And so Fortescue says: "This Law of Nature all the laws of the Old and New Testament approved, diminishing nothing therefrom; nay, the Lord says of it, as of the rest of his law, 'I came not to destroy the law, but to fulfil [it]'"[3]

Consistent with this exalted standing of the law of nature is its relationship to the eternal law (*Lex Eterna*). Fortescue accepts the identity of the eternal law and divine providence, defining Providence, in dependence upon Boethius, as "the manifold method" laid down by the divine mind for the ordering of all things subject to movement and change. He offers St. Thomas's understanding of the law of nature as the "participation of the Eternal Law in a rational creature" whereby "it hath a natural inclination to its rightful action

1. Ibid., 100.
2. Ibid., 83.
3. Ibid., 67.

and end."[1] He concludes that, just as men "by grace of participation of Divinity . . . are counted worthy to be called, not sons of God only, but gods" (according to the Psalmist), so the law of nature "is worthy to bear the name of Divine Law, by way of imitation, indeed, and not of equality."[2]

This analogy raises the question, the answer to which is enshrouded in ambiguity in Fortescue's thought, as to the role of the law of nature in man's salvation. St. Thomas is clear that conformity to the law of nature does not bring man to eternal bliss, but only conformity to the divine law revealed in the Gospel of Jesus Christ, which is the law of grace—of faith, hope, and love. For St. Thomas the revealed law of the New Testament comprehends the law of nature, but transcends it in its new demands, embodying a fuller knowledge of the eternal law. Unfortunately, he does not employ St. Thomas' succinct categories of "eternal," "natural," "divine," and "human" law, but rather blurs the distinctions between the eternal law and the divine law, the law of nature, and the Gospel law of grace. Thus, in treating of human laws, Fortescue says that they are all "instruments whereby the Divine Law develops its virtues in human actions," without clarifying whether these virtues belong to saving grace or to fallen human nature.[3] The categorial distinctions are further collapsed in the opening chapters of *In Praise of the Laws of England*, where Fortescue, by way of exhorting Prince Edward to "the study of the laws," describes human laws as "rules whereby the perfect notion of justice can be determined," that justice which "is virtue absolute and perfect, and distinguished by the name of Legal Justice." In the acquisition of such "universal virtue" consists the greatest human happiness available in this life; consequently, "he who has attained this justice . . . has attained the *summum bonum* or beatitude," an attainment not effected by "the law itself . . . exclusive of divine grace," but only by the law "through the divine concurrence" (*preveniente et comitante gratia*).[4] Fortescue nowhere in this treatise distinguishes the complete virtue to which human laws conduce from the supernatural virtue of charity that fulfills the divine law. Everywhere there are indications that the rule of just human laws in civil society is the earthly anticipation of Christ's eternal rule.

We are not, therefore, prepared for his occasional contrasting of the divine law with the law of nature and with human law. In one place he contrasts the divine law and the law of nature by means of the Thomistic-Augustinian distinction between spiritual contemplation and the practice of

---

1. Ibid., 107, quoting Thomas Aquinas, *Summa Theologiae*, 1a2ae, q. 91, art. 2.
2. Ibid., 107.
3. Ibid., 109.
4. J. Fortescue, *De Laudibus Legum Angliae*, in *The Works of Sir John Fortescue*, 340.

justice. The divine law he calls "the greater light which rules the day of our spiritual life, wherein we contemplate God, and enjoy Him here on earth," while the law of nature is "the lesser light . . . which rules the dark night of this our temporal conversation, wherein we sojourn far from the Lord, doing justly in this life by His grace alone."[1] In the following chapter of *On the Law of Nature*, he expounds the diverse ends of divine and human law. Whereas human law directs man to those virtues whereby earthly peace and love "may be nourished and preserved," divine law directs him to his ultimate beatitude, consisting in "the divine vision . . . alone" (*in sola visione divina consistit*).[2] Here divine law is synonymous with divine providence, under which name, says Fortescue, we also speak of "the New as of the Old Testament."[3] Finally, Fortescue develops the implications for political authority of the epistemological subordination of the law of nature to the divine law , proposing that the "rulers in the law Divine" ought to rule the "rulers in human law," correcting their defects and effecting their amendment. Notwithstanding the necessity for the secular judge to be "well versed" in the divine law, "in doubtful matters he [ought to] follow the decree of the supreme Pontiff" (*Summi Sacerdotis*).[4]

Perhaps the most revealing of Fortescue's thought on the relationship among the different types of law is his method of proceeding toward a resolution of the urgent, practical issue concerning the right of succession to the English throne. His defense of the claim of Lancaster against York hinges on the argument that the right of succession in a sovereign kingdom cannot descend to a woman, or through her, to her male offspring, owing to her exclusion from the right to govern by the law of nature and the law divine.[5] In developing his argument he shows how the divine law "approves" and "confirms" the law of nature, "under the form and with the effect of positive decree." God's promulgations of the law of nature in the Old and New Testaments comprise a double benefit, in that they eliminate "every suspicion of error" in respect to the law, and as well, strengthen the duty of observance

---

1. Ibid., 107.
2. Ibid., 111, quoting pseudo-Thomas Aquinas, *De Regimine Principum*, bk. 3.
3. *The Works of Sir John Fortescue*, 111.
4. Ibid., 113.
5. S.B. Chrimes is right to emphasize the centrality to Fortescue's argument of "the rules of succession to real property." The superior title to the kingdom of the late king's brother over the daughter rests on the public nature of the property. The inheritance was attached to an office, the duties of which only a male heir could perform. Interestingly, Chrimes regards Fortescue's lengthy argument for such a public property rule of succession as testifying "to the absence of any accepted legal principles of royal succession." See S.B. Chrimes, *English Constitutional Ideas in the Fifteenth Century* (Cambridge, 1936), 10-13.

by the force of command, rendering the penalty for violation more severe.[1] The Biblical evidence for the subordination of the woman illustrates this relationship. According to the Book of Genesis, "human law has enacted that the woman be subject to the man", and, in order that she "may never throw off that yoke, Divine law has constituted the man her master; so that if she refuse to do willingly what nature hath decreed, she may be compelled to do it by the power which the Divine law has conferred."[2] Thus, in aspiring to rule a kingdom, a woman is guilty of the graver sin, and susceptible of the heavier punishment, for violating God's express command than for violating the enactment of nature's law.

If, as Fortescue demonstrates, the divine judgment resolves the legal issue in question more certainly and forcefully than the law of nature, why does he argue his case from the law of nature? The answer lies in the epistemological and ontological priority of this law. Without the prior enactment of the law of nature, he explains, God's sentence on Eve would be groundless and unintelligible; its validity and intelligibility for us depend on our rational subjection to nature's law. He states the case for moral rationalism with unusual clarity: ". . . the things which are forbidden by the moral commandments are not on that account sins . . . but because they were before found to be sins by the law of nature they were also forbidden by Divine edict. . . ."[3]

B. THE CASE FOR ROYAL AND POLITICAL RULE

As the law of nature has established all forms of just rule over men, so it is empowered to decide the best form of human rule. According to Fortescue, "the kingly dignity" *as such* was created, and continues to be governed, by the law of nature; however, the form of kingly rule that embodies the law most fully is the "political rule" of kings. Following St. Thomas, he distinguishes "royal rule" and "political rule," only to argue that their combination constitutes the best regime. He is chiefly concerned to contrast the historical

---

1. *The Works of Sir John Fortescue*, 143. Significantly, in Fortescue's thought the relationship between human custom and statute law parallels that between the law of nature and positive divine command. That is, custom becomes statute by being committed to writing on the order of the king, with the command that it should be observed; and this conversion both places the subjects under greater obligation of obedience to the law, and calls for stiffer penalties for its violation, the offense now being against the king's command. See generally, Fortescue, *De Natura Legis Naturae*, chap. 30 and discussion of statutes in Fortescue's theory in Chrimes, *English Constitutional Ideas*, 201-203.
2. *The Works of Sir John Fortescue*, 143.
3. Ibid., 146.

origins, controlling forms, and merits of royal rule and royal-political rule, paying little attention to political rule as a discrete form.[1]

In *On the Law of Nature*, Fortescue introduces his distinction of types in the context of defending kingship against the objections to it expressed in I Samuel 8 and 12. In I Samuel 8, the Lord interprets the Israelites' petition to Samuel for a king as a rejection of his own reign over them and commands Samuel to declare to the people the evil, exploitative "manner" of the king whom they desire. To clarify the divine judgment, Fortescue, in dependence on Giles of Rome's *De Regimine Principum*, distinguishes regal and political government: whereas "the head" of a regal government rules "according to the laws which he himself lays down and according to his own will and pleasure," the head of a political government "governs the citizens according to the laws which they have established." He quickly passes on to the third type of government, illustrated by the "kingdom of England," wherein "the kings make not laws, nor impose subsidies on their subjects, without the consent of the three Estates of the Realms." This third regime is "political" because "regulated by the administration of many" and "royal" because "the subjects themselves cannot make laws without the authority of the sovereign, and the kingdom is possessed by kings and their heirs successively in hereditary right. . . ."[2] Now the Israelites under the judges were subject to "royal and

---

1. Chrimes' exposition of Fortescue's theory of "mixed dominion" (*dominion regale et politicum*)—its sources in St. Thomas, its meaning and historical importance—is highly illuminating. Especially instructive is his distinguishing of Fortescue's conception from later formulations of constitutional monarchy (e.g., by Algernon Sidney and John Locke), in that he interprets Fortescue's apparent discounting of the *dominion politicum* option. According to Chrimes, Fortescue, in expounding the origin of mixed dominion, "completely confused the origin of political society and the formation of the monarchical state by treating them as one phenomenon. In his view, the people, when joining together in political society, necessarily (*semper oportet*) established at the same time one ruler over them, and this ruler was king. He did not conceive, as Locke did, that the people might agree to unite first, and later, by some further compact, appoint a ruler to rule according to an agreed code of laws. His social contract was also itself the political one. . . . The act of incorporation and the establishment of the monarch were part and parcel of the maintenance of law; there could be none of these without the others, any more than in a physical organism the head, heart, and nerves could live without one another. Without the incorporation of the people and the establishment of the ruler, law could not be maintained; and law unmaintained is not law. But the purpose of law was to protect the people in their lives and goods, and therefore the king, when established, had no power to change the law or to seize the property of the people. King and law were bound up together; no king, no law—no law, no king. . . . For the only power the king had was from them, and he had it for the maintenance of law. But he did have this power, and he had it absolutely. Once given, it could not be taken away without the dissolution of the body politic. . . ." Chrimes, *English Constitutional Ideas*, 319-20.

2. *The Works of Sir John Fortescue*, 77.

political" rule, in that God Himself ruled Israel "as His peculiar kingdom," while their judges "administered everything for their common advantage" (*omnia ad eorum commune . . . ministrabant*).[1] The kingly rule appointed for them by God as a punishment for their rebellious spirit was to be a "royal" rule, rule by the selfish and arbitrary will of an unrestrained monarch. Such a tyranny, while not a complete violation of the law of nature, is an insufficient form, it would appear, because it neglects the common good and lacks the consent of the governed. The common good (we may assume) is defined by the principle of natural justice that commands men to do unto others as they would have others do unto them. Fortescue implies that knowledge of natural justice is obtained by the counsels of many, that exceed in prudence the counsels of a few. And so his full conception of royal-political rule combines the principles of public consent to laws, public involvement in their construction, and the laws' conformity to natural justice. "The law of a king ruling royally and politically," he says in summary, "is always subject to the rules of the law of nature. . . ."[2]

It is clear from Fortescue's discussion of types of rule that the basis of political and legal authority—the law of nature—has manifold elements. This diversity is sharply expressed in the opposing origins of "royal" and "royal and political" rule. Royal rule, he tells us, originated in the evil designs of powerful men who, by means of conquest and forceful subjection of peoples, "assured and usurped to themselves" the royal title. By contrast, royal and political rule originated in the common recognition of the necessity for a governing head by a people, that is "a body of men joined together in society by a consent of right, by a union of interests, and for promoting the common good."[3] Here, the shared interests that give content to the "common good" (and hence to the principle of natural justice) concern the protection of "lives, properties, and laws." The mutual agreement to erect a government takes the form of a "compact."[4] The unity of the political body that forms the head is at once volitional and organic, even "mystical" (*mysticum*). It is constituted by the people's intention (*intencio populi*) regarding "the prudential care and provision for the public good" (*provisionem politicam utilitati populi illius*), which is transmitted to the head, and via the head to all the corporeal members, as the blood is pumped by the heart to the brain, and via the brain, to the rest of the body for its subsistence and invigoration. Extending the organic analogy is Fortescue's well-known comparison of "the

1. Ibid., 78.
2. Ibid., 91.
3. Ibid., 346.
4. Ibid., 347.

law under which the people is incorporated" to "the nerves or sinews of the body natural" by which "the whole frame is fitly joined together and compacted," "the bones and all other members of the body" preserving their functions and discharging their offices by the nerves. "And as the head of the body natural," he continues, "cannot change its nerves or sinews, cannot deny to the several parts their proper energy, their due proportion and aliment of blood, neither can a king, who is the head of the body politic, change the laws thereof, nor take from the people what is theirs by right, against their consents."[1] Such is the original subordination of the king, reigning royally and politically, to the legal constitution of his kingdom.

Thus, on the one hand, the basis of kingly authority in "royal rule" is simply the natural necessity, divinely decreed, for a power-wielding head to preserve a rudimentary order in society, so that it does not perish in the conflict of private and particular interests waged by sinful men.[2] On the other hand, the basis of kingly authority in "royal and political rule" is the free, rational, and united intention of a people to preserve and promote the common good. The continuity between them lies in the *telos* of safeguarding the material structures of collective human life. However, these two bases of political authority stand in tension in Fortescue's thought, being in no way systematically related. There is evidence that they are aligned with a theological division between the sovereign lordship of God over His creation, wherein His Will of itself is Law, and the lordship of Christ over "the Blessed reigning together with [Him] . . . in their native country, in that peace which they long for . . . where there shall not be wanting the consent of all the citizens in every judgment of the King."[3] *In Praise of the Laws of England* leaves us with the impression that the rule of the English king over his subjects, exercised with the wise counsel of many and the consent of all (in parliament), is indistinguishable from the rule of Christ over His saints. At least it is indistinguishable, we are told, from the law by which "all mankind would have been governed, if, in the Paradise, they had not transgressed the command of God."[4] Such is the unity of nature and grace in the kingdom of England!

1. Ibid., 346-7.
2. Ibid., 80.
3. Ibid., 84.
4. Ibid., 345.

Four

WILLIAM TYNDALE AND THE LUTHERAN DIALECTIC

Among the first generation of English Protestants William Tyndale (c.1494-1536) stands out as a figure of legendary proportions. Like Wyclif, whose labor he continued, Tyndale is the reformer to an archetypal degree: ambitious, tireless, and self-sacrificing in his undertakings, temperamentally austere and judgmental, fanatical in unmasking the intellectual and moral hypocrisy of others. Unlike Wyclif, who passed his youthful career in the scholarly calm of Oxford, Tyndale plunged into the turbulent and menacing waters of public controversy early on. An exile and a hunted man for most of his lamentably few productive years, it is no wonder his thoughts turned incessantly on the persecution of God's prophets by the pharisees of the day.

Although his theological treatises attracted much attention and were influential in their day, the more significant portion of his legacy is comprised of his Bible translations. The successive editions of his English translation of the New Testament, Dickens tells us, "provided a text at once splendid and homely in character" that would dominate all subsequent translations "until our own day," constituting the basis "for nine-tenths of the Authorised Version itself"[1] It is arguable that even in Tyndale's own generation, the

---

1. A.G. Dickens, *The English Reformation* (London, 1964), 71.

availability to the literate laity of a philologically careful, yet moving, translation of the New Testament did more to foster adhesion to Reformation principles than all the instruction of his Lutheran tracts. Tyndale's doctrinal writings are not particularly distinguished by theological originality, penetration, or synthetic power. They drive home interminably the conviction of the sinner's justification "by faith of Jesus Christ," extending this principle in manifold and diverse criticisms of righteousness by works. The Lutheran opposition of law and gospel is a much labored theme, with predictable implications for Tyndale's political thought, with its overall Lutheran cast. However, his development of the meaning and scope of the category of law breaks out of the Lutheran mold in one notable respect, linking up with a tradition of incontestably English pedigree. In placing obedience to God's law (evangelical and natural) at the heart of the life of faith, Tyndale is following in the footsteps of Wyclif and Fortescue, for whom faith in Christ and law-abidingness stand in no tension. To know how Tyndale interprets the claim of the law, especially the civil law, in its actual demands, we should not despise the illumination of his teaching offered by his conduct. So let us turn to the broad details of his tempestuous career.

Educated at Oxford, where he excelled chiefly in the knowledge of languages and of the Scriptures, Tyndale studied briefly at Cambridge, probably drawn there by Erasmus' lectures on Greek.[1] About 1520 he found employment as tutor in the household of Sir John Walsh, an eminent Gloucestershire gentleman. His frequent and severe criticisms of the Scriptural ignorance and doctrinal error of his local clergy gave much offense to his clerical colleagues in the diocese and incurred the wrath of the bishop's chancellor, from whose harassment he fled. This unhappy encounter with the church convinced Tyndale of the necessity of putting the vernacular Scriptures into the hands of the laity, so that, by direct acquaintance with "the process, order, and meaning of the text," they might defend themselves against the exegetical "sophistry," invention, and "juggling" of ecclesiastics.[2] Refused patronage for his translating work by the conservative Bishop Tunstall of London, he was allowed to labor in the home of a rich cloth merchant, where he was introduced to "the obscure world of the 'Christian Brethren'"[3] Up to this time, the term "Christian Brethren" had loosely designated the heretical Wycliffites, or Lollards, but it was coming to be used of "the secret society of London merchants engaged in subventing and import-

---

1. "Biographical Notice" to *Tyndale's Doctrinal Treatises*, ed. Rev. Henry Walter, for the Parker Society (Cambridge, 1848), xiv-xv.
2. Ibid., xx.
3. Dickens, *The English Reformation*, 70.

ing books by English Protestants on the continent."[1] We have already remarked, in connection with early Tudor Lollardy, that the continuity in the public consciousness between the Wycliffite and the English Lutheran heresies was neither historically nor doctrinally unfounded. On the one hand, according to Dickens, Tyndale's patron and his associates "belonged to the international world of Lutheranism," while "on the other, they were certainly linked with men of Lollard background in the distribution of these forbidden books from abroad."[2]

After six months in the household of Henry Monmouth, Tyndale decisively resolved to remove himself to the continent, apparently with the mixed motives of evading the law-enforcement agencies at home, consulting with Martin Luther, and facilitating the printing of his English New Testament. In going abroad with the intention of translating the New Testament for English readership, Tyndale was violating English ecclesiastical and secular law alike. Church regulation "prohibited anyone from issuing a translation of the Bible without the endorsement of his bishop," while "a statute of the realm forbade ordinary subjects to leave the country without the royal consent."[3] Tyndale's defiance of both spiritual and temporal authority in the cause of propagating the true faith exhibited the limits of his duty to be subject to the powers that be, heralding, in the view of M. M. Knappen, "years of Puritan insubordination and 'reformation without tarrying for any.'"[4] Yet Tyndale's disregard for human authorities never transgressed the boundaries of passive resistance. While "he proposed to flood his homeland with unsanctioned and even prohibited books, . . . he did not intend to use force against his sovereign." And although as a fugitive exile, "he was taking every precaution to avoid detection and capture, should he be apprehended, he was prepared to submit to whatever punishment the authorities might ordain." Knappen points out that: "With one or two notable exceptions this doctrine of passive resistance was the burden of Puritan sermon, petition, and pamphlet throughout the century."[5]

Owing to the sustained monetary assistance of Monmouth, Tyndale succeeded in visiting Luther, and in completing his translation of the New Testament, aided in the final stages of the labor by a Cambridge-trained, ex-Observant Friar, William Roy, sent to him by Monmouth. The entire New

1. Ibid.
2. Ibid., 71.
3. Marshall M. Knappen, *Tudor Puritanism: A Chapter in the History of Idealism* (Chicago, 1963), 3.
4. Ibid.
5. Ibid., 4.

Testament was printed in 1525 at Worms, a Protestant city where Tyndale was currently residing, having been forced to flee the local magistrates at Cologne. By the spring of 1526 copies were entering England in such numbers and with such enthusiastic reception as to elicit a fit of suppressive activity by the ecclesiastical authorities. The same year witnessed a great burning of these heretically tainted books outside St. Paul's Cathedral, presided over by the Lord Chancellor Wolsey, and a proclamation issued by the zealous Bishop Tunstall "calling in all copies of the offending work under pain of excommunication and suspicion of heresy."[1] However, no perseverance in repressive measures could stem the tide of contraband New Testaments, fed by successive editions, with revisions in 1526, 1534, and 1535.

The "quarto edition" of Tyndale's New Testament (1525) carried a prologue of his own composition that was reprinted in an emended version before 1532 under the title *Pathway into the Holy Scripture*. This piece contains in germ the range of his principal ideas on the interpretation of Scripture, on law and Gospel, faith and love, authority and obedience. After relocating in 1528 to the English house of the Merchant Adventurers at Antwerp, Tyndale published two more treatises that enjoyed wide circulation together. *The Parable of the Wicked Mammon* (1528), although a belabored statement of the doctrine of justification composed from a sermon of Luther, contains several noteworthy (if not original) remarks on natural equity and social structure. *The Obedience of a Christian Man* (1528) offers a considerably more developed social teaching on such germane subjects as the political function of the law, the form and scope of the secular and the spiritual jurisdictions, the duty of civil subjection and the prerogatives of the king, especially with respect to the clerical estate. All these subjects are addressed within the framework of a defence of the vernacular Scriptures against the prelates' charge that the availability of God's Word to the laity is an incitement to civil insurrection, illegality, and abuse. Tyndale continued his polemical rejoinder to the prelates in a further controversial treatise entitled *Practise of Prelates* (1530), wherein he enlarged upon the justifying necessity for "princes to resume authority over ecclesiastics, and to humble the usurping hierarchy."[2] Concurrently he was working on a translation of the Pentateuch, with the assistance of Miles Coverdale, a former Austin friar from Cambridge, who had joined him in Hamburg for this purpose in 1529. With Coverdale, Tyndale returned to the English House at Antwerp, where he resided until

---

1. Ibid., 20.
2. "Biographical Notice" to *Tyndale's Doctrinal Treatises*, xli.

1535 when he was apprehended, imprisoned, and condemned to the stake for "obstinate heresy." Before his death in 1536 he had contrived to print his translation of the Pentateuch and the Book of Jonah.

In the realm of Biblical translation, Tyndale's legacy extends beyond his own monumental accomplishments to comprehend the distinguished work of his protégés and disciples, most notably that of Miles Coverdale (1488-1568) and John Rogers (c.1500-1555). During Tyndale's imprisonment Coverdale published a complete translation of the Bible that virtually incorporated his master's New Testament and utilized his Old Testament translations, together with current German versions. Owing to the tireless persuasions of Henry's chancellor Thomas Cromwell, this became the first English Bible to circulate in the kingdom with royal authorization. It was quickly rivalled by Rogers' translation, the so-called "Matthew Bible" after his pseudonym, also owing a generous debt to Tyndale, and promoted by Archbishop Cranmer. Coverdale went on to execute a masterful revision of the Bible at Cromwell's behest, published in 1539, that came to be called variously "the Great Bible" and "Cranmer's Bible," the latter on account of Cranmer's impressive preface.

A. THE SCRIPTURE AS LAW AND GOSPEL

Tyndale's theological conviction of the urgent need for Biblical translation is intimately bound up with his Lutheran hermeneutic of law and gospel. From his 1525 preface onward, he unceasingly set forth law and gospel as the controlling principles of Biblical interpretation. The law in its most generic meaning is "the ministration of death," the ministration of God's wrath and condemnation, whereas the Gospel is "the ministration of life," "the ministration of the Spirit and of righteousness (II Cor. 3)." "The law," says Tyndale in *A Pathway into the Holy Scripture*, "was given to bring us unto the knowledge of ourselves . . . [of] what we are, of nature. . . . For it killeth our consciences, and driveth us to desperation; inasmuch as it requireth of us that which is unpossible for our nature to do. It requireth perfect love, from the low bottom and ground of the heart, as well in all things which we suffer, as in the things which we do." But "when the law has passed upon us, and condemned us to death . . . , then we have in Christ grace, . . . favour, promises of life, of mercy, of pardon, freely, by the merits of Christ. . . ."[1] Thus, "'the end of the law', or the cause wherefore the law was made, 'is Christ, to justify all

---

1. W. Tyndale, *A Pathway into the Holy Scripture*, reprinted in *Tyndale's Doctrinal Treatises*, 10-11.

that believe'": the office of the law is "to bring to repentance, and to drive unto Christ."[1]

In this typical dialectic, the Gospel overcomes the work of the law, emancipating sinful man from its bondage. Nevertheless, the meaning of the law is not exhausted for Tyndale by its function of condemnation preparatory to faith, for he also reserves a role for the law within faith, and a decisive one at that. Indeed, he conceives the work of faith primarily in terms of law. In faith, the "Spirit of Christ" enables us to "consent to the law, and love it inwardly in our heart, and desire to fulfil it, and sorrow because we cannot: which will . . . is sufficient, till more strength be given us; the blood of Christ hath made satisfaction for the rest. . . ."[2] Salvation does not come by faith's free subjection to God's law, he is careful to point out. On the contrary, salvation comes only by "believing the promises" ("by faith alone"), for the law, of necessity, "requireth perfection . . . and damneth all imperfectness," while "the promises . . . damn not, but give pardon, grace, mercy, favour, and whatsoever is contained in the promises."[3] God's law, then, is intrinsically good, its validity in no measure diminished by the grace of Christ, although without grace it avails nothing to sinful man. Of itself the law effects no righteousness, but it gives outward form to the inward goodness bestowed by the Spirit of Christ.

As to the content of the law and its internal divisions, Tyndale's account is neither systematic nor precise. "The law" typically refers to the Mosaic legislation, chiefly the Decalogue, the commandments of which specify the meaning of the Great Commandment to "love thy neighbour as thyself." The law of love appears to be one with the law of nature, which, in Tyndale as in Fortescue, is expressed in the Golden Rule.[4] Thus, God's law seems to be a seamless garment or unbroken thread that exhibits no inner tension or dialectic: whether "natural" or "revealed," it is a single, unified, and unchanging set of imperatives.

A similar continuity characterizes the relationship between divine law and human law. The ordinances by which civil society is governed are God's ordinances, in so far as they do not contradict "His commandment." They comprise the "inferior" law, that at all times and in all places is to be "judged" and "interpreted" by "the higher law" revealed in the Scripture.[5] In what the inferiority of the civil law consists Tyndale does not tell us, as, presumably, it

---

1. W. Tyndale, *The Obedience of a Christian Man*, reprinted in ibid., 192-193.
2. Tyndale, *A Pathway*, in ibid., 15.
3. Ibid.
4. W. Tyndale, *The Parable of the Wicked Mammon*, reprinted in ibid., 69.
5. Tyndale, *A Pathway*, in ibid., 25.

coincides at points with God's express commandments. It is probable that it represents a partial and less stringent formulation of the divine imperatives.

This view of the civil law is suggested by Tyndale's passing remarks about lordship and possession. On the one hand, he sets out the natural commonality of all earthly goods among those who participate equally in the lordship of Christ, emphasizing even more than Wyclif the theft involved in witholding one's excess wealth from a needy brother. In that "Christ is Lord over all; and every Christian is heir annexed with Christ . . . everyone [is] lord of whatsoever another hath. If thy brother or neighbour therefore need, and thou have to help him, and yet shewest not mercy, but withdrawest thy hands from him, then robbest thou him of his own, and art a thief."[1] Further, drawing out the mystical, eschatological aspect of Christological community, Tyndale argues: "But Christ is all in all things. Every Christian man to another is Christ himself; and thy neighbour's need hath as good right in thy goods, as hath Christ himself, which is heir and lord over all.[2] On the other hand, Tyndale, unlike Wyclif, does not follow the tradition of degrading civil possession to a species of sin on account of its relative incompatibility with evangelical possession. Rather, he implicitly repudiates any idea of incompatibility by attributing civil possessions to Christ and his disciples. In explaining Christ's and Peter's payment of tribute in Matthew 17:24-27, he proposes that "the cause, why Christ paid, was because he had a household, and for the same cause paid Peter also: for he had a house, a ship and nets, as thou readest in the gospel."[3] Although the civil law does not, in strict conformity to Christ's law, require the charitable donation of all excess wealth (that is, wealth beyond the provision of daily necessities), it is not wrong in establishing and protecting civil ownership, for the latter, in Tyndale's view, is clearly the presupposition of charitable giving. Furthermore, the law of Christ and the civil law agree that provision for another's need must begin with caring "for thine household . . . as that is thy part committed to thee of the congregation."[4] Thus it is that God's law, revealed in the Scripture, instructs us in our natural and civil duties, commanding us to obey the regulations necessary to civil order.

Above all, it is the false and pernicious teaching of priest and prelate about God's law that renders urgent the translation of the Bible for the laity. The ecclesiastics, serving the ends of their own insatiable covetousness, systematically misconstrue its purpose and content. They set forth God's law,

1. Ibid., *The Parable*, in ibid., 97.
2. Tyndale, Ibid., 98.
3. Tyndale, *The Obedience*, in ibid., 190.
4. Tyndale, *The Parable*, in ibid., 98.

interpreted, promulgated, and enforced by the church, as the divine instrument of man's salvation, made efficacious by the merits of Christ's atoning passion. It is by complying with the church's manifold regulations for extorting wealth and inflicting spiritual servitude that the Christian layman procures his eternal happiness. But, in conspiring to "bind violently" the laity with their arbitrary and secretive laws, the priests "a thousand things forbid . . . which Christ made free," their laws being nothing but pharisaical inventions, the hypocritical creations of greed and craft.[1] They prove the insincerity of their regulations by "dispensing with them again for money," while pretending to exercise their power of exemption over ordinances that really are from God, as well as those from men that carry divine authority.[2] In perverting God's laws, they pervert His Gospel, usurping for themselves the place and work of Christ; even aspiring to do what Christ could not, namely, exempt sinners from the law's judgment.

Only the right understanding of the Scripture is able to emancipate beguiled cleric and layman alike from the tyranny of deception practiced by the pope and his prelates, the "Antichrist" and his "false prophets."[3] The *ordo cognoscendi* of scriptural truth, manifest in the plan of Scripture itself, runs as follows. First is the law's demand: the obedience required of us by God to all "authorities" and "superiors" and the obligation laid on us to "love one another." Next is the law's condemnation: its demonstration of our rebellious will and depraved nature, of our incapacity to be "righteous in the sight of God," for which we are damned. Then, in the wake of the law's judgment come to us "the testament and promises which God hath made unto us in Christ," which comprise "the principles and the ground of [our] faith." Finally, on the basis of these principles and this ground is revealed the meaning of the sacraments. If this order of teaching the Scripture is followed, says Tyndale addressing the clergy, "the Spirit [shall] work with thy preaching. . . ."[4] It is just this *ordo cognoscendi* that renders plain the "literal" truth of the words of Scripture; for, "God is a Spirit, and all his words are spiritual. His literal sense is spiritual. . . ."[5]

---

1. Tyndale, *The Obedience*, in ibid., 147.
2. Ibid.
3. Ibid.
4. Ibid., 156.
5. W. Tyndale, *Four Senses of the Scripture*, reprinted in ibid., 309.

B. Two Offices and Authorities: To Preach and To Judge

The office of priest or elder is simply and exhaustively to preach the law and the gospel of God. The office is "spiritual" and not "carnal," entailing no coercive jurisdiction or mediatorial power. The priest neither judges in God's stead nor sacrifices on behalf of the church, having no authority to determine and pronounce the guilt, the punishment, or the remission of sins, or to intercede for the sinner before God. The "literal" meaning of the authority of the keys is its "spiritual" meaning: "nothing else save knowledge of the law, and of the promises or gospel."[1] Only by a "carnal" interpretation of God's law and promises do the priests "bind with their own law" and "loose and justify with pardons and ceremonies."[2] St. Paul makes clear in II Corinthians 3 that "true binding" is preaching the law, wherein "all men are found sinners, and therefore damned," while "true loosing" is preaching the "glad tidings" wherein "are all, that repent and believe, found righteous in Christ."[3] By preaching the law we rebuke our sinful brother, and by preaching the gospel we forgive him his sins, as God forgives them.[4] Even in administering the sacraments, whether of baptism or of the Eucharist, the priest accomplishes nothing but proclamation of the promise that alone justifies: the promise "that God hath made unto us in Christ . . . . that we are cleansed with Christ's bloodshedding; which was an offering, and a satisfaction, for the sin of all that repent and believe, consenting and submitting themselves unto the will of God."[5]

Whereas the elder possesses the authority of the Word, the civil magistrate possesses the authority of the sword, the monopoly of coercive judgment. The divinely appointed office of princes, says Tyndale, is "to take vengeance of evil doers" in the execution of which they "are in God's room."[6] For God reserves to Himself the authority to judge and to punish the wicked, forbidding man the exercise of vengeance, on the grounds of his incapacity to "be a righteous, an egal or an indifferent judge in his own cause, lusts and appetites so blind [him]." But He chooses to execute His judgment through the instrumentality of human judges, and so "in all lands hath put kings, governors and rulers in his own stead, . . . and hath commanded all causes to be brought before them, as thou readest [in] Exod. xxii."[7] All unauthorized

---

1. Tyndale, *The Obedience*, in ibid., 205.
2. Ibid., 243.
3. Ibid., 269.
4. Ibid, citing Matt. 18 and John 20.
5. Ibid., 253.
6. Ibid., 175, 180.
7. Ibid., 174.

taking of vengeance by private individuals is a usurpation of the divine prerogative, a refusal to give "room unto God to . . . be judge over thee."[1]

With the representative authority to judge, God has given to temporal rulers laws by which to judge. Although few men are "under the everlasting testament of God in Christ," yet are all nations "under the testament of the law natural, which is the law of every land made for the commonwealth there, and for peace and unity, that one may live by another."[2] All men are bound by this law of natural equity, embodied in human laws, and will be rewarded by God with earthly blessing and prosperity or earthly deprivation and "the loss of this life" according as they are obedient or disobedient to it.[3] The one exception is the king himself, who is "in this world, without law; and may at his lust do right or wrong, and shall give accounts but to God only."[4] The king may live lawlessly in this world with impunity, but he must rule lawfully in one respect at least, lest he be rendered impotent: he must punish evil-doers universally, not exempting anyone. The "greatest tyrant," says Tyndale, "though he do wrong unto the good," is, nevertheless, "a great benefit of God," in that he "punisheth the evil, and maketh all men obey." The king who does not uniformly enforce his law with punishment is but a "shadow," "grievous unto the realm."[5] Having offered an undiscerning account of tyranny,[6] Tyndale goes on to make a hardly justified pronouncement on the damnation of all princes who "give liberty or licence unto the spirituality to sin unpunished" and to enable others to escape punishment by the provision of "sanctuaries," "privileged places," and so on.[7] His overriding concern in emphasizing the coercive aspect of royal authority appears to be with the temporal subjection and discipline of the clergy. In his hatred of clerical arrogance, of the pretensions of priests to be above the law and the common lot of their fellow Christians, Tyndale equals if not exceeds Wyclif. "With what face," he demands, "durst the spirituality, which ought to be the light and an ensample of good living unto all other, desire to sin unpunished, or to be excepted from tribute, toll, or custom, that they would not bear pain with their brethren to the maintenance of kings and officers, ordained of God to punish sin?"[8] To spurn secular subjection is the most heinous of sins: it is the

1. Ibid., 176.
2. Ibid., 204.
3. Ibid., 175.
4. Ibid., 178.
5. Ibid., 180.
6. The tyrant who rules in the interests of his own lusts and passions is surely arbitrary in applying his laws and in punishing offenders.
7. Ibid., 180.
8. Ibid., 178-179.

pharisaical refusal to be under God's law while claiming the righteousness of the law.

Despite his preoccupation with the avenging authority of the king, Tyndale does not entirely neglect the other duties and virtues of kingship. The Christian king, conforming to Christ's example, should be a selfless servant of the common good, sacrificing himself ceaselessly to his subjects' welfare with true parental devotion, "never avenging his own wrongs, but suffering all things; bearing every man's weakness, teaching, warning, exhorting, and ever caring for them, and so tenderly lov[ing] them, that he desire[s] God either to forgive them, or to damn him with them." When the king is not required to sit in judgment, executing "the sharp law of vengeance," he, too, is a "minister in the kingdom of Christ." Though the church and the realm be a single polity, Tyndale, with unflinching Lutheran dualism, sets over the public domain a law that shows no mercy, that "preacheth no gospel."[1] In his own case the law was merciless indeed.

---

1. Ibid., 203.

Five

St. Germain and Henry VIII's Church Take-Over

The diversity of training, careers, personalities and allegiances presented by Wyclif, Fortescue, and Tyndale provides us with sufficient evidence of the comprehensiveness of the Erastian position. Such evidence speaks against any attempt to associate Erastian sentiments too closely and exclusively with a particular social class, vocational group, theological persuasion, or personality disposition. Throughout the Henrician period, the widespread tendency to integrate ecclesiastical structures into the secular legal and political edifice continues unabated, gathering increasing momentum.

However, we can also draw attention to the longstanding tradition of Erastian and even anticlerical sentiments among the common lawyers. The expanded powers of parliament and the secular courts had fuelled rather than dampened their animosity toward ecclesiastical jurisdiction, rendering it increasingly influential. It is hardly surprising, then, that the statesman who masterminded Henry's VIII's revolutionary legal program for reforming the English Church, namely, Thomas Cromwell and the writer who provided the most comprehensive theoretical justification of it, St. Germain, were both common lawyers, with the instincts and outlook of their profession.

A. St. Germain: Doctor and Student

Born about 1460, a barrister of the Inner Temple, Christopher St. Germain was well into old age when he launched his career as publicist for Henry VIII's legal reformation of the English church. The succession of pamphlets and treatises he produced between 1530 and 1540 were propagandist to the extent of keeping apace with "the evolution of anti-clerical opinion" during this period.[1] His most influential apology for English law and the legal supremacy of King in Parliament, entitled *Doctor and Student: or Dialogues Between A Doctor of Divinity And A Student in the Laws of England* (1531), appeared during the second session of the Reformation Parliament. The reforming intent of this publication was confined to diminishing the legislative and judicial power of the clergy. The same scope of intention characterized his treatise of the following year, *Spirituality and Temporality*. But his subsequent writings of 1534-35, most notably *A Treatise Concerning the Power of the Clergy and the Laws of the Realm* and *An Answer to a Letter*, adopted the more blatantly secularist program of transferring to the temporal sovereign "the entire *potestas jurisdictionis* of the clergy, including the right to define doctrine."[2]

These later treatises offered a thoroughly Marsilian apology for the king's claim, legislated by the Act of Supremacy of 1534, to be "the Supreme Head of the Church of England." They took over the Italian master's redefinition of the division between "spiritual" and "temporal" power, aimed at restricting the priestly authority to the realm of piety, consecration, and sacrament (the *potestas ordinis*), and relegating all external and juridical aspects of ecclesiastical order (the *potestas jurisdictionis*) to the secular authority. Their argument is predicated on the radically antipapal understanding of the church as comprising the whole community of believers. With respect to the doctrinal authority of the secular rulers, St. Germain slavishly reiterates Marsilius' reasoning: "All men agree," he says, "that the Catholic Church may expound scripture: and if the clergy can prove that they be the Catholic Church, then it belongeth to them to expound it. But if the emperors, kings, and princes with their people, as well of the clergy as of the laity, make the Catholic Church and the clergy but a part of that Church; then may the emperor, kings, and princes with their people expound it."[3] While his earlier writings do not

---

1. Franklin Le van Baumer, *The Early Tudor Theory of Kingship* (New Haven, 1940), 66.
2. Ibid.
3. Christopher St. Germain, *An Answere to a Letter*, Giiii-Gv, quoted in Le van Baumer, *The Early Tudor Theory of Kingship*, 48. See also Christopher St. Germain, *A Treatyse Concerninge the Power of the Clergye and the Lawes of the Realme*, Diiii-Diiiib, quoted in ibid.

confidently propound this revolutionary principle, they, nevertheless, pave the way for it, as is manifest from the framework of legal theory and practice laid down in *Doctor and Student*, which merits careful consideration.

As its full title indicates, this publication is a multiple composition, comprised of two earlier dialogues—a dialogue of 1523 translated from its original Latin, and a dialogue of 1530 in the vernacular—together with an appendix of thirteen "Additions." The first dialogue sets out a comprehensive theory of law and equity and demonstrates in numerous cases the conformity with it of English law and the English courts. The second dialogue extends this demonstration in a discussion of diverse other cases. The "Additions," with a more revolutionary bent, defend the right of the Parliament to legislate against the Spirituality in various ecclesiastical domains. We shall direct our attention to the theoretical foundations of the first dialogue and their practical legal consequences outlined in the "Additions."

1. Laws of Man and Laws of God

In his handling of the traditional fourfold typology of law, St. Germain is instructed by the earlier formulations of John Fortescue and Jean Gerson. Following in their footsteps, he affirms the primacy of the law of nature (or reason) over the law of God in the determination of human conduct. The law of reason is the one eternal, immutable, divine law "written in the Heart" of man, to which all "Prescriptions," "Statutes," and "Customs" must conform, lest they be "things void and against justice."[1] Not only does the law of reason have epistemological priority over the law of God revealed in Scripture (of which Fortescue makes much), but it has ontological priority in the decisive respect that it orders men to felicity in this world rather than in the world to come. Whereas Fortescue emphasizes the coincidence of the law of reason and the law of God, conceiving the latter chiefly as a clarifying and strengthening repromulgation of the former, St. Germain, under the influence of Gerson and Marsilius, emphasizes the diversity of the two laws according to their different ends. Like Marsilius, he prefers a teleological to an epistemological understanding of the law of God, holding that it "is not properly [so] called . . . because it was shewed by Revelation of God, but also because it directed a Man by the nearest Way to the Felicity eternal."[2] From this position he repudiates the equation of the canon law and the law of God, arguing that the former is concerned not only with "the Declaration or Conservation of the Faith" necessary to eternal life, but also with "the

---

1. Christopher St. Germain, *Doctor and Student*, 15th ed. (London, 1751), 5-6.
2. Ibid., 8.

political Rule and Conservation of the People." Entailed in this repudiation is the denial that "all the Goods of the Church [are] spiritual," as belonging to "the Spirituality" and leading to "the Spirituality." Rather, he argues, the Goods of the Spirituality are "things mere temporal, and keeping the Body." He sets this argument within the conceptual framework of a unitary civil society ("the whole political Conversation of the People"), composed of "Spiritual Men . . . deputed and dedicated to the service of God" and "Secular Men or Lay Men" who, "though they walk in the Way of God," are yet "occupied about such things as pertain to the Commonwealth and to the good Order of the People."[1] Within civil society all laws touching the political ordering of temporal goods are "civil," whether these goods belong to ecclesiastical or lay persons.

By the "Law of Man," St. Germain means chiefly the civil law, although this category includes all positive law, ecclesiastical and secular. The principal function of the law of man is the regulation of right of possession: "For whatsoever [Lands and Goods] a Man hath by such Laws of Man, he hath righteously."[2] Ignoring completely the idea that righteous possession presupposes a divine grant, St. Germain simply asserts the unqualified competence of the civil law to establish right to property. He further characterizes the law of man by its conformity to right reason and its relation to coercive authority. Not only does the law of reason command respect for private and property rights, but the positive law protecting them carries the binding force of the sovereign legal body of the land. St. Germain is clear that the legal sovereign is "the King in Parliament," and not the king acting on his royal prerogative alone. And the legal authority of the King in Parliament is, apparently, absolute and infallible.[3] To "the parliament" he ascribes "an absolute power as to the possession of all temporal things within this realm . . . to take them from one man, and give them to another without any cause or consideration."[4] Moreover, parliamentary statute has precedence over "general customs" and even constitutive power over the courts of law, to alter them and their names.[5] St. Germain's account of human positive law places him squarely behind the movement of legal centralization characterizing the reigns of Henry VII and Henry VIII, in which the legislative organ of the King in

---

1. Ibid., 9.
2. Ibid., 12.
3. Le van Baumer, *The Early Tudor Theory of Kingship*, 156.
4. Christopher St. Germain, *Spirituality and Temporality*, 228, quoted in ibid., 156.
5. St. Germain, *Doctor and Student*, 21.

Parliament was absorbing the medieval liberties (e.g., of church, town corporation, and guild) and subordinating all other law to itself.[1]

Given St. Germain's theoretical framework, we are hardly astonished at the matters "concerning the spirituality" that fall within the legislative powers of Parliament. In his *Additions*, he asserts that Parliament "hath good Authority to Make Laws" to set mortuary dues,[2] to prohibit the transference of properties into mortmain (that is, into inalienable church land),[3] to curtail appropriations by religious houses of advowsons (of the right of appointment to ecclesiastical benefices),[4] to stipulate the conditions of sanctuary and the locations of sanctuaries,[5] to transfer suits of delapidation concerning church property to secular courts,[6] to determine the legitimate pope in the event of schism,[7] to regulate admission to the priesthood to ensure "sufficiently learned" men,[8] and to prohibit episcopal charging of visitation fees on religious foundations.[9] In addition, Parliament may legislate that all suits respecting "any loss or worldly Hindrance" (including theft and murder) be prosecuted "at the Common Law," and that a range of clerical crimes be prosecuted in like manner rather than dealt with in Chancery.[10] Likewise, it may restrict the awarding of penances by the church courts to "spiritual" (as opposed to monetary) ones.[11] In summary, "the Parliament may ordain many good Laws for Strength of Faith, and for the good Order of all the People as well Spiritual as Temporal, though it judge not upon the Right of things that be more Spiritual."[12] To prescind from passing judgment on purely spiritual matters is not, as it turns out, a serious impediment to parliamentary control over ecclesiastical affairs. It does not prevent Parliament from conducting its own inquiry into the ecclesiastical causes of heretical "Sects and Opinions" in the Realm, from directing its reforming zeal against the excesses of wealth,

---

1. Franklin Le van Baumer summarizes the threat to the common law thus: "The fact remains that under Henry VIII, [courts of] chancery, star chamber, and requests were interpreting and extending and, indeed, sometimes reversing the decisions of the common law in the interests of strong government and equity." Le van Baumer, *The Early Tudor Theory of Kingship*, 176-77.

2. Christopher St. Germain, *Additions to the Second Dialogue*, chap. 1, in id., *Doctor and Student*.

3. Ibid., chap. 2.
4. Ibid., chap. 3.
5. Ibid., chap. 4.
6. Ibid., chap. 6.
7. Ibid., chap. 8.
8. Ibid., chap. 11.
9. Ibid., chap. 13.
10. Ibid., chaps. 7, 9.
11. Ibid., chap. 6.
12. Ibid., chap. 11.

privilege, and power among "Spiritual Men" that incite clergy and laity alike to embrace rebellious and unorthodox views.[1]

B. THE HENRICIAN STATUTES 1529-1539

When Parliament convened in November 1529, it displayed its intention to exercise the legislative power over the spirituality that St. Germain would claim for it two years later. It was clearly set on a course of ecclesiastical reform, without, however, anticipating its revolutionary magnitude. The legislation enacted over the next six years represents a coalition and compromise of the interests of Parliament and Crown. By the end of 1535 the English Church had received its legislative, judicial, and financial emancipation from Rome and had become subordinate in all respects to the monarch. While Parliament had gained some share in the direct control of ecclesiastical temporalities, it benefited primarily from the government's sympathy for its criticisms of clerical wealth, administration, and jurisdiction. It was primarily the king's sovereign power and financial self-sufficiency that was pronounced in the legal reform of the church. Let us glance briefly at the legislative milestones of the Reformation Parliament, drawing out their theoretical impetus.

The initial spirited attack on the legislative and juridical power of the clergy came from the Supplication of the Commons against the Ordinaries, drafted first in 1529 and revised in 1532. In the style of St. Germain, the Commons open their attack by awarding blame for the recent "discord, variance, and debate" in the realm, not only to certain seditious and unorthodox books but also to "the extreme and uncharitable behaviour and dealing of diverse ordinaries" in their "examination . . . upon the said errors and heretical opinions."[2] The document proceeds to enumerate the contentious powers and practices of the ecclesiastics that include: the power of Convocation to legislate without the assent of the king or the laity; the delays of the Canterbury courts of Arches and Audience; the heavy exactions of the church courts; the unedifying conferring of ecclesiastical benefices on unfit minors; and the unscrupulous methods of interrogation in heresy cases.[3] The king, dissatisfied with Convocation's answers to these complaints, himself commanded that henceforth: (1) they make no new canons without the royal "licence," "assent," and "authority"; (2) they submit for examination all heretofore enacted canons to the king and a commission appointed by him; and (3) they retain in force only the canons approved by the majority of the

---

1. Ibid., chap. 8.
2. *Tudor Constitutional Documents, 1485-1603*, ed. J.R. Tanner (Cambridge, 1951), 21.
3. Ibid.

commission, "abrogating" those failing to obtain this endorsement.[1] In May 1532, Convocation acceded to these demands in a document known as the Submission of the Clergy, and their submission received statutory embodiment in the Act for the Submission of the Clergy (1534). According to Dickens, Convocation's surrender of their legislative function to royal control was a prudent maneuver to avert the more terrible hazard of "the wholesale destruction of their courts and their legal privileges at the hands of Parliament."[2] The maneuver proved successful, as Henry VIII, once in possession of the Church's legislative power, ignored the remaining lay grievances and "refrained from the radical overhaul or abolition of ecclesiastical jurisdiction to which the Commons aspired."[3]

The Act in Restraint of Appeals (1533) is the most historically consequential piece of legislation devised by Thomas Cromwell. Its famous preamble "embodies a view of the relations of Church and State on which all subsequent legislation has proceeded, down to modern times."[4] Significantly, this preamble also represents the zenith of the influence of Marsilius' *Defender of the Peace* on English society. In it Cromwell sets forth Marsilius' leading doctrines regarding the body public, ecclesiastical and secular jurisdiction.[5] Occasioned by Henry VIII's determination to have his divorce suit against Catherine of Aragon settled in the English ecclesiastical courts without appeal to an apparently intransigent Pope, the Act stipulates that all causes lying within "the spiritual jurisdiction of this realm," including "causes testamentary, causes of matrimony and divorces, tithes . . ." shall be from henceforth "finally and definitively adjudged and determined, within the King's jurisdiction and authority and not elsewhere, in such courts spiritual and temporal . . . as the natures, conditions, and qualities of the causes . . . shall require. . . ."[6] The political rationale of this stipulation is contained in the preamble, which declares the sovereign self-sufficiency of the English Crown and the "body politic" subject to it.

On the testimony of "divers sundry old authentic histories and chronicles," the realm of England is described as "an empire . . . governed by one

---

1. Ibid.
2. A. G. Dickens, *The English Reformation* (London, 1964), 116.
3. Ibid.
4. *Tudor Constitutional Documents*, 40.
5. We should note that the *Defensor pacis* shaped secularizing and anticlerical opinion in powerful and respectable circles of English society under Henry VIII, despite the stigma of papal condemnation attached to it. Cromwell sustained its influence by financing the first English translation in 1535. This, as we have observed, was an emended text, edited to suit the circumstances of hereditary monarchial rule.
6. *Tudor Constitutional Documents*, 43.

Supreme Head and King having the dignity . . . of the imperial Crown of the same," and "institute[d] and furnished by the goodness and sufferance of Almighty God with plenary, whole, and entire power, pre-eminence, authority, prerogative, and jurisdiction to render and yield justice and final determination to all manner of folk [residents] or subjects within this his realm. . . ."[1] Here the king's title to plenary civil jurisdiction, so central to Marsilius' concept of rule, is granted not by the human but by the divine legislator. The body politic under the royal jurisdiction is divided into two parts: (1) the Spirituality, or the English Church, empowered to interpret "the law divine," adjudicate in matters "of spiritual learning," and administer spiritual "offices and duties," being endowed "with honour and possessions" by "the King's most noble progenitors, and the antecessors of the nobles of this realm"; and (2) the Temporality, empowered to administer, adjudge, and execute "the laws temporal" for the regulation of property and the conservation of civil "unity and peace."[2] Notwithstanding that the sufficiency of the Spirituality and the Temporality for the performance of their respective offices, together with the royal sovereignty, has been established by successive "ordinances, laws, statutes and provisions," appeals "out of this realm to the see of Rome" continue to cause "great inquietation" and "vexation" to the king and his subjects, on account of the high costs, dangers in travelling, and delays in settlement. Henceforth all such appeals are proscribed, and their prosecutors punishable under the Statutes of Provisors (1351, 1390) and Praemunire (1383, 1393).[3] The structure of appeal in ecclesiastical suits is now from the archdeacon to the diocesan bishop's court, and from there to the archiepiscopal court, except in causes touching the king, "his heirs or successors," in which case the appeal is directly to the upper House of Convocation. Finally, to counter disciplinary action from Rome, it is provided that all ecclesiastics in the realm may rightfully administer the sacraments and "divine services," notwithstanding papal "inhibitions," "interdictions," or "excommunications."[4]

The legal elaboration of a state church continued apace with the passing of three further pieces of legislation in 1534: the Act in Restraint of Annates, the Dispensations Act, and the Act of Supremacy. The Act in Restraint of Annates not only stops the payment to Rome of annates or first-fruits by those presented to bishoprics and archbishoprics, but also institutes a procedure for episcopal elections that exalts the royal prerogative to the exclusion

1. Ibid., 41.
2. Ibid.
3. See Chapter II, note 9.
4. *Tudor Constitutional Documents*, 44.

of papal influence.¹ It provides that at each episcopal vacancy, the king will nominate a candidate to the cathedral chapter in a "letter missive," accompanying the royal licence to elect (*congé d'élire*), and that failure to elect the king's choice will subject the dean and chapter to the penalties of Praemunire. The Act thereby reaffirms the traditional claim of the king to be chief patron of the English church. The Dispensations Act, besides accomplishing the final cessation of all payments to Rome, declares that dispensations (licenses to depart from the canon law) shall be obtained, not from the pope, but from the Archbishop of Canterbury, "for causes not being contrary or repugnant to the Holy Scriptures and laws of God."² However, the visitation of monasteries, hitherto a papal privilege, is assigned to a commission of the king's appointment.

The Act of Supremacy, described by one historian as "an ornamental coping-stone" to Henry's edifice of reforming legislation, recognizes the king and his successors to be "the only Supreme Head in earth of the Church of England."³ While professing to be the "corroboration and confirmation" of an already existing Headship, the Act gives the "imperial Crown" *explicit* authority to visit the clergy, to "repress, . . . reform, . . . correct, restrain, and amend" their "errors, heresies, abuses, . . . [and] contempts," both for "the increase of virtue in Christ's religion" and for "the conservation of the peace, unity, and tranquility of this realm," the united religious and political ends of the civil community.⁴ Although the king's headship of the national church does not entail the claim "to consecrate bishops or to administer the sacraments in person," it nevertheless indicates his intention to "exercise certain spiritual functions hitherto pertaining to the Papacy and the bishops."⁵ In retrospective fact, Dickens tells us, the "jurisdictions" and "authorities" herein "annexed and united to the . . . Crown" included "the power to correct the opinions of preachers, to supervise the formulation of doctrine, to reform the canon law, to visit and discipline both regular and secular clergy, and even . . . to try heretics in person."⁶ Within months, continues Dickens, Henry produced a "striking demonstration" of "the personal exercise of caesaro-papalism" in appointing Cromwell "his vicegerent, vicar general and special commissary," vested with "unlimited ecclesiastical jurisdiction" and

---

1. Annates or first-fruits are the whole revenue of one year's occupation of an ecclesiastical "dignity."
2. *Tudor Constitutional Documents*, 35.
3. Ibid., 47.
4. Ibid., 47-8.
5. Dickens, *The English Reformation*, 119.
6. Ibid.

"official precedence over the whole episcopate," after the extravagant fashion of Wolsey.[1] Thus, even before he turned his hand to dissolving the monasteries, Henry showed glaring signs of incarnating the most sinister features of Wyclif's pontifical king, steering the church into a new epoch of servile freedom.

Admittedly, the Henrician Statutes left somewhat uncertain whether the English church's new master was to be the king alone or the King in Parliament, for the constitutional relationship between Parliament and Convocation that they effected was an ambiguous one.[2] On the one hand, there was a tendency to establish Parliament and Convocation as "two concurrent powers, each operating within its own sphere . . . in a direct relation with the King," (as exemplified by the preamble to the Appeals Act and the Act for the Submission of the Clergy). Reinforcing this tendency, "the King issued articles of faith . . . by the advice and assent of Convocation alone" and, through his vicegerent, "conducted monastic visitations and issued royal injunctions to the clergy without reference to Parliament." On the other hand, there was a tendency to establish the superior authority of Parliament over Convocation and of statute law over canon law. This was manifest in parliamentary legislation regularizing or restating acts of Convocation, confirming subsidies granted by Convocation, and deciding doctrinal and jurisdictional matters within the ecclesiastical realm "without reference to Convocation," (as exemplified by the Annates Acts and the Six Articles Act).[3] Whichever tendency had the upper hand, it is probably safe to conjecture that Thomas Cromwell contemplated both with the satisfaction of a farsighted statesman.[4]

C. Epilogue to Henrician Reform: The Constitutionalism of Thomas Starkey

While St. Germain undoubtedly promoted the partnership in rule of king and Parliament, he did so without dwelling on their respective rights and limitations. So concerted was their legislative action in the massive ecclesiastical reforms afoot (owing partly to Henry VIII's desire for parliamentary cover), that St. Germain saw no public benefit issuing from constitutional

---

1. Ibid., 120.
2. Ibid., citing Woodward, *Schweizer Beiträge zur Allgemeinen Geschichte*, Band 16 (1958), 56ff.
3. Ibid., 120-21.
4. Dickens suggests that Cromwell probably foresaw "with equanimity" the future ascendancy of parliament. Ibid.

reflections that might diminish the king's prestige. Hence, he was silent on the inflation of royal prerogative associated primarily with the king's assumed "headship" of the English church.

Not so with Thomas Starkey (c.1495-1538), who was equally committed to far-ranging church reform. He was too devoted a student of classical political philosophy and too much under the sway of Renaissance humanist and republican ideals not to give thorough public consideration to the composition of the best political order and the constitutional safeguards against the worst. Starkey had been educated in the tradition of civic Christianity represented in England by such eminent men of learning as Dean John Colet (c.1466-1519), Sir Thomas More (1478-1535), and Cardinal Reginald Pole (1500-58). He had probably encountered Colet during his period at Oxford before 1521, was undoubtably familiar with More's *Utopia*, in circulation since 1516, and had spent almost a decade in Italy in the company of his patron Pole by the time of his writing his compendium of political theory and reform entitled *A Dialogue between Reginald Pole and Thomas Lupset*.[1] Despite the considerable political gulf separating Starkey from his patron when the *Dialogue* was published in 1536 (Starkey being now a royal chaplain and Pole a dangerous papist abroad), it is Pole who articulates the political principles that emerge victorious under questioning, and, in all likelihood, with *some* measure of fidelity to his actual opinions.

Like More's *Utopia*, Starkey's *Dialogue* is primarily interested in determining the commonweal and those constitutions, customs, and laws best suited to creating and sustaining it. In the medieval constitutionalist tradition, taken up by Ockham and the conciliarists, it is the communal good that limits the authority and directs the actions of the ruler. Starkey combines this principle with the conviction that sovereignty belongs to the human community, invested by God with the power "to elect and choose him that is both wise and just, and make him a prince; and him that is a tryan[t], so to depose."[2] A lynchpin of Roman civil law, in which Starkey received a doctorate in 1531, the principle of popular sovereignty was also a long-standing feature of papalist thought utilized by Pole in his *Defence of Ecclesiastical Unity* (1536) written against Henry VIII's schismatic church reforms. But whereas Pole used the

---

1. In the introduction to his recent edition of the *Dialogue*, T. F. Mayer argues persuasively for a dating of its writing between 1529 and 1532, instead of the later dating of between 1533 and 1535 previously accepted by scholars. See Thomas Starkey, *A Dialogue Between Pole and Lupset*, ed. T.F. Mayer (London, 1989).

2. Thomas Starkey, *A Dialogue Between Pole and Lupset*, ed. Kathleen M. Burton (London, 1958), 153. We have chosen to quote from Burton's edition rather than Mayer's, because it is much more readable, and, it would appear from a textual comparison with Mayer's, quite adequate for our needs.

principle to reinforce the subordination of royal authority, of merely human institution, to papal authority, of divine institution, Starkey had no such papalist intention. Rather, his intention is to reinforce a secular constitution that owes more to Marsilius of Padua than to Pole.

In the *Dialogue* Starkey propounds his ideas on law and authority within a thoroughly Aristotelian account of public and private virtue that makes no concessions to the Franciscan-Augustinian tradition. For the Christian individual, he rejects the ascetical life of solitary contemplation, poverty, suffering, and self-denial in favour of the magnanimous life of wise administration of moderate abundance.[1] He admits no conflict between the virtuous enjoyment and use of earthly prosperity and the obedient love of God. Similarly, with respect to the Christian community, he admits no irreducible tension between divine and human justice and law. With more bluntness and less equivocation than Fortescue, he collapses the order of grace into the order of nature, identifying human perfection with harmonious existence according to natural law.[2] He views the whole body of positive law in its diversity and transitoriness as man's divinely ordained tutor in eternal and immutable equity, which never departs from frail and sinful humanity.[3] Boldly he credits the possibility that even the heathen, deprived of "the law of Christ," may "be saved" by earnest observance of "their civil ordinance and statutes . . . directing them to the law of nature."[4] Happily are divine decree and human consent wedded in the authority of positive law, which, though grounded in and ordered to transcendent nature, "hath his strength and power wholly of the opinion and consent of man."[5] For Starkey the principle of consent does not dictate any one form of government but is susceptible of embodiment in all three conventionally recognised forms: monarchy, aristocracy, and democracy. As the best regime varies with the nature of the ruled and their circumstances, Starkey dismisses as futile protracted dispute over the absolutely best form, while, nevertheless, accepting the judgment of "wise men" that "the state of a prince, whereas he is chosen by free election most worthy to rule," is most conducive to "the maintenance and long continuance of this common weal . . . in any commonality."[6] Oppositely, he regards the establishment of princely rule by natural succession as tending to "the most pestilent and pernicious state" of tyranny, "most full of peril, and to the

1. Ibid., 52.
2. Ibid., 30-35.
3. Ibid., 32.
4. Ibid., 35.
5. Ibid., 33.
6. Ibid., 64.

common wealth most dangerous. . . ."¹ Given the regrettable (but apparently historically necessary) fact that the princes of England "come by succession," Starkey emphatically advocates stricter limitations on the royal prerogative.² Chiefly, he advises the removal to "the common counsel of the realm and parliament" of the existing princely powers "to dispense with the common laws and with the transgressors and breakers of the same, to distribute all great promotions and office, and to make and break leagues and peace with other nations and princes about."³

Starkey's proposal for the transference of powers is a constitutionally innovative one of daring proportions. For by "the common counsel of the realm" he has in mind a permanent body of fourteen persons appointed by the assembled parliament and invested with its authority during the period of its dissolution.⁴ Instituted to defend the laws and liberties of the realm against "hurtful and prejudicial" policies of the King and "his proper counsel" and to remedy corruption and injustice within the commonwealth, this "little parliament" would have, in addition to the above mentioned powers, authority to call to account, discipline and punish inferior officials, secular and ecclesiastical, for negligent and criminous conduct of their duties; to appoint the King's "proper counsel"; and to summon the "great parliament" to decide matters of political moment affecting the whole commonwealth.⁵

With such an effective curbing of royal self-interest, irresponsibility, and misgovernment, and with the balance of power in the hands of civic-spirited public servants, Starkey is confident that beneficial reforms can move apace in all sectors of communal life. As to religious and ecclesiastical reform, Starkey's recommendations demonstrate nationalist, conciliarist, and Lutheran sympathies: embracing an English episcopacy and ecclesiastical judicial system largely independent of Rome; a limited, constitutional papacy; and a Bible and liturgy in the vernacular, with sound preaching and virtuous living from an educated clergy.⁶

Although Starkey's constitutionalist interpretation of "mixed rule," with its clear bias toward parliamentary supremacy, sounded a somewhat discor-

1. Ibid., 100.
2. Ibid., 104.
3. Ibid., 100-101.
4. Ibid., 156-7, 166.
5. Membership of the permanent counsel, that is successor to the historically earlier office of "Constable of England," includes: "four of the greatest and ancient lords of the temporality" (namely, the Constable, the Lord Marshall, Steward and Chamberlain of England), four of the chief judges, two bishops (of London and Canterbury), and four distinguished citizens of London (the site of the counsel).
6. Ibid., 127-30, 178-179, 189-90.

dant note within the predominant monarchistic and centralist tune of Henrician reform ideology, it was nonetheless widely and appreciatively heard. It played its part in mediating the English natural law tradition to the younger generation of classical humanists who would ascend under Edward VI, paving the way by its subtle transformations of the tradition for the militant Protestant political response to Queen Mary's persecution.

Six

Thomas Cranmer and the Dilemma of the Erastian Reformer

In striking contrast to Thomas Cromwell, whose life is a paradigm of maddening consistency, stands his contemporary, Thomas Cranmer (1489-1556), whose life has presented subsequent generations with a fascinating enigma. The apparent ambiguities and contradictions of Cranmer's character and career have provided endless fodder for the wildly contradictory propagandist interpretations of Protestant and Catholic biographers alike. Set against the traditional Catholic portrait of Cranmer as "an unprincipled opportunist and a tool of royal tyranny" is the traditional Protestant portrait of "an honest Papist who gradually saw the light."[1] Cutting through the skein of polemical exaggeration and suppression is the more balanced and subtle picture that emerges from the meticulous detail of Jasper Ridley's biographical study. While not dissolving the enigma of the man, Ridley's study reduces it to the scale of the ordinary by placing it in proper perspective. The picture of Cranmer drawn by Ridley is of a man disposed equally to tentativeness of judgment and to courage of conviction, led down occasionally opposite paths by his dual loyalty to the supreme truth of Scripture and the supreme public authority of the monarch, and haunted by a dread of popular uprising and revolutionary disorder. Such a constellation of

---

1. Jasper Ridley, *Thomas Cranmer* (Oxford, 1962), 11.

loyalties and anxieties goes far to render intelligible the periodic episodes of scandalous conduct of which this wise and noble theologian and statesman stands accused: for example, his granting of three divorces to Henry VIII on spurious grounds; his constant compliance with Henry's tyrannous arbitrariness, especially in the prescription of official religious doctrine; and his condemning as heretics colleagues whose views he secretly endorsed. It may justifiably be said that the issue of authority is the stumbling block of Cranmer's intellectual and moral career, never to be resolved unambiguously. Cranmer was so circumstanced that his conduct as well as his thought was bound to be a vital and consequential working out of this thorny issue.

A. Cranmer's Life and Works

Born in 1489, Cranmer was educated at Cambridge, and appointed a Fellow of Jesus College around 1514. Compelled to resign his fellowship upon his marriage, he was remarkably reinstated after the early death of his wife. After taking holy orders, he became a Doctor of Divinity in 1526 and remained a Cambridge divine for five more years. His scholarly life was devoted to intensive study of the Scriptures and to the digesting of illegal Lutheran tracts. He pursued his investigations into Lutheranism quietly, keeping his distance from its more outspoken sympathizers among his colleagues, such as Thomas Bilney (1495-1531), Robert Barnes (1495-1540), and Hugh Latimer (c.1485-1555).

Cranmer first attracted the king's attention by his novel suggestion that the issue of his divorce from Catherine was a theological one that should be settled by divines in the universities and not by canonists in the ecclesiastical courts. On the basis of a preference for Leviticus over Deuteronomy, he publicized the view that Henry's existing marriage violated the law of God and so could not be validated by papal dispensation.[1] His argument proved so persuasive with his Cambridge colleagues that Henry soon enlisted him to wrest a favorable judgment from the Italian universities—an enterprise necessitating less scrupulous tactics. The relative futility of his diplomacy did not prevent his being appointed as chaplain to Anne Boleyn, and then to the king.

Of considerable consequence for his future life and thought was his sojourn at Ratisbon throughout 1532 as resident ambassador at the court of

---

1. The issue, as Cranmer saw it, was whether marriage of a man to his brother's widow was prohibited merely by canon law, from which the Pope could dispense, or by the law of God, from which the Pope could not dispense. The key Biblical passages were Leviticus 18:21 and Deuteronomy 25:5 that stood in tension, Leviticus prohibiting intercourse with one's brother's wife and Deuteronomy requiring a man to marry his brother's widow.

Emperor Charles V. During these months Cranmer had his first taste of Lutheran civic culture, made secret contacts with Lutheran luminaries, and was wedded, apparently by Andreas Osiander (1498-1552), to his wife's niece, thereby cementing a covert but compelling alliance with Lutheranism. In November 1532, he received from Henry VIII an urgent summons to return to fill the vacant archiepiscopal see of Canterbury. Apparently, the king was eager to consecrate an archbishop with papal authorization before embarking on his schismatic course in the pressing matter of his divorce. Cranmer later testified before his Oxford judges to his grave reluctance to accept this unorthodox advancement, probably out of his growing conviction of the morally reprehensible character of Henry's conduct toward Catherine. Nevertheless, he was consecrated archbishop in time to annul Henry's marriage and crown the new Queen before the arrival of the Princess Elizabeth. At his consecration Cranmer swore the customary oath of obedience to the Roman Church and pope, promising to "defend" and "promote" their "honour, privileges and authority," and to "persecute and denounce heretics, schismatics and rebels." But he proceeded to subject his oath to a novel protestation that qualified it to the point of nullifying it, by denying that any oath to the pope was binding which ran against "the law of God," "the King of England or the Commonwealth," "the laws or prerogatives of his realm," or the monarch's interest in reforming "the Christian religion and the government of the Church of England."[1] Ridley puts in perspective the offensive duplicity of Cranmer's public performance by reminding us that the traditional oath of allegiance to the king in respect of temporalities had required archbishops for over four centuries to renounce and repudiate all "clauses, words, sentences and grants" contained in the papal bulls of the archbishopric of Canterbury that were, are, or may be "hurtful or prejudicial" to the king and his successors, and to acknowledge themselves as taking and holding the archbishopric "immediately and only of your Highness and of none other"![2] It is hard to resist Ridley's judgment that the scope of the oath for temporalities was such as to render the protestation theoretically superfluous.

The first years of Cranmer's archiepiscopacy saw the dismantling of the papal power structure and the erection of the royal supremacy over the English church. This revolution entailed a vast enlargement of the jurisdiction of Canterbury, with the transference to it of such papal prerogatives as the judgment of final appeals in ecclesiastical causes, the issuing of mandates for the consecration of bishops, and the granting of dispensations from the

---

1. The consecration oath and formal protestation are described in Ridley, *Thomas Cranmer*, 55.
2. Ibid., 55-56.

canon law. The wielder of these powers proved to be a perfect public agent of the royal despotism, authorizing antipapist propaganda and suppressing dissent by convicting for heresy and treason, while directing Convocation to recognize the king's wisdom. The intellectual basis of Cranmer's orientation comes most clearly to light in the argument by which he hoped to persuade Sir Thomas More (1478-1535) to swear the oath required of the whole population by the Act of Succession of 1534. When More, without condemning his colleagues for swearing, refused to take the oath to uphold the succession established by Henry's divorce in explicit defiance of papal authority, Cranmer argued that More's reluctance to condemn his clerical brothers evidenced his "unsure conscience on the propriety of taking the oath," and that in such uncertainty he should "take the sure way of obeying his Prince by swearing it."[1] Allowing for the element of sophistical rhetoric in Cranmer's argument, it still expresses his most stubborn conviction that the monarch's will defines truth and error, good and evil for the community. More's resistance to this attack on the public claim of the Catholic conscience, that brought about his martyrdom for the "old faith," rightly assumed the role of Cranmer's Achilles' heel to the end of the Archbishop's life.

Cranmer's continual subjection of his convictions and scruples to Henry's official policy never exhaustively defined his relation to the king. In private intercourse he occasionally opposed, criticized, and instructed Henry, especially on doctrinal and theological matters. An amusing, if ominous, instance of Cranmer's presumption was his critical commentary on Henry's revisions to "the Bishops' Book," officially titled *The Institution Of A Christian Man*. This formulary of faith was originally issued by a party of bishops and divines under Cranmer's editorial guidance in 1537 and was about to be reissued in the king's name upon his approval of the text. When Henry invited Cranmer to comment on his 250 emendations, Cranmer wrote objections to 82 of these, chiefly opposing the king's incorrigible works-righteousness and his sometimes willful, sometimes innocent, derogation from the authority of the words of Scripture. The Bishops' Book, Henry's revisions, and Cranmer's comments together comprise a revealing statement of Henrician political theology, to which we shall return.

Cranmer's quiet crusade for the authority of the Scriptures advanced a step when he arranged with the king on behalf of Convocation for the preparation of an English translation of the Bible. The rather unproductive result of this committee effort was shortly to be compensated for by Cromwell's successful negotiations for the authorized issue of Coverdale's Bible, published in

---

1. Ibid., 73.

1537. In apparent ignorance of these negotiations, Cranmer sought, through Cromwell, and obtained the king's license permitting another English translation, namely, the Matthew's Bible, to be read with impunity throughout the realm.

In 1538 Henry's interest in an alliance with the German princes offered Cranmer the opportunity to oversee on the English side the construction of a joint formulary of faith with the German Lutherans. A draft statement of Thirteen Articles containing agreements on the controversial doctrines of justification, the Real Presence, confession, and civil authority was developed, but never officially issued, owing to Henry's refusal to acquiesce in the Lutherans' condemnation of private mass, communion in one kind, and clerical celibacy. Nevertheless, the formulary remains significant as a source document for the Articles of Faith issued in the reigns of Edward VI and Elizabeth.

To Cranmer's dismay, the king proceeded to demonstrate a wild fluctuation of judgment in favour of a retrenched Catholicism in his attempt to abolish religious diversity with the Six Articles. Under close royal scrutiny, the Lords constructed a reactionary defense of the "abuses" condemned by the Lutherans, which, after obtaining Convocation's assent, was enforced by parliamentary act. Cranmer's capitulating endorsement of practices and positions, known to contradict his firm convictions (and secret conduct),[1] has been universally regarded by admirers and detractors alike as a betrayal of his Christian obligation not to sin at the prince's command but to refuse to comply and suffer martyrdom. Whatever his sufferings from moral self-reproach, he was soon consoled in his practical defeat by Henry's re-opening of doors to a German alliance, again for reasons of political expediency. A little more than a year later, he had the gratification of arranging the publication of the third authorized translation of the Bible, commonly known as the "Great Bible," that bears his preface.

During the unpromising last years of Henry's reign, beset by Catholicizing retractions, Cranmer's greatest accomplishment was to survive the bitter opposition and plots to discredit him—as Cromwell did not. No doubt his survival was largely due to the king's enduring regard for him. Nevertheless, he had many causes for discouragement, the most formidable being Henry's growing disapproval of the Great Bible and of Bible-reading by the laity, which he legislatively curtailed in 1543.

As is well known, the ascent to the throne of Edward VI, under the protectorship of the Duke of Somerset, unleashed reforming impetus with

---

1. Cranmer was at this time illicitly cohabiting with his wife, Margaret.

momentous consequences. The most thorny problem threatening reform was the potential crisis of authority owing to the king's minority, and this necessitated a concerted effort by the reformers on the king's council to secure the royal headship over the church. Serving this end (though not exclusively dictated by it), Cranmer's coronation speech is an unguarded apotheosis of the royal supremacy over church and realm. He dispels the false opinion that the royal dignity is bestowed by the church in the coronation rites, conditional on the keeping of promises made by the monarch to the Archbishop, and insists instead that the king's power rests solely on divine ordination, election, authorization, and equipment, the ceremony having merely admonitory force.[1] Fortunately, the supreme ruler proved susceptible of wise persuasion and allowed the reformation of religion to proceed apace.

It is Cranmer's contributions in this phase that establish him as the founding father of Anglicanism. His first (and least) contribution is his promulgation in 1547 of a Book of Homilies, all of which he approved and authorized, three of which he authored. His Homilies "Of Salvation," "Of The True, Lively, And Christian Faith," and "Of Good Works Annexed Unto Faith" form a continuous exposition of the doctrine of justification by faith alone, which, nevertheless, shuns any tendency to diminish the authority for faith of God's law.

Cranmer's second and most revered contribution is his Book of Common Prayer, which is the fruit of a decade of thought and five years of labor. His first draft of the new liturgy is commonly associated in time with his English Litany, composed for King Henry in 1544. It provides a common service for the realm, based on the familiar Sarum Use, conservative in tone and entirely in Latin. His second draft, probably of the following year, more adventurously reduces the eight traditional Hours to Morning and Evening Prayer and translates focal parts of the service. Only his final draft of 1548 offers a complete liturgy in the vernacular, embodying a radical theological reorientation as regards the Communion Service, that "eliminat[es] as far as possible the idea of the mass as a sacrifice."[2] Cranmer's revolutionary accomplishment had been called forth by the bold action taken by the Parliament and Convocation of the previous year to institute communion in both kinds for the laity and to abolish private masses. Even this liturgy, however, proved insufficiently reformed to satisfy the sympathizers of Calvin and Zwingli, so that in 1552 it was subjected to a thoroughgoing revision (undertaken probably by Cranmer)

---

1. *Miscellaneous Writings and Letters of Thomas Cranmer*, ed. Rev. John E. Cox, for the Parker Society (Cambridge, 1846), 126. All page references to Cranmer's works are to the above volume.
2. Ridley, *Thomas Cranmer*, 287.

to excise Romish doctrines and practices from the entire corpus of services. By this revision the Prayer Book was rid of such suspect features as prayers for the souls of the deceased, extreme unction in the visitation of the sick, the delivery of the chalice and paten to the priest on ordination, a range of vestments, and every prayer and rubric suggesting belief in the Real Presence.

Imposed by an Act of Uniformity that lacked episcopal support,[1] the Book of Common Prayer of 1548 excited widespread conservative religious revolt, fuelled by social discontent. This tide of rebellion drove Cranmer to forceful pronouncements on ecclesiastical and secular authority and the Christian duty of obedience that have the clear ring of theological sincerity.

Cranmer's third contribution was his Articles of Religion that gave official doctrinal circumscription to the Edwardian reformation. His original Forty-five Articles, composed in 1552, were issued in 1553, with certain minor modifications to his intentions. Although a somewhat polemical and negative statement, designed to repudiate equally Popish and Anabaptist errors, the Articles, nevertheless, make positive declarations of lasting theological value. They concern, among other things, the sufficiency of Scripture as the source and measure of saving truth and the constitutive authority for the church,[2] the election of men in Christ and their justification by faith in Him,[3] the permanent validity of the moral law,[4] the effectual character of the Sacraments as signs of grace,[5] and the perfection of Christ's satisfaction for the sins of the world made once upon the cross.[6] Naturally, the occasion is taken to assert the king's supreme headship under Christ of the Church of England, the divine ordination of civil authority, and the *civil* duty of obedience.[7] Civil ownership is reinforced by an unequivocal denial of the commonality of property among Christians, an exhortation to almsgiving notwithstanding.[8] Cranmer's Articles, of course, form the basis of the Thirty-Nine Articles, promulgated under Elizabeth I in 1563, to which the Church of England still formally subscribes.

Within two months of the publication of the Articles, Queen Mary was on the throne and Cranmer in disgrace—imprisoned on a charge of treason for his support of Edward's appointed successor, Lady Jane Grey. His reluc-

---

1. The Act of Uniformity was carried against the dissenting votes of the conservative bishops in the House of Lords. Ibid., 289.
2. Arts. V, VI, VII, XII, XXI.
3. Arts. XI, XII, XIII, XIV, XVII.
4. Art. XIX.
5. Arts. XXVI, XXVII.
6. Art. XXX.
7. Arts. XXXIII, XXXVI.
8. Art. XVII.

tant acquiescence in Edward's "divise" to vest the Crown in his cousin, against Mary's hereditary and statutory claims to it,[1] exposed the theological foundation of the prince's unconditional demand to be obeyed: namely, that he was the Lord's elect, regardless of how he had come by the throne. Hence, the duty of "submission to any *de facto* King."[2] To be accused of treachery to the Crown was the harshest conceivable punishment of Cranmer's almost boundless devotion to it. He enthusiastically embraced Mary's eventual decision to make heresy rather than treason his crime for its obvious justice. He had courageously provoked her religious indignation by publicly repudiating as a Satanic invention the "Latin satisfactory mass" that she was plainly intending to restore. In so doing he, ironically, came closer to seditious conduct than he ever had before. This repudiation, bearing the archiepiscopal seal and affixed to every church door in London, stands as an authentic witness to the church's civil responsibility that overshadows the much discussed later recantations of an harassed, ill-treated, and bewildered old man. It is interesting to observe, however, how thoroughly Cranmer's subsequent appeals against his excommunication and degradation, as well as his subsequent endorsements of Catholic doctrine and practice, are declarations of the monarch's sovereign authority to define the faith of her subjects. A petition for pardon to Mary expresses with epitaphic eloquence the deeply-rooted sentiments for which Cranmer is rightly remembered: ". . . it lieth not in me, but in your grace only, to see the reformation of things that be amiss. To private subjects it appertaineth not to reform things, but quietly to suffer that they cannot amend." Fortunately, the Christian duty of the bishop-theologian does not end here. Cranmer continues: "Yet nevertheless to shew your Majesty my mind in things pertaining unto God, methink it is my duty, knowing that I do, and considering the place which in times past I have occupied."[3] Mary refused him "licence" to show his mind; and Cranmer was sent to the stake, after two years of further agony, without the consolation of being condemned by the legitimate authority of his sovereign queen rather than the usurped authority of the antiChrist in Rome.

---

1. Not only had Henry VIII provided in his will for Mary's succession to the throne in the event of Edward dying childless, but a parliamentary act of 1545 had made it high treason to dispute the succession thus established.
2. Ridley, *Thomas Cranmer*, 345.
3. Cranmer to Queen Mary (December 1553), in Cranmer, *Miscellaneous Writings*, 444.

B. THE UNRESOLVED PROBLEM OF LAW AND AUTHORITY

Cranmer, the theologian, upheld consistently and unequivocally the two touchstones of Reformation doctrine: *sola scriptura* and *sola gratia*. He professed the Scripture to be the sole revelation of God's truth and righteousness, salvation and law, with the authority to interpret itself to the faithful reader. He likewise professed the salvation of the sinner by the sole justifying grace of Jesus Christ, working through a "true" and "lively" faith. These two doctrines were constitutive for his treatment of law and authority, as they were for Tyndale's, but they lacked the conclusiveness for Cranmer that they properly had for his Lutheran contemporary. Tyndale never doubted that the claim of God's truth and law in the Scriptures to be heard and obeyed surpassed and qualified the claim of civil rulers to the loyalty and obedience of their subjects, whereas Cranmer never, apparently, got beyond doubt in this regard. His inconclusiveness more resembles that of Wyclif, without, however, springing from the soil of fateful theological tensions. To what then is it attributable?

To an overweening predilection for public diplomacy and the art of the possible? In part, no doubt. But also, there is evidence of the seductive influence of Marsilius' resolution of theopolitical issues, mediated, most probably, by Gerson. Cranmer's public pronouncements and formulations in the course of his episcopacy exhibit striking features of Marsilius' settlement:[1] most notably, his conceptions of the dual basis (divine and human) of priestly authority and the contingency of priestly inequality and papal power on human exigencies, together with the purely "spiritual" character of ecclesiastical jurisdiction that removes it from the realm of law enforcement by material penalties. Indeed, his close association of law with coercive jurisdiction inclines him to represent as law only that enacted by the civil authorities.

In addition, Cranmer's attempts at liturgical reform furnished abundant opportunities for reiterating the principle that the church's worship is, for the most part, the outcome of man-made traditions, without direct divine authorization. He relished the occasion for pitting the idolatrous righteousness of the pope's cultus, that promulgates human laws as divine laws, against the true righteousness of the civil law, that upholds God's laws, by inducing men to observe them, without claiming to promulgate them.[2] Admittedly, this opposition owed more to Lutheran polemic against religious works

---

1. Here are included public statements constructed under his supervision with multiple authorship, such as *The Institution of A Christian Man* (1538).
2. T. Cranmer, *An Homily Or Sermon Of Good Works Annexed Unto Faith*, in Cranmer, *Miscellaneous Writings*, 146-7.

righteousness than to Marsilius' evaluation of the status of ecclesiastical law. Equally Lutheran in inspiration was his depiction of his royal master as the successor of "Josaphat, Josias, and Ezechias," who "put away" all the "pharisaical and papistical leaven of man's feigned religion" to reinstate God's "holy commandments" and "Christ's pure religion."[1] Whatever the modest demeanor Cranmer sometimes wished to ascribe to the civil laws, his public conduct invariably spoke their identity with God's laws. The decisive point of identity for Cranmer was the very demand for obedience to temporal rulers, which in the Bishop's Book he allowed to be found in the Ten Commandments under the rubric of honoring thy father and mother.[2] The obedience required by the king's law to itself was an obedience required of all subjects by God. So exalted was the authority of the king's law that the king himself was bound by it—not as a subject is bound but as its maker and executor. In reply to Henry's claim to be above his own law, Cranmer boldly defended the law's claim upon his sovereign will: "Princes," he counsels, "must also do all things with justice, which otherwise cannot be known, than by their laws and ordinances institute for the ministration thereof: and when Princes give pardons, placards, protections, and licences, contrary to the common order of their laws, yet that also is done by the law, so that it be never done against justice and equity between party and party."[3] Evidently, this formal authority of the ruler's law for his own action does not oblige him to legislative consistency: he is always at liberty to alter, or even reverse, the law's commands if he should see fit. Thus, neither God's law nor man's law provides an institutional restraint on the sovereign's legislating: his political will carries absolute authority, even when it contravenes the teaching of Scripture and the tradition of the realm. It is Cranmer's lamentable judgment that the divine author of truth and righteousness continues to entrust their presence in the civil community to a single supreme arbitrator. Here again we encounter the Henrician face of Marsilius, which simply substitutes the plenary power of the Crown for that of the pope.

---

1. Ibid, 148.
2. The Bishops' Book of 1538, compiled under Cranmer's direction, extends the meaning of father in the Fifth Commandment to cover "spiritual" and "temporal" authorities. It should not be overlooked that Cranmer resisted Henry's determination to exclude "spiritual fathers" (ecclesiastics) from the honor commanded. See *Corrections of the Institution of a Christian Man by Henry VIII, with Archbishop Cranmer's Annotations*, in ibid., 103-4.
3. Ibid., 105.

Seven

The Marian Exiles and the Puritan Option

Two groups of exiles shaped Elizabeth's religious settlement: foremost were the English Protestant exiles to the continent during Queen Mary's reign; before them, the continental Protestant exiles to England during the Duke of Northumberland's reformation under Edward VI. The Marian exiles are our chief concern, but the Edwardian exiles deserve passing comment as a backdrop of some importance.

A. THE EDWARDIAN EXILES

From 1547 to 1550 England received an influx of eminent Protestants, who came in response to Archbishop Cranmer's warm invitation, assured of Northumberland's Protestant sympathies, and disinclined to tarry under the unacceptable religious compromise imposed by the Emperor in his territories.[1] Among their numbers were included the distinguished Italian divines, Pietro Martire Vermigli (Peter Martyr) (1500-62) and Bernardino Ochino (1487-1564), fresh from the Protestant intellectual ferment of Strassburg; the

---

1. The Interim of Augsburg, imposed in May 1548, conceded to the Protestants clerical marriage and communion in both kinds, while retaining an essentially Catholic worship that included transubstantiation and the seven sacraments.

adventurous Polish theologian John à Lasco (1499-1560), from the Reformed city of Emden, with his "advanced Zwinglian and Calvinist views"; and the pre-eminent German Reformer, Martin Bucer (1491-1551), disciple of Luther and Zwingli, intimate friend of Calvin, and "acknowledged patriarch" of the international Protestant community at Strassburg.[1] With the exception of à Lasco, who superintended the foreign Protestant congregations in London, these visiting dignitaries were placed by Cranmer in esteemed academic and ecclesiastical posts which allowed them to pursue and expound their Protestant learning. Their influence, although not dramatic or far-ranging, was present as a guiding force in the government's framing of ecclesiastical policy, notably in the Second Edwardian Prayer Book of 1552, in Cranmer's own theological development, and in the orientations of both universities. The fates of leading Cambridge Protestants under Edward VI provide a most striking testimony to the longer-term impact of the sojourn of Bucer and Martyr in England. The humanists and classical scholars, Thomas Smith and John Cheke, both powerful university administrators and previous members of Edward's Privy Council, followed the revered Martyr to Strassburg in flight from Mary's regime, with a contingent of young Protestant students. They were joined there by a host of early Cambridge associates who had occupied important governmental and ecclesiastical positions under the Protector Somerset, had been firmly behind Cranmer's reforms, and had welcomed and learned from the illustrious continental émigrés. Many of these associates, who included Sir Richard Morison, Sir Anthony Cooke, Oliver Wrothe, former archbishop Edwin Sandys, Edmund Grindal, Richard Cox, former bishop John Ponet, and Thomas Becon, were destined to be the executors of Elizabeth's religious legislation. The exposure of these humanistic Anglicans to the forces of international Protestantism at home prepared them for the immersion of exile, laying a foundation for the future consolidation of a Reformed stance.

It is undoubtedly the case that the continental émigrés of Edward's last years helped to shift the balance of reform from a Lutheran to a Calvinist footing. Their views on the sacraments and on discipline and authority were more under the sway of Geneva than Augsburg. They presented the attraction of a Biblically-educated, apostolically simplified, and self-disciplining ecclesial community, guiding the commonwealth and subject to the magistrate in a manner compatible with its evangelical mission and authority. On the subject of civil rule, Peter Martyr was pre-eminently the exponent of Calvin's scholas-

---

1. A convenient description of these continental reformers is given in A. G. Dickens, *The English Reformation* (London, 1964), 231-34.

tic doctrines, which, although by no means popularist and republican, were morally sympathetic to the victory of constitutionalism over royal absolutism.

Of equal importance with such theological scholarship in fashioning the English reforming consciousness, both positively and negatively, was the working model of "fullfledged" Puritanism provided by à Lasco's foreign congregations in London.[1] Under one constitution, three congregations (French, German, and Italian) formed a church organized, not "upon episcopal or even sacerdotal principles, but . . . upon a powerful group of ordained and elected 'elders' or 'presbyters'," of whom some "supervised discipline" and others "preached and taught."[2] This international, self-governing and relatively democratic church, to which admittance was conditional,[3] subjected its members to "two hours of expository sermons every Sunday and instructional classes called 'prophesyings' during the week," and, in addition, to "compulsory services of preparation" for the monthly communions, wherein candidates were examined for their fitness to receive the sacrament.[4] An object of admiration and suspicion alike to the English reformers, à Lasco's church would in days to come be imitated, not only by the more strictly Calvinist Marian exiles, but also by their more nationalistic and self-consciously Anglican compatriots.

The picture of immigrant theological influence in Edward's reign must be completed by mention of the Scottish Protestant, John Knox (1505-1572), who, before joining the continental exiles escaping Queen Mary's persecution, was exiled in England. Following his release from political captivity in Scotland, he preached uncompromising reform from English pulpits, determined to purge the English church of its vestiges of Romish idolatry.

B. THE MARIAN EXILES

During their period of continental exile, the English Protestants formed eight geographically separate congregations, with the assistance of their returned European guests: originally at Emden, Wesel, Frankfurt, Strassburg, and Zürich; subsequently at Basel, Geneva, and Aarau. All except Wesel (which proved inhospitable), were Reformed cities, the Lutheran states being

---

1. A.G. Dickens and M.M. Knappen concur in the impact on English Protestants made by this striking example of Puritan congregationalism. See ibid. and M. M. Knappen, *Tudor Puritanism: A Chapter in the History of Idealism* (Chicago, 1939).
2. Dickens, *The English Reformation*, 239.
3. Potential members were required to "show a knowledge of the Reformed faith and undertake to lead a Christian life." Ibid.
4. Ibid.

reluctant to welcome the refugees out of theological disapproval and political caution.[1] Although each congregation had its own distinctive complexion, the eight were broadly divisible along ecclesiological-liturgical lines, according to whether they upheld Anglican orthodoxy as embodied in Cranmer's 1552 Prayer Book or opted for a more stringently Calvinist mode of worship and organization. Whereas the congregations at Zürich and Strassburg were models of Anglican probity, those at Frankfurt and later Geneva occupied the vanguard of radical reform.

The notorious factional strife at Frankfurt was remarkable for its sharpening of past controversies under Edward and foreshadowing of future ones under Elizabeth. Here were manifest for years to come the battle lines between Anglican orthodoxy and Reformed radicalism, later to be known as "Puritanism."[2] Under the leadership of William Whittingham (1524-79), the Frankfurt community initially adopted a Calvinized 1552 Prayer Book, "abolishing vestments, the Litany, the oral responses and other features which savoured of the unreformed religion."[3] To strengthen their reforming intent, they appointed John Knox as their senior minister, contrary to the advice freely proffered by their Strassburg brethren. The orthodox protest, such as existed, was kept in rein until galvanized by the arrival of the formidable Dr. Richard Cox (1500-81), former tutor and Prayer Book commissioner of Edward VI. Assisted by John Jewel (1522-71), among others, Cox battled with Knox to reinstate "an English Church," and precariously succeeded, with the

---

1. Lutheran divines disapproved of the Zwinglian doctrine believed to prevail among English Protestants, while Lutheran magistrates feared the political repercussions of offering such hospitality.

2. This view is upheld by the vast majority of scholars who have written on Tudor Puritanism and its relationship to Anglican orthodoxy. See, e.g., Dickens, *The English Reformation*; Knappen, *Tudor Puritanism*; P. Collinson, *The Elizabethan Puritan Movement* (Berkeley, 1967); R. G. Usher, *The Reconstruction of the English Church*, 2 vols. (New York, 1910); and E. H. Emerson, *English Puritanism from John Hooper to John Milton* (Durham, 1968). However, it has been challenged by some scholarship, most notably that of M. A. Simpson, who views the Frankfurt battle lines as actually drawn up almost twenty years later. In *John Knox and the Troubles Begun at Frankfurt* (Edinburgh, 1975), Simpson argues that the primary source text for the Frankfurt controversy, entitled *Brieff discours off the troubles begonne at Franckford*, allegedly written by the "Knoxian" William Whittingham, does not originate in the Frankfurt period, but was produced in Protestant circles close to the time of its publication in 1574, its purpose being to discredit the Book of Common Prayer and Richard Cox, whose harsh repression of nonconformity, as Bishop of Ely, invited considerable Puritan resentment in the early 1570s. While taking seriously some of Simpson's reservations about the complete authenticity of the source document, this author judges that he overstates his case, having proved no more than that an early reliable account of the controversy underwent editorial revisions at a later date. Consequently, he exaggerates the discontinuity between earlier and later controversies.

3. Dickens, *The English Reformation*, 289.

aid of an underhanded political stratagem to bring about Knox's expulsion.[1] Ironically, though Cox's victory preserved the Prayer Book liturgy and ceremonies, it resulted in a Book of Discipline owing more to Geneva and à Lasco's London congregations than to previous English church practice. Moreover, after Cox's departure to Zürich and further leadership broils, the community endorsed a new order of discipline erected squarely on principles of democratic congregationalism. This order, Dickens tells us, "made the Frankfurt congregation 'a particular visible Church', in fact a self-governing body politic, owing no allegiance to monarchs or bishops and fully subordinating the authority of the minister to that of the congregation, the sole source of law."[2]

Given the fate of discipline at Frankfurt, we cannot regard the dissension between more conservative and more radical factions as fully anticipating the terms of the Elizabethan and Jacobean church struggle, which was over discipline as much as ceremonies. However, it is worthy of note in this connection that the superintendents of the Frankfurt congregation, on the eve of their return from exile, refused Knox's proposal that "a Genevan order [be] established as soon as possible in England,"[3] thereby indicating the limited and transient character of their experiment with an independent, congregational organization. As Dickens himself points out, the Calvinism of the influential moderates among the exiles proved compatible with a high tolerance of episcopacy and Erastian church government. It is out of such a subtle interweaving of Reformed theology and English ecclesiastical tradition that the future of Anglicanism was spun. Unless we grasp this subtlety, we cannot properly understand the orientations to law and authority characteristic of Elizabethan churchmen. Of the two most seminal and original political thinkers of the period— John Ponet and John Knox—the latter is susceptible of being read, without undue distortion, as a Genevan revolutionary, but the former defies any such straightforward hermeneutic.

With symbolic appropriateness, the Frankfurt episode resulted in the formation of a Genevan congregation, headed by Whittingham and Knox. This community proved a hotbed of Calvinist literature, both scholarly and propagandist. Its most monumental contribution to the furthering of the Reformed religion in England was the production in 1557 of a new English Bible translation, drawing on solid Reformed scholarship, as well as partisan

---

1. A member of Cox's party revealed to the Frankfurt authorities an indiscreet and libellous attack on Mary, Philip of Spain, and the Emperor Charles published by Knox, thereby forcing them to expel him out of prudential considerations.
2. Dickens, *The English Reformation*, 292.
3. Ibid., 293.

commentary and exegesis. The "Geneva Bible" had unrivalled popularity during Elizabeth's reign, and continued to attract readers for several decades after the publication of the Authorized Version of 1611, textually indebted to it. On the tail of the Genevan Bible appeared two vigorous political addresses: Knox's *First Blast of the Trumpet against the Monstrous Regiment of Women* (1557) and Christopher Goodman's *How Superior Powers Ought To Be Obeyed of Their Subjects* (1558). These Genevan communications were closely associated with the earlier, equally impassioned political tract of the Strassburg exile, John Ponet.

1. John Ponet: A Shorte Treatise of Politike Power

Perhaps the most fascinating detail of this treatise's fate is that its authorship had become obscure within 40 years of its publication in 1556. When in 1593 Richard Bancroft (1544-1610) undertook to expose the "seditious and rebellious" implications of Puritan doctrine in his *Dangerous Positions and Proceedings* (1593), he produced 16 quotations from a book cited under the title of *Obedience*, which is unmistakably Ponet's treatise. Significantly, Bancroft identified the book with the detestable writings of the Genevan exiles. Although a timely 1642 edition of the treatise bore Ponet's name, unlike the earlier editions which had borne merely the cryptic initials D. I. P. B. R. W., the book's authorship remained generally unknown until publicized by John Strype in the early eighteenth century. The revelation of the mysterious author to be Dr. John Ponet, Bishop of Rochester and Winchester, gave scandal to many and was credited only reluctantly.[1]

The obscurity of Ponet's authorship and the reluctance with which it was finally admitted suggests the implausibility of the connection between this book and this man. Readers continue to wonder how such views on civil authority and obedience could have been espoused by an Henrician scholar, Edwardian bishop, and intimate protégé of Thomas Cranmer. That a radical Calvinist of Genevan stripe should advocate popular sovereignty and civil resistance, though scandalous, was grimly comprehensible to defenders of Elizabeth's church establishment and to their Anglican successors; but a once highly-placed episcopal supporter of Cranmer's legacy was expected to think otherwise. No other English dignitary of the time, ecclesiastical or non-ecclesiastical, so blatantly repudiated the absolute right of the king and the absolute wrong of civil rebellion.

---

1. W.S. Hudson, *John Ponet (1516?-1556): Advocate of Limited Monarchy* (Chicago, 1942), introduction, 205-211. Hudson's presentation of Ponet's life and writings is followed by a reproduction of the 1556 text of *A Short Treatise of Politic Power*, which is used herein.

And yet Ponet, despite his appearance of historical incongruity and precocity, is quite intelligible as a theological humanist and classicist, student of Plato, Aristotle, and Cicero, and of the late medieval Schoolmen. He owes an obvious debt to the English natural law and constitutional tradition powerfully synthesized by Thomas Starkey, and, within a Catholic framework, by Cardinal Pole. This is not to diminish the influence of Calvin, mediated in part by Ponet's venerated teacher Peter Martyr, or the stimulus afforded by even an expurgated Marsilius, whose unexpurgated *Defender of the Peace* was available in Latin. It is only to point out the continuity of direction and development that situates Ponet's radicalism within a firmly established English context of ideas.

It is noteworthy that Ponet's radical action also had an indigenous context. There is evidence that his flight to Strassburg followed immediately upon a period of imprisonment imposed for his involvement in Wyatt's unsuccessful Kentish rebellion. This Protestant and anti-Spanish uprising, provoked by Mary's Catholicizing measures and her marriage alliance with Philip of Spain, had the object of capturing London and the queen. In his biographical introduction to *A Short Treatise* Hudson offers illuminating motives for Ponet's participation in the ill-fated enterprise from the standpoint of his subsequent writing.

> On the death of Edward, from [Ponet's] standpoint, it was impossible for a loyal subject legally and justly to oppose the coronation of Mary. Since the succession had not been altered with the consent of Parliament, . . . she was the rightful heir to the throne. But, after assuming the royal office, she had become a tyrant whom all true subjects were duty-bound to resist. By seeking the subversion of the gospel, she had violated divine law; by re-establishing the Latin Mass, she had disregarded positive law; and by the signing of the marriage treaty, it would appear to him that she had broken her coronation oath not to diminish any of the rights of the crown.[1]

Let us now proceed to render explicit, in the terms of *A Short Treatise*, the understandings of law and authority, civil rule, and civil duty implied in these compelling motives.

a. The Origin, Purpose, and Form of Civil Rule. According to Ponet, political power has its origin in God's post-deluvian decree to Noah that institutes capital punishment for the human crime of murder.[2] God's ordinance,

---

1. Ibid., 64.
2. Ponet, *A Short Treatise*, 7 ("He that sheddeth the blood of man, his blood shall be shed by man. For man is made after the image of God (Gen. 9:6)."). In all quotations we have substituted modern spellings.

requiring life for life, establishes man's authority over "the body and life of man," and over "goods, lands, possessions and all such things as might breed controversies and discords."[1] This authority is essentially that of making laws, and its bestowal stipulates the principles governing its practice: the proportionality of punishment to crime and the indifferent execution of the law on the meek and the mighty alike. The origin of civil rule, then, dictates its chief end to be the just punishment of wrongdoing.

However, Ponet indicates that the telos of political power embraces the broader good of maintaining the common "wealth and benefit," understood as conformity to the law of natural justice, contained in Christ's twofold command, that "Thou shalt love thy lord God above all things, and thy neighbour as thyself."[2] The laws should provide "for everyone doing his duty to God, and one to another,"[3] in order that the whole may "serve and glorify God."[4] Man's natural duty is further elaborated in the Decalogue, which defines both the content of the common good and the limitations of political authority, so that the means do not exceed the end. Accordingly, the power of "kings, princes, and other governors" over their subjects is not "absolute"; but rather is bound absolutely by divine law, with which they are in no way entitled to dispense.[5] Political authority, therefore, is intrinsically just: where justice is lacking, so is authority. This is Ponet's controlling theological-political principle, under which he frames his doctrines of sovereignty and obedience.

His concept of popular sovereignty is related to the form of civil rule. He argues in a manner reminiscent of Ockham that, while the power to make and execute laws is ordained by God, the form of this power is left to human ordinance: "But whether this authority . . . shall be and remain in one person alone, or in many, it is not expressed, but left to the discretion of the people to make so many and so few, as they think necessary for the maintenance of the state."[6] "The people" are divinely authorized to determine, instate and alter the form of government. Here Ponet, drawing on Fortescue's distinction between "royal" and "royal-political" rule, differentiates two types of "kings, princes, and governors": "the one who alone may make positive laws," being invested by the body politic with its entire law-making authority, and the other "unto whom the people have not given such authority, but keep it

1. Ibid., 8.
2. Ibid., 4.
3. Ibid., 22.
4. Ibid., 5.
5. Ibid., 22-25.
6. Ibid., 8.

themselves."¹ Following Fortescue, he identifies the first as "a tyrant," and the second as the monarch of a "mixed state" who shares political power with the nobility and commons in parliament. It is clear that, although the people are formally entitled to choose between a tyranny and a mixed state, only their choice of the latter respects the divinely ordained limitations of political authority. This is because Ponet assumes that only positive laws made by the people, as represented in the parliamentary estates, will embody to an acceptable degree the natural law of justice, to which the monarch's authority is subject. He repeatedly suggests that a monarch whose power is not bridled by parliamentary law will rule lawlessly. A just absolute ruler is for Ponet a contradiction in terms, for just political practice requires, apparently, a constitutional division of powers, under which kings are "but executors of God's laws, and men's just ordinances," being "also not exempted from them, but . . . subject and obedient unto them." To argue that a king, on account of his divine appointment, is exempt "from the laws . . . to do what him lusteth" is to imply that God allows his inevitable oppression of his subjects, and so, blasphemously, to make "God the author of evil."²

b. *The Civil Authority of the Individual Conscience.* Contrary to the direction in which his opening exposition of political authority leads, Ponet does affirm an absolute political authority: invested not in the hereditary monarch, the collective will of "the people," or parliamentary law but in the individual conscience. The individual conscience is the ultimate arbiter of political right and wrong, of civil justice and injustice. By means of its deliberations, the subject ascertains God's commandments, in the doing of which the commonweal consists, and measures against them the commandments of men. The conscience alone, and no temporal authority, justifies and acquits a man, or accuses and condemns him, before God. For its sake he obeys his ruler's good and virtuous commands, and resists his evil and wicked ones. His conscience teaches that the civil duty of obedience to God's laws requires him "to seek [his] own salvation: not to maintain evil but to suppress evil: for not only the doers but also the consentors to evil, shall be punished. . . ."³ Moreover, it instructs him in the true meaning of the Scriptures, against the crafty and deceitful expositions of ruthless tyrants, who bend God's Word to their evil designs of robbing their subjects of land, life, and labor. So when the king deviously construes Samuel's warning to Israel about royal tyranny in I

---

1. Ibid., 25-26.
2. Ibid., 43.
3. Ibid., 100.

Samuel 8:10-18 as a catalogue of God-given monarchial rights, the subject's Christian conscience loudly protests "No!"

Where the Scriptures do not pronounce, the subject's conscience does, revealing the demands of natural justice. Thus does it testify to the lawfulness of deposing and punishing an evil ruler, its testimony being confirmed by "manifold and continual examples" from the political histories of Israel, England, and other nations, and supported in addition by the judgment of the Roman canonists in favour of the lawfulness of depriving wicked popes.[1] In the case of king as of pope, the decisive principle is that divinely appointed authority is intrinsically just and virtuous and so cannot belong to unreformably evil men. The tyrannous pope or king holds his false authority from the erroneous act of men (constituting the body politic or the universal church), and not from God. His vice proves to the people the error of their choice, putting them in mind of Christ's exhortations about casting out unsavory salt and the eye that offends, in order that the "whole body" may escape destruction.[2] Such is the reciprocity of lawful authority between the ruler and the ruled, that each is divinely commissioned to correct and punish the other's wrongdoing, even to the point of taking life.

As to who of the people should undertake to depose and punish the tyrant, the Christian subject, respecting the public goods of orderliness and discretion, concedes the right and duty to the nobility first, then to the commons in parliament, finally to the "private man" only when "the whole state" conspires to neglect the execution of just punishment. In this last event, the executor of divine and human justice must either "have some special inward commandment or surely proved motion of God" or "be otherwise commanded or permitted by common authority upon just occasion and common necessity to kill."[3] This extraordinary latitude in regard to violent resistance bestowed by Ponet on the individual conscience is comprehensible in the circumstances of Mary's rule, given his theoretical starting point. For if he judged that Mary had forfeited her claim to political authority and that the nobility and commons were unlikely to exercise theirs, he might reasonably conclude that God would raise up a Moses or Ahud to save the English body politic from the absence of natural justice, that would be its perdition.

2. The Prophetic Addresses of John Knox in 1557-58

Whereas, as we have argued, Ponet's revolutionary ideas were deeply rooted in English political traditions and institutions, Knox's are more mani-

1. Ibid., 101-106.
2. Ibid., 104.
3. Ibid., 112.

festly of continental extraction. They echo theological categories and principles abstracted from the indigenous features of either English or Scottish political life. They have been described as partaking in an historically novel perspective on society and politics constructed out of a radicalization of Calvin's scholastic political doctrines.[1] Their theoretical similarities with Huguenot political treatises of the 1570s have been duly noted.[2] However, apart from the issue of distinguishing Calvinist and Lutheran sources for Knox's revolutionary theology,[3] it must also be remembered that Scotland had a tradition of aggressive, factious, and rebellious nobility, with certain of whose exploits Knox was already thickly implicated. Indeed, as recently as 1555-56, he had found himself back in Scotland carrying on a zealous Protestant missionary work among receptive congregations, under the protection of nobles who were thoroughly disaffected with their French Queen Regent and her French advisors. Rebellious sentiments were undoubtedly widely voiced in aristocratic circles, and religious justifications close to hand. What is still remarkable about Knox's political thought, given this sympathetic setting, is its thoroughgoing theological radicalism, involving an original constellation of Protestant social doctrines. This constellation unfolds in the four prophetic addresses of 1557-58 that bear the titles: *The First Blast of the Trumpet Against the Monstrous Regiment of Women, Letter to the Regent of Scotland, Appellation to the Nobility*, and *Letter to the Commonality of Scotland*. The leading themes combined in Knox's addresses with such powerful effect are the permanent political office of the prophet, the systemic opposition of man's law to God's law, the universal civil duty of suppressing idolatry, and the plurality of civil vocations directly authorized by the Word of God.

a. The Prophet and the Law. In calling Knox's addresses "prophetic," we are classifying them, not only in respect to their literary form and theological

---

1. In *The Revolution of the Saints: A Study in the Origins of Radical Politics* (London, 1966), Michael Walzer portrays English Puritanism as the original form of modern political radicalism, and interprets Knox's ideas within this coherent theoretical orientation.
2. See ibid., chap. 3 ("Two Case Studies in Calvinist Politics") and J.W. Allen, *A History of Political Thought in the Sixteenth Century* (London, 1928), pt. 3, chap. 4 ("The Huguenots and their Allies").
3. It is arguable that the most important continental source for Knox's position is the startling manifesto published at Magdeburg in 1550 that offers a theological justification of that city's refusal to accept the Emperor's Interim, and bears the signature of eight Lutheran clergymen. A comparison of Knox's doctrines with those propounded by the Magdeburg *Bekenntnis* gives an overwhelming impression of its influence on him, just as traces of its influence assert themselves in Ponet's formulations. The existence of this Lutheran document tells against attempts to make a rigid and sharp division between Lutheran and Calvinist political thinking in the second half of the sixteenth century.

content, but also, and chiefly, in respect to the self-understanding they convey and the office they explicitly claim. For Knox, as preacher of God's Word and pastor of Christ's flock, is first and foremost a prophet, whose office is "to preach repentance, to admonish the offenders of their offenses, and to say to the wicked, 'Thou shalt die the death, except thou repent'"[1] Having cast away the priest's vestment of sacramental grace, the minister of God puts on the prophet's mantle of saving admonition. Unlike the popish priest who administers God's law, the prophet simply proclaims it. And the law which he proclaims is, above all, God's violated and avenging law, that condemns the sinner and prescribes his punishment. In this blind, corrupt, and reprobate world, Christ's evangelical law of forgiving love is overshadowed by the accusing law of offended righteousness. The former law is assimilated to the latter, such that the first exercise of charity is the conviction of consciences and the pronouncement of divine sentence.

Knox's four addresses all interpret the command, judgment and sentence of God's righteous law that binds rulers and subjects alike. In so doing they impart a "hidden" knowledge of His law-giving and providential Will, concealed both from "the magistrates" and "the multitudes" of the age.[2] They publish His commandments for His people, convict the two nations and their royal houses of grievous offenses, and disclose the historical form of divine punishment on them. Throughout, the prophetic assault invokes a theological-epistemological polarity: between the plainness of God's law, made visible in nature, history, and the testimony of Scripture, and the blindness of man's depraved vision, manifest in the waywardness of all merely human laws, whether civil or ecclesiastical.

In Knox's view, the foremost part of divine law prescribes the right worship of God and the just punishment of idolators. As Scripture is the locus of this law, so it is man's highest juridical authority. Armed with Old and New Testament passages, he concentrates his accusations on the violation of religious law by the civil rulers and church authorities of England and Scotland. His controlling interest is strikingly remote from Ponet's more English concern with the regulation by natural law of political structures, authorities, and rights. Only in his *First Blast* is the law of nature accorded a typically forceful exposition, with an overall argument remarkably similar to Fortescue's in *On the Law of Nature*. Inveighing against the civil rule of women, Knox argues that, given their frail, feeble, foolish, and inconstant

---

1. J. Knox, *The First Blast of the Trumpet Against the Monstrous Regiment of Women*, in *The Political Writings of John Knox*, ed. with intro. Marvin A. Breslow (Washington, 1985), 39. All quotations from Knox's writings are taken from this collection.
2. Ibid., 38-41.

nature, women were originally subordinated to man by God's created ordinance, and, further, that their subordination became subjection "by constraint and by necessity" on account of "the curse and malediction pronounced against the woman by the reason of her rebellion."[1] Thus a female ruler, in sinning against nature, also violates God's express command, standing "in contempt of his punishment and malediction."[2] Even here, the case from nature is superseded by God's revealed Word in Scripture concerning the form of political rule (a matter not left to the discretion of the people!), as in Deuteronomy 17:14-15, where He commands the Israelites to appoint a king (not queen) from among their brethren. Significant is Knox's assurance that in Israel "the election of a king and appointing of judges did neither appertain to the ceremonial law, neither yet was it mere judicial, but that it did flow from the moral law as . . . having respect to the conservation of both tables [of the Decalogue]. For the office of the magistrate ought to have the first and chief respect to the glory of God. . . ."[3] Right civil rule belongs to man's duty to God, because its chief end is to promote His glory among men. Moreover, the ruler occupies "the throne of God," sitting in His place.[4]

Civil tradition, custom, and legal statute that permit the reign of a woman are without authority, being contrary to divine law, which alone authorizes human legislation. Knox goes so far as to deny even the existence of "order where God's appointment is absent. . . ."[5] In all his communications, he repudiates every attempt to justify and claim obedience for human ordinances contradicting God's revealed will. Especially is he intent upon denying validity to Catholic legislation designed "to suppress Christ's Evangel, to shed the blood of the saints of God, and to erect that most devilish idolatry—the papistical abominations and his usurped tyranny. . . ."[6] Neither councils nor emperors, says Knox in his *Appellation to the Nobility*, have authority to invest the pope and his prelates with "prerogatives" and "privileges" against "the ordinance and statutes of God," nor have civil statutes the authority to confirm such unlawful donations.[7] These abuses of jurisdiction are unequivocally the object of God's severest condemnation and punishment. Together with crimes against right worship, they have called

---

1. Ibid., 45-6.
2. Ibid., 46.
3. Ibid., 61. See also, J. Knox, *Appellation to the Nobility*, in Knox, *The Political Writings*, 114.
4. Knox, *The First Blast*, in ibid., 60. See also Knox, *Appellation*, in ibid., 115.
5. Knox, *The First Blast*, in ibid., 55.
6. Knox, *Appellation*, in ibid., 135.
7. Ibid., 135, 140-44.

down the manifold plagues by which He is chastising the English and Scottish nations.

In pronouncing God's judgment upon the two polities, Knox is compelled to render divine providence scrutable. He embraces this compulsion with unshakable prophetic confidence, boldly asserting that, for their idolatry, England and Scotland have been betrayed "into the hands of strangers." "Under the title of marriage," their mad and tyrannous Queens, Mary Tudor and Mary Stuart, have "translated" the "liberties, laws, commodities, and fruits" of their realms to "the power and distribution of others," respectively, to the Spaniard Philip and to the French Dauphin.[1] Giving theological form to the repugnance felt by nobles and commoners alike to these foreign alliances, Knox claims that they contravene God's justice by establishing unlawful possession, analogous to the possession attained "by theft, murder, tyranny, violence, deceit, and oppression."[2] Not only, then, does he discern God's providential law in the rights of historical peoples, but also in their political fates. With Knox, profane history has become a fully intelligible and unerring witness to God's eternal purposes.

b. Universal Civil Duty and Particular Civil Vocations. In his letters of 1558 Knox increasingly departs from his earlier view, still prevalent in *The First Blast*, that Christian subjects are called to suffer patiently, with imprisonment and martyrdom, their ruler's idolatry and the ensuing plagues against their commonwealth. Rather, he becomes persuaded that the sin which God is visiting with evil upon the subjects of England and Scotland is not only their monarch's idolatry, stemming from the past coolness of their reforming zeal; but also, and perhaps chiefly, their neglect of the duty to resist idolatry wherever it infects the body politic. Knox proclaims the radical equality of all Christians in their public obligation to resist actively, even forcibly, the perpetrators of idolatry.[3] As each stands equally under God's judgment and His redeeming love, so each stands equally under His law—that is, the law promulgated to Israel by Moses requiring the preservation of true religion and

---

1. Knox, *The First Blast*, in ibid., 71.
2. Ibid.
3. The equality of Christians in their faith and in their duty is the central theme of Knox's *Letter to the Commonality of Scotland*, in Knox, *The Political Writings*, 150-55. It is tempting to discern in Knox's concept of the universal Christian duty to suppress idolatry the influence of Ockham's concept of the universal duty to correct *errantes* within the church. Although Ockham's influence at this point has no scholarly documentation, it is highly plausible, given that Knox studied theology for four years at St. Andrews under Ockham's student, John Mair, whose ecclesiology owes much to his master. See Q. Skinner, *The Foundations of Modern Political Thought*, 2 vols. (Cambridge, 1978), 2: 43-4 and Jasper Ridley, *John Knox* (Oxford, 1968), 15-17.

the suppression of idolatry. There is no question here, as in Cranmer's thought, of competing loyalties to God's law revealed in Scripture and the temporal sovereign's law: the claim of the former on every believer's will is final and absolute.[1]

This does not mean that there are no civil duties specific to the separate parts of the commonwealth. The universality of the civil duty to uphold God's law does not, Knox assures us, undermine the "ordained distinction and difference betwixt king and subjects," nobility and commonality.[2] To the three civil orders belong reciprocal rights and obligations, complementary in degree, and derived directly from divine appointment. Thus Knox advises the Regent of Scotland that she has been "promoted to high dignity" "above" her commonwealth to effect the reformation of religion and the administration of "a justice inflexible . . . against murderers and common oppressors," albeit she is by nature unfitted to the task.[3] Likewise, he advises the Scottish nobles that they are "princes in that people," after the example of the princes of Judah in the time of Jeremiah, with the especial duty of delivering God's innocent prophets (preachers) from the unjust sentences passed on them by malicious, false, and corrupt ecclesiastics.[4] But, further, they are God's "appointed heads in [their] commonwealth," occupying His "chair," ruling "above" their brethren as His chosen "lieutenants," to the end that they promote His glory by providing that their subjects "be rightly instructed in his true religion, . . . be defended from all oppression and tyranny, . . . [and that] such as blind and deceive the people, . . . rob and oppress the flock may be removed and punished as God's law prescribeth."[5] Conspicuously, Knox says nothing to mark the nobles' authority as being inferior to the king's. On the contrary, he belies his earlier intimation of political hierarchy by explicitly subjecting the monarch to their religious jurisdiction.[6] The nobles are commanded and empowered by God to correct and repress their monarch's idolatry, not only by counsel and admonition but also by capital punishment

---

1. J. Knox, *Letter to the Regent of Scotland*, in Knox, *The Political Writings*, 88 ("But heavy shall the judgment be which shall apprehend such blasphemers of God's majesty who dare be so bold as to affirm that God hath commanded any creature to be obeyed against himself. Against God it is that for the commandment of any prince, be he never so potent, men shall commit idolatry, embrace a religion which God hath not approved by his word, or confirm by their silence wicked and blasphemous laws made against the honour of his majesty.").
2. J. Knox, *Letter to the Commonality of Scotland*, in Knox, *The Political Writings*, 150.
3. Knox, *Letter to the Regent of Scotland*, in ibid., 92.
4. Knox, *Appellation*, in ibid., 108-111.
5. Ibid., 114.
6. Knox's nobles perform the same public function as the *untere Obrigkeit* (lesser magistrates) of the *Bekenntnis* of Magdeburg.

in the event of royal obduracy, the execution of which would inevitably be preceded by armed rebellion. To shrink from exercising their proper authority (as have the justly chastised English nobles shrunk from putting to death their wicked Jezebel) is to consent to the evils tyrannously perpetrated—a reiteration of Ponet's logic.[1]

The commonality are assigned the more modest duty of providing for the true preaching of Jesus Christ and the right administration of His sacraments among themselves. In performing this duty they may, firstly, require of their "superiors" that they furnish true preachers and expel false ones; secondly, instate true teachers themselves in the event of their superiors' negligence; and, thirdly, withhold from corrupt bishops and clergy demanded dues until such time as they reform.[2] All the same, it must be said that Knox regards with sanguine eye the divine commissioning of a tyrant-slayer from among the lowly. To this extent he, like Ponet, trusts in the final authority of the individual conscience. Nevertheless, it is the historic nobility who wield the instruments of public justice with the most established authority; and they do so without claiming to represent the people.

3. Christopher Goodman: How Superior Powers ought to be Obeyed of their Subjects

Christopher Goodman was broadly experienced in the differences of outlook and resulting tensions among and within the continental refugee communities, having resided successively in Strassburg, Frankfurt, and Geneva. At the time of writing *How Superior Powers ought to be Obeyed*,[3] he was fellow pastor with Knox of the Genevan congregation. Contemporary with Knox's *First Blast*, Goodman's tract takes up his colleague's promised political agenda for a future work.[4]

In his treatise Goodman is chiefly concerned with the limits of political obedience arising from the divinely decreed nature and purpose of the political community. His argument manifests the spirit of theological-political radicalism associated with Geneva publications, but is a somewhat less compelling example of the species than those penned by Ponet and Knox, demonstrating neither the systematic political reflection of Ponet, nor the systematic theological reflection of Knox. Accordingly, we shall confine our

---

1. Ibid., 135.
2. Knox, *Letter to the Commonality of Scotland*, in ibid., 155.
3. Christopher Goodman, *How Superior Powers Ought to be Obeyed* (Geneva, 1558). We have substituted modern spellings in all quotations from Goodman's treatise.
4. As M. M. Knappen points out, the *First Blast* had promised a subsequent discussion of the social compact theory. Knappen, *Tudor Puritanism*, 146.

treatment of it to summarizing the common themes with the other writings and presenting several points of interest in their development.

Goodman's axiomatic premise, shared by Ponet and Knox, is the absolute authority of God's law, revealed and natural, to circumscribe the subject's duty of obedience to superior powers. With a prophetic urgency close to Knox's, Goodman stresses the active character of this required obedience, especially over against the commands of apostate and tyrannous rulers. When oppressed by their idolatrous and lawless demands, he insists, ". . . it is not a sufficient discharge for us before God, when we deny to accomplish their unlawful demands and threatenings, except we do the contrary, every man in his vocation and office, as occasion is offered, and as his power will serve."[1] In his appeal to the Scriptures, Goodman repeats the noteworthy hermeneutical principle that the Apostle Paul's exhortation to obedience in Romans 13 must be understood in the light of the Apostles Peter's and John's defiance of the Jewish magistrates in Acts 5.[2] Ordered by the priestly council to desist from preaching in the name of Christ crucified, they bluntly answered that "in all things God is to be obeyed before men," only to continue preaching after their release.[3] When the Apostles' example is allowed to control the meaning of Romans 13, its clear intention is to exhort obedience to the God-fearing, lawful, and equitable commands of government.[4]

Furthermore, Goodman concurs with Ponet and Knox that the subject's dutiful resistance to idolatry and tyranny is not even confined to doing the contrary of what is commanded and suffering for it, but extends to restraining and punishing the guilty authority. He is adamant that "where as the kings or rulers are become altogether blasphemers of God, and oppressors and murderers of their subjects, then ought they to be accounted no more for kings or lawful magistrates, but as private men: and to be examined, accused, condemned and punished by the Law of God. . . ."[5] While the responsibility for defending religion and for executing God's laws lies primarily with the nobility and inferior magistrates,[6] the common people too have "a portion of the sword of justice," to "execute the judgments which the magistrates lawfully command" and, where the magistrates "would wholly despise and betray the justice and Laws of God," to "maintain and defend the same Laws against them. . . ." Perhaps Goodman's most penetrating theological insight is

1. Goodman, *How Superior Powers*, 43.
2. Ibid., 37-39.
3. Ibid., 39.
4. Ibid., 111-13.
5. Ibid., 139.
6. Ibid., 34, 122-23.

that God's Word reveals to those who are ruled the political liberty or right they "may lawfully claim" and "are bound at all times to practice."[1] Failure to claim this divinely granted right invites tyranny both as natural consequence of and as divine punishment for the people's public cowardice and indifference.[2]

---

1. Ibid., 160.
2. Ibid., 150.

Eight

The Elizabethan Settlement and Its Detractors

During their continental sojourn, the exiled English Protestants were determining, wittingly or unwittingly, their future careers. From the outset, Queen Elizabeth gave signs of inclining to a conservative (that is, Edwardian) Protestant position. Given her inclination (for whatever motives), she was bound to cast an ambivalent eye on the returning refugees. On the one hand, they attracted her favor as victims of her sister's persecution; on the other, their European experience rendered them suspect. They, after all, had tasted the heady wine of self-governing churches in self-governing cities and had managed their own congregational autonomy.

While Elizabeth's doctrinal and theological commitments were, for the most part, opaque, the exceptions were her strong attachments to royal sovereignty and a hierarchically ordered realm. She plainly expressed her hatred of such radical theological-political doctrines as the unlawfulness of female rule and the duty of subjects forcibly to resist their ruler's idolatry. But she quickly elevated to ecclesiastical positions of authority and responsibility Protestant leaders and divines who had proved their patriotic, conservative stripe by their allegiance to the 1552 English Prayer Book and by their public profession of political orthodoxy. For example, her handpicked committee of 1559 to revise the Edwardian Prayer Books included three Frankfurt exiles who had sided with Anglican forms in the original controversy: namely,

Richard Cox, David Whitehead, and Edmund Grindal. Along with them was James Pilkington, who had headed opposition to Knox's Genevan proposals for reconstructing the English church. All went on to assume episcopal office, as also did the Anglican stalwarts, John Jewel and Edwin Sandys. Two of their number were further promoted to archbishoprics—Sandys to York and Grindal to Canterbury. By contrast, their Genevan associates were received coolly, if at all, and, for the most part, were debarred from ecclesiastical promotion on account of official animosity towards both them and their Reformed scruples. Knox was denied entrance into the realm; Goodman, after a furtive few weeks in his homeland, joined his fellow Genevan in Scotland; the distinguished Coverdale was never restored to the bishopric of Exeter; Whittingham was only allowed the deanship of Durham after five years of neglect.

Elizabeth was scarcely more receptive to Puritan attempts in 1559 to develop a political alternative to Knox which would correct his more glaring errors.[1] John Aylmer's *An Harbor for Faithful and True Subjects (against the First Blast)* (1559), with its exalted conception of the rights of parliament, fell on deaf ears in government circles and failed to rally powerful Protestant support. Laurence Humphrey's *On the Conservation of Religion and its True Reformation* (1559), which combined a strict separation of secular and religious jurisdiction with a constitutional theory of parliamentary sovereignty, met with the same lack of enthusiasm, as did his slightly earlier *The Nobles*, a Knoxian-style appeal to the reforming authority and leadership of the English nobility. While these treatises did not emanate from the odious Genevan group, they were, nevertheless, tainted by association with its radicalism, and so, along with their authors, were kept at arm's length by prudent Protestants.

A. THE LEGISLATION OF 1559

The legislated religious settlement of 1559 has recently been interpreted as the product of an alliance of intention between Elizabeth's government and

---

1. Consistent with standard scholarly usage of the term "Puritan," we have, with reference to the first decade of Elizabeth's reign, applied it generally to dissenting Protestant positions of Reformed inspiration from the established church. With reference to succeeding decades, following the emergence of Separtist conventicles, we have confined its application to Reformed dissent that refuses to break with the established church, setting up rival organizations to it. In the latter usage, the term "Puritan" is equivalent to Presbyterian. It is worthy of note, however, that Separatism, in origin and orientation (doctrinal and ecclesiological), is a sub-species of Puritanism. For a confirmation of this point, see Stephen Brachlow, *The Communion of Saints: Radical Puritan and Separatist Ecclesiology 1570-1625* (Oxford, 1988).

the moderately Protestant House of Commons, overcoming Catholic resistance in the Upper House. This interpretation, carefully documented by Norman L. Jones,[1] purports to correct the previously accepted theory that the legislation of 1559 embodied a compromise struck by Queen Elizabeth and her Secretary, Sir William Cecil, with the militant Protestant contingent in the Commons.[2] However modest and inconsequential in fact was the parliamentary voice of militant Protestants, it is certain that returned exiles were represented in their ranks—not, of course, the Genevan extremists, but the "Coxian or Prayer Book exiles," led, apparently, by Sir Anthony Cooke and Sir Francis Knollys, arrived from Strassburg and Basel respectively. The settlement took shape in 1559 in the Act of Supremacy and the Act of Uniformity, which combined features of Henrician and Edwardian law.

The Act of Supremacy was chiefly necessitated by Mary's Second Statute of Repeal (1555) that had reinstated papal jurisdiction in England by "repealing all Statutes, Articles, and Provisions made against the See Apostolic of Rome since the 20th year of King Henry the Eighth."[3] Elizabeth's measure of 1559 repealed the Marian statute and revived specific Acts of her father's, including the Act in Restraint of Appeals (1533) and the Act Concerning Ecclesiastical Appointments and Absolute Restraint of Annates (1534) which established the election of bishops by royal *congé d'élire*. The measure went on to annex to the Crown the "jurisdictions, privileges [etc.] . . . exercised or used for the visitation of the ecclesiastical state and persons, and for reformation, order, and correction of the same. . . ."[4] But the Crown was authorized to exercise such "jurisdictions" and "privileges" through subjects appointed "by letters patents" (that is, through royal commissioners) whose "power to order, determine, or adjudge any matter or cause to be heresy" was circumscribed by "the authority of the canonical Scriptures, . . . the first four General Councils, . . . [or previous judgments of] the High Court of Parliament of this realm with the assent of the Clergy in their Convocation."[5] Finally, the Act required of all public officials, ecclesiastical and temporal alike, an oath testifying that "the Queen's Highness is the only Supreme Governor of this realm . . . as well in all spiritual or ecclesiastical things or

---

1. *Faith By Statute, Parliament and the Settlement of Religion 1559* (London, 1982) (Royal Society Studies in History Series, No. 32).
2. A. G. Dickens, *The English Reformation* (London, 1964), 297, summarizing the argument of J.E. Neale in *Elizabeth I and Her Parliaments* (New York, 1953).
3. *Tudor Constitutional Documents A.D. 1485-1603*, ed. J.R. Tanner (Cambridge, 1951), 125.
4. Ibid., 132.
5. Ibid., 135.

causes as temporal . . .," with forfeiture of office or benefice for refusal to swear.[1]

Elizabeth's substitution of the title "Supreme Governor" for that of "Supreme Head" claimed by her father was not an entirely empty symbolic concession to the liberty of the church. Rather, in conjunction with the stipulated manner of exercising her jurisdiction, it portended a reduced and indirect royal control of ecclesiastical affairs. She surrendered the loud prerogative of "a crowned theologian, confounding Parliaments and bishops with God's learning," for the comparatively discrete management of "an adroit and devious politician, operating through the interstices of Statute Law."[2] It is probable that the Queen's less overtly domineering demeanor was equally welcome to Catholic and Protestant conservatives, given their common reservations about the lawfulness of female rule over the church.

Likewise, the Act's explicit invocation of "the Canonical Scriptures" as the first (and, by implication, highest) standard of public religious truth was a significant and unprecedented disclaimer of royal absolutism in the realm of belief and worship. The Queen, through the agency of her Commissioners, was prohibited from disciplining the clergy and laity according to arbitrary doctrinal canons resting solely on the authority of her own will. This was an official step in the direction of emancipating the church from the legacy of Henry and Cranmer.[3] But the step would have been less equivocal had the Commissioners not been presented so completely as agents or instruments of the royal jurisdiction. As it was, they were civil servants carrying out the ecclesiastical policies of the Queen (or the Queen in Parliament). The status of civil functionary was widely accorded to all ecclesiastical dignitaries under Elizabeth: indeed, bishops themselves invoked it when trying to enforce royal policy on recalcitrant Puritan clergy. Thus, the national church established by the Act of Supremacy was still an Erastian institution, perhaps more expressly and systematically conformed to the requirement of an ommicompetent state than any previous English church had been. Whether the civil government of the church rendered the authority of the Scriptures "a kind of legal fiction,"

---

1. Ibid., 134.
2. Dickens, *The English Reformation*, 303.
3. Edwardian ecclesiastical legislation had occasionally invoked Scriptural authorization of its requirements, without giving such legal prominence to Scriptural authority or bringing it to bear directly on the matter of the royal jurisdiction. The theological significance of this legal-Scriptural limitation of the High Commission's authority escapes the notice of such a capable scholar as N.L. Jones, owing to his preoccupation with uncovering the factional interests served by the proviso and amendment which originated in the Upper House. See Jones, *Faith By Statute*, 142-3.

as one historian has claimed, is a question that can only be decided in the light of subsequent controversies.¹

The second government-sponsored bill, the Act of Uniformity, legislated the form of "Common Prayer and Divine Service" contained in the 1552 Prayer Book with a few important revisions, two of which were to prove momentous for the future of Anglicanism. Firstly, to the 1552 words of the administration of Holy Communion were prefixed the 1549 words of administration. The former implied a Zwinglian understanding of the eucharistic act as purely commemorative of Christ's sacrifice on the Cross: "Take and eat this in remembrance that Christ died for thee, and feed on Him in thy heart by faith with thanksgiving." The latter preserved belief in the "Real Presence" of Christ's Body in the sacrament: "The Body of our Lord Jesus Christ which was given for thee, preserve thy body and soul unto everlasting life."² This combined rubric was diplomatically conceived to accommodate the broad sprectrum of eucharistic doctrine found within the post-Marian church.

Secondly, for the 1552 stipulation on vestments was substituted the confusing "Ornaments Rubric" that intended to reinstate the practice of 1549. Whereas the second Prayer Book had required the officiating priest to "wear a surplice only," forbidding the use of "albe, vestment, [or] cope" at "the Communion and all other times in his ministration,"³ the earlier stipulation, prefacing the 1549 Communion Service, had required "a white Albe plain, with a vestment or Cope."⁴ The offensiveness of the rubric to Protestant sentiment was exacerbated rather than mitigated by its mystifying demand that

---

1. J.W. Allen, *A History of Political Thought in the Sixteenth Century* (London, 1928), 172. Allen states his case persuasively: "It was fully admitted that the Supreme Government of the Church was bound by the text of Scripture. Yet, if you accepted the Elizabethan system, you could not deny that it was for the Queen, or for the Queen in Parliament, to declare authoritatively what doctrines and what sacraments are indeed in Scripture. 'The Word of God cannot speak', said Bishop Andrewes to Henry Barrow: 'which way should it decide our controversies?' Law recognized that the determinations of civil authority concerning religious belief and observance must be consistent with the Word of God; and law proceeded to assume that they always were so. The authority of the Scriptures became a kind of legal fiction. But the lawyers went even further; as indeed they could not help doing. They maintained that appeal to the text of Scripture was, if not quite irrelevant, at least not admissible. John Penry complained that if one were summoned before judges or royal commissioners for the cause of religion, these authorities declared that the question whether this or that were supported by the Word of God was not before the court. All they had to do was to see to it that the Queen's law was not broken and that her supremacy was recognized in word and in deed." Ibid., 172-3.

2. These words of administration are still in use in current editions of the Anglican "Book of Common Prayer."

3. *The First and Second Prayer Books of Kind Edward VI*, intro. Douglas Harrison (London, 1968), 347.

4. Ibid., 212.

"such ornaments of the church and of the ministers thereof shall be retained and be in use as was in the Church of England by authority of Parliament in the second year of the reign of King Edward the Sixth, . . ."[1] as the 1549 Prayer Book had been authorized in the third year of Edward's reign. Compounding the obscurity of its intent, the rubric appended to its requirement the qualifying clause: "until other order shall be therein taken by the authority of the Queen's Majesty, with the advise of her commissioners. . . ."[2] Placing an overly sanguine construction on this clause, the Reformers decided that their Supreme Governor did not intend to force upon her clergy the pernicious vestments of 1549. Their expectations were, however, quickly disappointed by the official policy of the royal visitation that followed upon this legislation. The Injunctions of 1559, issued for use by the commissioners, laid down further conservative regulations for clerical dress and discouraged as well clerical marriage, forbidding priests to take a wife without the consent of their bishop and the two nearest justices of the peace.[3]

It is generally supposed that Elizabeth's position on vestments reflected her personal preference for a distinctive and ornamental clerical garb as much as the exigencies of a divided religious polity. Whatever her reasons, her government's policy in this regard invited incessant ecclesiastical quarrelling and discontent. It "sorely tried the consciences" of even the most conservative, establishment, and English-minded reformers, dividing the Protestant leaders into those whose scruples permitted them to accept preferment and those whose scruples did not.[4] The former, installed in their bishoprics, expended their theological talent and pastoral energy in trying to sustain an administrative double-dealing, without undue compromise of their integrity. They engaged one half of their public persona in subverting the Queen's law on vestments by relaxing the requirements in practice, while they engaged the other half in theologically defending the Monarch's right to legislate on the matter and to be obeyed. As for the Puritan hardliners, they occupied pulpit after pulpit with their protest, and labored endlessly to rally Convocation and the Commons behind their *idée fixe* through a series of exasperating defeats.

---

1. This demand is reiterated in the Act of Uniformity. See *Tudor Constitutional Documents*, 139.
2. Ibid.
3. Ibid., 140.
4. Knappen, *Tudor Puritanism*, 179.

B. Theological Opposition to the Settlement of 1559

The theological and ecclesiastical controversies ensuing from Elizabeth's religious settlement continued the thematic struggle characteristic of the earlier phases of the English Reformation. Now, as before, the pivotal issue concerned the basis and scope of the ecclesiastical and civil authority and jurisdiction. On the Catholic side, the supreme (if no longer plenary) authority of the pope and his juridical system over Christ's Church continued to be defended against Elizabeth's heretical regime, but defended, for the most part, by theologians in exile at Louvain and Douai, who had a much clearer conception of the church universal than was reflected in the typical English Catholic's attachment to traditional rites and doctrine.[1] On the Protestant side, the supreme authority of God's Word in the Scriptures, as mediated by the enlightened consciences of preaching clergy and instructed laity, was asserted against the unscriptural and idolatrous pretentions of the queen and her episcopate to legislate the church's belief and practice. The Protestant protest, framed along Knoxian lines, was one with the Catholic in setting God's law above man's law as its judge, and in entrusting the binding interpretation of God's law to some other authority than the temporal sovereign. The two protests likewise converged in affirming the legislative independence of the visible church as the custodian of God's saving commandments. Needless to say, these broad concurrences of theological principle did nothing to mitigate the fierce hatred of Catholic and Protestant protesters for each other, rooted in their fundamental disagreements over the epistemological mediation and the saving substance of God's law.

On the subject of salvation, however, it is essential for understanding the battlelines of Elizabeth's church to realize that the Reformation principle of "*sola gratia*," which had theologically dominated Henrician Protestantism, played no ostensible role in the Anglican-Puritan dispute. Rather, it belonged to a common fund of doctrine that claimed the allegiance of both sides and was beyond serious debate. Jewel was perfectly justified in aggressively asserting the theological unity of Elizabeth's Protestant church against the Roman accusation of massive sectarian division. He could truly insist that the different reforming streams "vary not betwixt themselves upon the principles and

---

1. The leading Catholic writers in exile during Elizabeth's reign who defended the separate earthly headship and juridical structure of the church universal were: Nicholas Sanders and Thomas Harding at Louvain; William Allen, John Feckenham, and Thomas Stapleton at Douai; and, subsequently, Robert Parsons at Rheims. Louvain was the dominant center of exiled English Catholics until Allen established the English seminary college at Douai, that transferred to Rheims in 1578. See the summary of this English Catholic literature in Allen, *Political Thought in the Sixteenth Century*, 199-209.

foundations of our religion, nor as touching God, nor Christ, nor the Holy Ghost, nor of the means of justification, nor yet everlasting life. . . ."[1] Nor even as touching, he might have said, the other great Reformation principle of "*sola Scriptura.*" For both establishment Anglicans and dissenters acknowledged the unconditional authority of the plain word of Scripture in matters of faith and worship. They differed only on the narrower issue of the plainness of the Scriptural word in particular cases, and occasionally on the plain content of its word. In the realm of theological controversy, the authority of the Scriptures was treated with the utmost gravity, however fictional its treatment in the political-legal realm. The scope of this consensus is evident in the three foci of Protestant opposition to the settlement of 1559: the official vestments requirement, legislation of the Prayer Book, and the civil hierarchy of the church.

At issue in the vestiarian controversy was the civil ruler's right to legislate church order either without or against the explicit authorization of Scripture. The majority of Protestant opponents of the prescribed vestments agreed with their defenders that they did not in themselves violate any explicit Scriptural injunction. Rather, they were condemned as things "corrupted by idolatrous associations," such that to wear them was "to seem to consent" to the Pope's "blasphemies."[2] As with the food offered to idols about which St. Paul speaks in I Corinthians 8:19-20, Catholic vestments wounded the consciences of those incapable of dissociating them from the pope's religion, seducing them back into idolatrous habits of mind, or else giving constant offense to deeply felt Protestant sentiments. In view of their taintedness, the use of these "ornaments" should be left to the discretion of individual clergy and not imposed indiscriminately by the secular arm. Even if they were things indifferent to salvation (*adiaphora*), as Archbishop Parker and his episcopal administrators were fond of arguing, this did not entitle the civil sovereign to dictate to the church the details of its discipline and order. These were for the clergy to decide, and, in this instance, the majority judged the queen's prescriptions to be unedifying to the church and inimical to the cause of proper reverence and decency within it. Thus ran the objections of the original protagonists in the vestiarian dispute: Thomas Sampson and Laurence Humphrey at Oxford, William Whittingham at Durham—all

---

1. John Jewel, *An Apology of the Church of England*, ed. J.E. Booty (Charlottesville, VA, 1963), 48.
2. See the summary of Whittingham's argument in Knappen, *Tudor Puritanism*, 191.

Genevan schooled exiles of radical ecclesiastical (and in Humphrey's case, political) leanings.[1]

In the wake of Archbishop Parker's *Advertisements* of 1566 and the heavy-handed tactics of the ecclesiastical commissioners in dealing with the London clergy, a harder-line Puritan opposition to the required vestments appeared in print, which made their use a violation of God's Word.[2] For, argued the influential London pluralist Robert Crowley, obedience to God requires that we do nothing not commanded by Him, except that which edifies His Church. An unedifying Commandment of "the Prince" must be disobeyed, and the civil consequences suffered.[3] Likewise, the Puritan controversialist Anthony Gilby, reiterated the traditional dissenting argument that even the Sovereign, being bound by God's Word, cannot command evildoing. To require "one piece of popery as a matter of policy" was to offend the glory of "an exacting God."[4] Gilby's objection entailed the accusation that Catholic vestments actually contradicted the prescriptions of God's Word for right worship.

From its inception in King Edward's reign, the battle over vestments was bound up with the battle over the Prayer Book. In the Elizabethan phase of the battle, however, the Puritan offensive had the ultimate goal of replacing the Prayer Book, rather than the earlier, more modest aim of purging it of Catholic residue. Let us recall that the Calvinist radicals at Geneva, and probably at Frankfurt, had abandoned the Second Edwardian Prayer Book along with Edwardian clerical costume, substituting Reformed liturgies composed under the supervision of Gilby and Goodman, Whittingham and Knox respectively. These resembled the forms of worship employed by à Lasco's London congregations, while manifesting the more immediate influence of Calvin. They provided simplified services of worship and administration of the sacrament, the regular weekly worship consisting chiefly of prayers and psalm-singing arranged around a sermon, with conspicuous omission of Scripture readings and the Litany.

---

1. It is instructive to note the close alignment of the positions in the vestiarian controversy of the 1560s with those advanced a decade earlier in the dispute between Ridley and Hooper, following the issuing of Edward's 1549 Prayer Book and the accompanying Act of Uniformity.
2. The *Advertisements* were a set of formal regulations for clerical attire and "other matters connected with church worship and discipline" published by the Archbishop in 1566, in an attempt to effect stricter clerical conformity to the Act of Uniformity. Knappen, *Tudor Puritanism*, 192.
3. Ibid., 198-9.
4. Ibid., 202.

Significantly, the exiles' adoption of Reformed liturgies went hand in hand with adoption of a Reformed ministry of "elders," "ministers," and "deacons," charged respectively with government and discipline, preaching and administration of the sacraments, and care of the poor. In Geneva all church officials underwent painstaking examination for fitness prior to their election by the congregation and were further subjected, along with their flock, to weekly sessions of mutual criticism and discipline organized on a regional basis. While in the opening years of Elizabeth's reign the majority of returned exiles did not press for the complete conversion of the English Church to the Genevan pattern, the more scrupulous among them continued to regard as inseparable the defects of the established Prayer Book and the defects of the established ministries of the church.

By the close of Elizabeth's first decade, a new generation of reform had arisen to reinvigorate the Protestant attack on the "Prayer Book system" and its incorporated church structure. Their ranks were drawn up in the continental training-ground of the Cambridge colleges, where once more, as in King Edward's time, intellectually commanding teachers were nurturing a body of "keen-minded young enthusiasts" in a tradition of reform.[1] The leading lights of Cambridge Puritanism were Edward Dering, Fellow of Christ's College until his departure for a London lectureship in 1570, and Thomas Cartwright (1535-1603), who in the same year was elected Lady Margaret Professor. Of the two voices, Cartwright's was the more theologically consequential for focusing reforming impetus on the issue of church polity. His sensational lectures of 1570 on the Book of Acts laid out the apostolic standard of church organization by which the English system was to be judged and corrected. The norm was essentially a presbyterian polity, comprised of a "purely spiritual" episcopacy, governing "presbyteries" or "congregational sessions," parochially elected ministers, and deacons. While his brash proposals cost him his professorship and resulted in his removal to Geneva, they, nevertheless, made the desired impact, as the momentous Puritan eruptions of the next two years would testify. For Puritan lay agitation was to reach a Parliamentary climax in a frontal assault on the Prayer Book and the church hierarchy.

Disaffected with the episcopally-controlled and Catholic-inclined Convocation, Puritan leaders, in the second decade of Elizabeth's settlement, channelled their efforts into amassing Parliamentary support for their program of ecclesiastical reform. In the 1571 Parliament, Puritans in the Commons pushed for the passage of a range of bills to suppress Catholicism

---

1. Ibid., 219.

and correct manifold perennial ecclesiastical abuses.[1] Passing on from this relatively uncontentious legislation, they introduced a bill for revision of the Prayer Book, which encountered insurmountable opposition from the bishops and the queen's representatives. Undaunted by this defeat, they attempted in the following year to legalize the nonconformity of Puritan clergy to the Act of Uniformity.[2] This maneuver was thwarted in a spectacular manner by the queen's confiscation of the offending bills in the course of their readings, accompanied by the order that "in the future no bill concerning religion should be introduced into the House unless previously approved by the clergy."[3] In the face of such a decisive political routing, the Puritan leadership decided on recourse to the public press, authorizing two of their number—namely, John Field and Thomas Wilcox—to write an explosive tract entitled *An Admonition to the Parliament* in the full prophetic style of John Knox. Broadly speaking, the *Admonition* appealed to the secular authorities to institute God's law for His Church against the proud and rebellious regime of the bishops. It exhorted the government to conduct a wholesale reformation of the ministry, worship, and discipline of the English church, bringing it into line with the best Reformed models. It formulated its attack on existing ecclesiastical corruptions as a defense of recent Puritan refusals to subscribe before the queen's commissioners to the Thirty-nine Articles—the revised Edwardian articles issued by Elizabeth in 1563 to give doctrinal reinforcement to the 1559 settlement. Not only did the *Admonition* provide a detailed statement of the Puritan platform, but it also gave a coherent theological framework to the diverse elements of the Puritan protest. This theological coherence was important for the weightiness it lent to concern with "externals" (that is, with symbolic practices of relative inconsequence) that constantly threatened to become disproportionate and obsessive.

The theological keynote of the treatise is sounded in an extensive contrast of the current English and primitive apostolic churches:

> Then the ministers were preachers: now bare readers. And if any be so well disposed to preach in their own charges, they may not, without my Lords licence. In those days known by voice, learning and doctrine: now they must be

---

1. These included "simony, benefit of the clergy, nonresidence, leases of benefices, and pensions from them." Ibid., 226.
2. They proposed that preachers in charge of congregations be permitted, with episcopal consent, "to abridge the required service" or to use alternative forms, such as were allowed to the foreign churches in London. Ibid., 233.
3. Ibid., 234.

discerned from other by popish and Antichristian apparel, as cap, gown, tippet, etc. Then, as God gave utterance they preached the word only: now they read homilies, articles, injunctions, etc. Then it was painful: now gainful. Then poor and ignominious: now rich and glorious. And therefore titles, livings and offices by Antichrist devised are given to them as Metropolitan, Archbishop, Lords grace, Lord Bishop, Suffragan, Dean, Archdeacon, Prelate of the garter, Earl, . . . High Commissioners, Justices of peace and Quorum, etc. All which, together with their offices, as they are strange and unheard of in Christ's church, nay plainly in God's word forbidden: So are they utterly with speed out of the same to be removed.[1]

The central ecclesiological principle herein expressed is the primacy of the preaching office within Christ's community. Free, learned, and sound preaching of God's Word revealed in the Scriptures is the foremost "outward mark" of "a true Christian Church."[2] On this mark depend the other two "outward marks," namely, "minist[e]ring of the sacraments sincerely, and ecclesiastical discipline which consisteth in admonition and correction of faults . . . ."[3] In the absence of capable preaching, the sacramental and disciplinary orders of church life fall prey to rank corruption. The sacraments are surrounded by idolatrous superstitions, the clergy by a priestly mystique (supported by ornamental vestments), and ecclesiastical authority by the tokens of worldly pomp and glory. Mindless of the true basis and forms of the church's action, clergy and laity alike invoke false apparatuses of power and influence: episcopal ordination; the buying and selling of benefices, pluralities, titles, and ranks; endless liturgical inventions; clerical attire; and, the combining of ecclesiastical and secular offices, notably in the functioning of church courts with their material, monetary, and corporal punishments.

Conversely, the restoration of preaching to its proper primacy effects a renewal of all aspects of church order. Organizational renewal comes about as Scripturally earnest congregations demand the right to search for and elect their pastors, rejecting the arbitrary and unscriptural patronage of bishops. Disciplinary renewal comes about as elders join forces with ministers to instruct, admonish, correct, and punish willful wrongdoers within their parishes, with the object of bringing the offenders to inward repentance and outward reform, without the involvement of episcopal favors and persecutions or court fees. And, finally, liturgical renewal comes about as mere reading of the Scriptures and unedifying "service saying" gives way to nourishing

1. *Puritan Manifestoes*, eds. W.H. Frere and C.E. Douglas (London, 1954), 11.
2. Ibid., 9.
3. Ibid.

"feeding" on God's Word,[1] public penitence, sincere prayers, and celebration of the sacraments according to Christ's intention and command, and without the "confusion" and "deformity" of "heathenish" garments and ceremonies.[2]

Here we have the Puritan plea for a completely reformed, apostolic church order to replace the disorder of the English Church. This fiery manifesto sparked a celebrated literary controversy between Anglican champion, Bishop Thomas Whitgift (1530-1603), and Puritan champion, Thomas Cartwright (1535-1605), that offers invaluable instruction in the conflicting theological treatments of law and authority in church and state. Cartwright's contribution to the controversy is most profitably read alongside the chief literary contribution of his like-minded friend and former Cambridge colleague Walter Travers (c.1548-1635). Together, these exhibit the developments in the Reformed alternative to Anglicanism twenty years after its first formulation by the Protestant exiles.

C. CARTWRIGHT AND TRAVERS ON THE FORM OF THE CHURCH

According to their Anglican opponents, Cartwright and Travers belonged to the ranks of preachers of dangerous political doctrines, in company with the Anabaptists and Papists. In repudiating this charge, Cartwright disowns the intention of meddling in political matters as unbefitting a divine.[3] This disclaimer immediately suggests the difference of vocational self-understanding between these two Cambridge Puritans writing in the 1570s and their exiled predecessors of the 1550s, Knox and Goodman. Whereas the older Genevan theologians were possessed by a prophetic self-consciousness, engaged in battle with the apostate forces in the civil commonwealth, and bent on the religious reformation of the whole nation, the younger Puritan divines were possessed by a clerical self-consciousness, struggling against apostate ecclesiastics for the restoration of integrity and good order to the church's ministry. The latter never allowed their theoretical attention to be deflected from the central issue of church polity (as distinct from secular polity), never making civil authority, offices, and duties a subject of systematic or protracted theological reflection. In their writings the theocratic vision

---

1. Ibid., 22-3.
2. Ibid., 35.
3. *The Second Reply of Thomas Cartwright against Master Doctor Whitgift's Second Answer, touching the Church Discipline* (London, 1575), 228. In his lucid exposition of Cartwright's theological-political doctrines, A.F. Scott Pearson takes Cartwright's disclaimer with theoretical seriousness, as we ourselves do. *Church and State: Political Aspects of Sixteenth Century Puritanism* (Cambridge, 1928), 1-8.

and temper of Knox has been replaced by Calvin's more moderate and differentiated constitutional sense. They evenly sustain a conception of complementary spheres of authority, focusing the theologian's vocational duty to instruct on the "spiritual" sphere. Undoubtedly, their distance from Knox is connected with the changed circumstances of the English Church under Elizabeth: they wrote as sanguine reformers temporarily abroad, rather than as persecuted exiles with a bleak and uncertain future. Nevertheless, this perspectival distance should not obscure the striking resemblances of their thought to his: they are heirs to fundamental elements of his theological orientation, together with their unresolved problems.

1. Command and Constitution

As the opposition to vestments has already demonstrated, the Puritans looked to God's "general or especial" Word for direction in all matters of faith and action. They repudiated the notion of "things indifferent," if taken to mean things not regulated by God's express law. For God's law omits nothing: argues Cartwright, it determines "the free use of [things]" (for, otherwise, there could be "no lawful use of them at all") and places this free use in the service of God's glory.[1] For Cartwright and Travers, God's law is, for the most part, identical with Scriptural commands, the particular command being the perfect form of law because it "leave[s] as little undetermined and without the compass of the law as can be." Cartwright assures us that "a conscience well instructed . . . seeketh for the light of the Word of God in the smallest actions," convinced that God's "good laws" leave "few things" to the discretion of fallible men.[2] Accordingly, he and Travers take the Mosaic legislation of the Pentateuch as the controlling locus of divine law, upholding the authority not only of its form, but also of its substance. "All these laws," says Cartwright of the Mosaic corpus, "moral, ceremonial, and judicial, being the laws of God and by his revealed will established, must so far forth remain as it appeareth not by his will that they are revoked.[3] The moral law retains its entire validity (a position in conformity with the whole tradition of the church, honored by Catholics and Protestants of every stripe). But the judicial (or political) laws also bind all governments by their "substance" or "equity," their perpetual "reason or ground," providing that they "hinder not the

---

1. Cartwright, *The Second Reply*, 59. We have substituted modern spellings in all quotations from Cartwright's and Travers' writings.
2. Ibid., 94.
3. Ibid., 96.

atonement of the Jews and Gentiles with God, or of one of them with another."[1]

Chief among the permanently binding judicial laws are those "which command that a stubborn idolator, blasphemer, murderer, incestuous person, and such like, should be put to death."[2] With Knox's vehemence, Cartwright proclaims the duty of the magistrate (if not of all civil orders) to punish with the utmost severity persistent transgressors against "the first table"—against "true religion and . . . the service of God," arguing that "the dishonour of his name" is the fountain of all criminality and lawlessness. It leads men "into wicked minds, to the committing of all kind of sins contained in the second table, be they never so horrible," and so comprises at one and the same time an assault on God's glory, man's salvation, and "the common wealth."[3] Compared with the suppression of religious vice, the purely civil duties of the magistrate, in the protection and distribution of lands and goods, are of minor importance, although indispensable to communal peace.[4]

Of equally minor importance from Cartwright's ecclesiological point of view is the political constitution of civil society. He is as remote as Knox from the concerns of English constitutionalism. On Scriptural evidence he argues that (1) God permits a diversity of political forms, "and all good," along with a corresponding diversity of "offices and dignities"; and (2) commonwealths are susceptible of "conversions, one form being changed into another."[5] No one regime is divinely prescribed, nor necessarily superior in performing the appointed duties of civil government. Yet Cartwright on occasion demonstrates his preference for a mixed polity, and he extols the liberal political principles of popular consent and elected representation.[6] But he voices his approval of these institutions in an entirely conventional manner, stressing his dependence on the authority of others for judgments outside the scope of his vocational competence. And, more importantly, he expresses these passing political opinions in the context of defending the constitutional principles of the presbyterian church polity, that are his overriding interest.

If God's law is flexible and pluralistic in the realm of civil polity, it is the opposite in the realm of ecclesiastical polity. Here, Christ, as prophet and king, expounds and promulgates God's universal and necessary, perpetual

---

1. Ibid., 95-7.
2. Ibid., 95.
3. Ibid., 117-18.
4. Ibid., 94. See also *Works of Archbishop Whitgift*, ed. J. Ayre, 3 vols. (Cambridge, 1851-53), 3: 416-17.
5. Ibid., 2: 356. See also Cartwright, *The Second Reply*, 579.
6. Whitgift, *Works*, 1: 390; Thomas Cartwright, *The Rest of the Second Reply* (London, 1577), 66-7. Cartwright appears conversant with the traditional Aristotelian arguments.

and perfect law for the ordering of His holy commonwealth.[1] Travers grounds Christ's unchangeable law for His earthly kingdom in the latter's eschatological relationship to His heavenly kingdom, arguing for a proportionality between them of "justice and equity," "obedience," "knowledge," and purity.[2] Cartwright grounds Christ's law in God's eternal elective designs before the world's creation. "The church," he says, "is the foundation of the world": the completion of its membership is "the cause why this world endureth."[3] They are in general agreement over the constitutional content of Christ's invariable discipline, as ordaining: (1) the permanent offices of elders, doctors, pastors, and deacons, with the respective functions of disciplinary enforcement; doctrinal and catechetical teaching; preaching, exhortation, and sacramental administration; and charitable distributions;[4] (2) the governing structure of parochial "consistory" or "council" (comprised of all church officials above deacon), and provincial, national, and general synods or "conferences" (with representation from the consistories), forming a hierarchy of appeal in cases of appointment, deposition, suspension, and excommunication; and (3) the "lawful calling" of all church officials, consisting of appointment by God and by church authorities: the former being the vocational assurance of the candidate's "conscience," the latter, his "election" and "ordination" by the consistory.

This threefold constitution of the church is divine, apostolic, and scriptural: eternally ordained by God in Christ, instituted by Christ's apostles, and witnessed authoritatively by the Scriptures. Cartwright constructs it chiefly out of the account in the Book of Acts and the epistles of the practice and dictates of the apostles and their helpers and successors, called "evangelists." Thus, it is not explicitly propounded by Christ, but indirectly authorized by Him, through His commissioning of the apostles to "found" the church, and their commissioning of the evangelists variously to erect and oversee the prescribed order. In their defence of the presbyterian structure, Cartwright and Travers are compelled to argue that the original offices of the church—of apostle, evangelist, and prophet—are not the "ordinary" and "perpetual" ones, but rather extraordinarily ordained by God for the time of the church's establishment, thereafter to cease.[5] Not only the original offices but also cer-

---

1. Walter Travers, *A Full and Plain Declaration of Ecclesiastical Discipline* (London, 1574), 9.
2. Ibid., 11.
3. Cartwright, *The Rest of the Second Reply*, 66.
4. Cartwright also admits bishops, intending a regional office with certain administrative duties, such as the calling of synods.
5. Cartwright, *The Second Reply*, 327, and Travers, *Declaration of Ecclesiastical Discipline*, 132-5.

tain aspects of their spiritual equipment (such as the apostolic power of conveying the Holy Spirit through the "laying on of hands"), are not a continuing part of the church's divine endowment.[1]

The "ordinary" constitution of the church is that of a mixed polity: a combination of monarchy, aristocracy, and democracy.[2] The church is a monarchy in respect of its theocratic headship: Christ, the lawgiver, maintains "all the parts of his kingdom" by his "decrees and ordinances" promulgated in the Scriptures.[3] The church is an aristocracy in respect of its government by "assemblies of elders" (that is, of elders, doctors, and pastors), which constitute "the church" from an official and juridical point of view, exercising the powers of appointment and discipline. The elder's authority is, however, representative, established by the congregation's original election or consent. And so the church is a "democraty" or "popular estate," ordered by the principle which equity, reasonableness, and convenience lays down, namely, "that which standeth all men upon should be approved of all men."[4]

The democratic component of presbyterian polity was an object of incessant propagandist exaggeration in the hands of such Anglican opponents of Cartwright and Travers as Whitgift and Bancroft, who harped on its seditious, insurrectionary, and tyrannous implications. In fact, both Puritan theologians restricted its scope to the realm of parochial appointments. The practical principle for which they fought was that of congregational approval of officials elected by the consistory. The governing elders exercised their powers of selecting, examining, electing, and ordaining officials, but the rest of "the saints" gave or withheld their consent, on the basis of their own experience of the candidate's "equipment" during his trial ministry among them. Only at the founding of a parish might all the eligible church members directly elect their pastors, teachers, and elders (as in the congregations of Marian exiles). In the ordinary course of parochial church government, concerning all matters other than appointments, congregational consent played no role, being required neither by the Scriptures nor by the testimony of the lawyers concerning natural equity. Thus, contrary to the accusations of their detractors, Cartwright and Travers were proponents of a theory of "delegated sovereignty" rather than "popular sovereignty."[5] Travers was especially clear in propounding the doctrine that "the people," in choosing their rulers, surrender their sovereignty to their elected representatives:

1. Ibid., 68.
2. Whitgift, *Works*, 1: 390; Travers, *Declaration of Ecclesiastical Discipline*, 177-9.
3. Ibid., 10.
4. Whitgift, *Works*, 1: 370.
5. A.F. Scott Pearson develops this point in *Church and State*, 50-1.

So it cometh to pass in the establishing of the church . . . that when as yet there were none set over them, all the authority was in all men's hands: but after that they had once given the helm into the hands of certain chosen men, this power no longer belonged unto all, but only to those who were chosen by them to steer and govern the church of God.[1]

In the commonwealth as in the church, says Travers, the authority to govern resides with the elected magistrates and not with the people.

2. The Unequal Partnership of Church and State

Similitudes between civil and ecclesiastical polity dominate the writings of Cartwright and Travers, despite their defensive protestations that no strict conformity of the former to the latter sphere is divinely prescribed. The concept of a legal ecclesiastical constitution, as well as its precise structural components, are mirrored in contemporary civil polities, English and European. Anglican critics, their polemical excesses aside, rightly perceived that the introduction of presbyterian orders into the church would strengthen the corresponding political institutions: chiefly, parliament as a representative body with legislative controls on monarchial power. More importantly, they perceived the subservience of the political to the ecclesiastical authorities in religious affairs demanded by the presbyterian scheme.

Although unjustly dismissing the sincerity with which Travers and Cartwright publicly professed the queen's supremacy and governorship of the English church, the Anglican bishops justly surmised that their opponents' interpretation of the royal supremacy derogated from its claim. For the magistrate's oversight of the church, recognized by the two Puritans, was in all matters to be guided by the church's own wisdom, his office being to confirm, maintain, and enforce the judgments of the elders on doctrine and discipline. Cartwright upheld the magistrate's regular authority to confirm ecclesiastical appointments, maintain the true teaching of God's ministers, legislate godly laws, and convene general church councils, while also allowing him a voice in the deliberation of church assemblies.[2] To these ordinary duties Travers added the provision of fit pastors and teachers, through the erection of schools and colleges, and the arrangement of church finances to ensure adequate remuneration of its officers.[3] As long as the church possessed a lawful ministry, the magistrate's authority was more or less at its disposal. Only in the absence of a lawful ministry was the magistrate entitled to "take

---

1. Travers, *Declaration of Ecclesiastical Discipline*, 55.
2. Cartwright, *The Rest of the Second Reply*, 153-168.
3. Travers, *Declaration of Ecclesiastical Discipline*, 101, 126-7.

order" in ecclesiastical affairs, lending his ear to prophetic counsel.[1] Albeit the civil authorities had to fear no interference from ecclesiastical officers in their secular duties, such was the strict separation of jurisdictions propounded by the Puritan theologians. With Wycliffite rigor Cartwright and Travers curtailed the church's authority to the spiritual realm, the province of the conscience, forbidding the confusion of responsibilities. Nevertheless, they intended the church within its own sphere to be a self-sufficient polity.

While not as manifestly implausible as Wyclif's Erastian plan for unfettering the church's liberty, the program of Cartwright and Travers is still beset by unresolvable contradictions. The root contradiction affects their understanding of Christian law and freedom: essentially, they want to safeguard the spiritual freedom of Christ's church with the law of Moses, with the resulting assimilation of the New Covenant to the Old. They interpret the Gospel law in terms of the legalistic, punitive Mosaic code of ceremonial and judicial law. Rather than seeking the principles of the church's discipleship, they seek a political constitution for it, erecting this structure into the vessel of salvation. As much as their papist enemies, they cast the city of God in the form of the earthly city, oblivious to the eschatological opposition of the two cities. They have even forgotten the Lutheran dialectic of Law and Gospel so close to the hearts of the Henrician reformers, Erastian though they were. Their undialectical concept of the church as a legally constituted polity brings it into inevitable rivalry and alignment with the secular polity. This ambiguous relationship leaves the magistrate in the unenviable position of remaining the coercive arm of institutional religion, while losing the full juridical authority won for this office. We cannot entirely blame Elizabeth for her violent revulsion at the spectre of reversion to an (albeit incomplete) Hildebrandine subjection of the civil sovereign to the ecclesiastical authorities.

The lasting theological validity of the Puritan program lay in its concept of a self-governing, disciplined community of faith with the institutional freedom and equipment to fulfil its apostolic calling of preaching the Gospel of Christ and administering the sacraments of man's salvation, in accordance with the word of Scripture. Its weakness lay in its failure to be satisfied with the apostolic equipment for this calling: faith in Christ crucified and resurrected, the boldness to proclaim His work of salvation, obedience to His law of love, and openness to the testimony of the written Word. Rather, it placed its trust in a particular institutional embodiment of this equipment, looking for the day of its civil establishment.

---

1. Cartwright, *The Rest of the Second Reply*, 165.

Nine

Hooker's Theological Consolidation of the English Church

A. Richard Hooker and the Status Quo

The morning and the evening of the English Reformation are marked by two theological syntheses of law and authority, both late medieval in theoretical inspiration: Wyclif's Franciscan-Augustinian synthesis and Hooker's Thomistic-Aristotelian one. Wyclif's synthesis is historically significant in its anticipation of sixteenth century positions, Hooker's in its consolidation of their peculiarly English features. From the vantage point of the post-Reformation maturation of the English Church, Wyclif's contribution appears as a somewhat fantastic and abortive early episode, a marvellous but fast-vanishing morning-star; Hooker's, by contrast, appears as the secure, if unastonishing, lodestar of Anglican thought and practice through four centuries. The enduring theological and ecclesiastical inheritance of the Henrician and Elizabethan reformers has remained untouched by both the brilliance and the waywardness of Wyclif's speculative penetration and dialectical extremes; while it has continually fed and clothed itself with Hooker's moderate reasonableness and limited, yet subtle, orthodoxy.

The Christian polity enshrined by Hooker is without the dramatic vitality and ironic wisdom bred by theological paradox; it is, however, amply endowed with the spirit of probity, moderation, and charitable compromise.

Though insensible of eschatological self-criticism, it allows scope for routine acts of self-denial and modest reform within unquestioned societal givens. In Hooker's religious commonwealth the judgment of God's righteousness and justice on human law and equity is not an incalculable revolutionary force, but a manageable goad to diligent self-correction.

At one point, however, Wyclif's and Hooker's syntheses partake of a continuous thread: the point of complete identity of church and realm. Whereas Wyclif presses this identity into his mould of total ecclesiastical reform, Hooker employs it to subvert any such comprehensive reforming enterprise. Their opposite uses of this identity are made possible by the different interests and prerogatives of the secular authorities vis-à-vis church affairs in the second halves of the fourteenth and sixteenth centuries. Wyclif and Hooker alike propound the supreme authority of the secular sovereign over the church, but with the contrary effects of fuelling and dampening the cause of ecclesiastical renovation. For the material benefits—political, legal, and fiscal—after which the secular magnates of Wyclif's day scrambled in their religious zeal, had long since fallen to the English Crown and nobility by the fourth decade of Elizabeth's reign. Elizabeth and her bishops were occupied in entrenching reforms rather than in launching them. And whereas Wyclif's masters were prudentially alert to the threat of destabilizing domestic resistance, Hooker's royal mistress was wholly obsessed with it. To uphold the identity of church and commonwealth after 1570 was tantamount to rendering unpatriotic all unsatisfied desire for ecclesiastical revision.

Indeed, given that the actual constitutional identity of church and realm rested in the queen's supreme dominion, who can seriously hold that vocal discontent with her ecclesiastical policy was untainted by disloyalty to the lawful monarch? Undoubtedly, Romanist nonconformity subsequent to the papal bull *Regnans in excelsis* (1570) that excommunicated and deposed Elizabeth portended more dangerously treasonous sentiment than could be reasonably imputed to Puritan unrest. In pronouncing anathema on all who would persist in loyal obedience to the queen's "laws and mandates," the bull "not only legalized rebellion but, by implication, positively commanded it."[1] And if the courageous ministrations of the "seminarist" missionaries from the English colleges abroad came under unjust political suspicion and censure, there was no want of evidence, as the sixteenth century drew to a close, for English Catholic involvement in internal and foreign conspiracy against Elizabeth's throne and life. In addition, the Roman recusants had in the Jesuit

---

1. J.B. Black, *The Reign of Elizabeth: 1558-1603* in *The Oxford History of England* (Oxford, 1936), 8: 136.

Robert Parsons (1546-1610) a preacher and publisher of sedition unequalled by even the Puritans' pseudonymous Martin Marprelate in his ribald and jocular assaults on the Queen's bishops and clergy.[1]

Nevertheless, neither of the chief Puritan spokesmen admitted the royal claim to supremacy over a unified ecclesiastical commonwealth. Moreover, both Cartwright and Travers advocated a system of church government that would seriously diminish the monarch's symbolic and legal authority. For the Presbyterian discipline comprised a republican hierarchy of self-government with which the queen was not entitled routinely to interfere. Theoretical justification of this autonomous arrangement involved both theologians in strenuously asserting the non-identity of civil and ecclesiastical polity; but, ominously for the secular authorities, the temporal maintenance of church discipline, in the face of papist idolatry especially, required the occasional waiving of this principle, at the discretion of the highest ruling clerical body. In the minds of Cartwright and Travers, the qualified separation of church and realm chiefly meant that the monarch "had only duties towards the Church, not rights"—a repetition of "the Hildebrandine claim," as F.J. Shirley points out.[2] It placed the secular ruler, in one sector of his subjects' common affairs, at the disposal of a superior jurisdiction.

The restriction of the Crown's right to command obedience entailed by this subjection was scarcely more tolerable to Elizabeth and her sympathizers than the pope's outright pronouncement of deposition. Indeed, in the queen's judgment, the subtle ambiguity of the Puritan position rendered it a more insidious attack on her prerogative. Her ecclesiastical defenders regarded the Puritans' repeated oaths to uphold the royal supremacy and their assurances of "tarrying for the monarch" as a dangerously arbitrary stopping-short of the Separatist cause. For, they argued, the Puritans' theological evaluation of church order as part of Christ's saving law committed them to "tarrying for no-one" in its establishment, at least at the parochial level. Anglican stalwarts saw the Separatists' angry indignation at the Presbyterians' timidity in action as a perfectly justified response to the logic of their theological stance. The leading Separatist Robert Browne (c.1550-1633) was right to accuse his mentor Cartwright of betraying his own fundamental principles.[3] Displaying

---

1. Between the close of 1587 and Christmas of 1589, when the authors had been disclosed and punished, seven satirical tracts appeared, popularly known as the "Marprelate Tracts."
2. F.J. Shirley, *Richard Hooker and Contemporary Political Ideas* (London, 1949), 26.
3. Browne made this accusation in replying to Cartwright's argument against Separatism contained in his circulated letter to Browne's colleague Robert Harrison. See M. M. Knappen, *Tudor Puritanism: A Chapter in the History of Idealism* (Chicago, 1939), 306 and

his famed astuteness, Hooker chose to expose the dangerous irrationality of the Presbyterian position by a lengthy quote from Browne's diatribe against the "falsehearted Scribes and Pharisees, [that] say, and do not."[1] Before the queen and her loyal clergy the Presbyterian renegades stood condemned by his embittered words:

> For adventuring to erect the discipline of Christ without the leave of the Christian magistrate, haply ye may condemn us as fools, in that we hazard thereby our estates and persons further than you which are that way more wise think necessary: but of any sin or offence therein committed against God, with what conscience can you accuse us, when your own positions are, that the things we observe should every of them be dearer unto us than ten thousand lives; that they are the peremptory commandments of God; that no mortal man can dispense with them, and that the magistrate grievously sinneth in not constraining thereunto?[2]

Timeservers Cartwright and Travers might possibly be, but politically innocuous they were emphatically not.

Moreover, Elizabeth was convinced, albeit on a prejudiced reading of the facts, that the Presbyterians had long since abandoned in practice the principle of "tarrying for the magistrate." In the 1570s she determined to crush as seditious a widespread movement of Puritan-minded parishes to introduce within the established ecclesiastical framework and with diocesan episcopal approval a system of educational, liturgical, and disciplinary gatherings for clergy and laity, the most contentious of which involved the clergy in lengthy public Biblical exposition under the scrutiny of their peers. Having suppressed these Presbyterian elements only by sequestering her recalcitrant Archbishop of Canterbury, Edmund Grindal, the queen was obliged in the next decade to strike with equal severity against a parallel movement to institute consistoral and synodal proceedings within the strict letter of her church law. The queen was never inclined to confuse legality with loyalty to herself!

While not wholly sharing Her Majesty's bias on this point, Hooker was disposed to concur in his superiors' general judgment about the rebelliousness inherent in Presbyterian strivings. Early in his career he had demonstrated stubborn resistance to the occupation by a Presbyterian of an influential public post. So when in 1585 he was nominated by Archbishop Edwin

---

Richard Hooker, *The Works of Richard Hooker*, 7th ed., ed. John Keble, 3 vols. (New York, 1970), 1: 174.

1. From Robert Browne, *A Treatise of Reformation without Tarrying for Any*, quoted in Hooker's Preface to the *Laws of Ecclesiastical Polity*, in Hooker, *The Works*, 1: 177.

2. Ibid., 1: 176-7.

Sandys (c.1516-88) for the Mastership of the Temple, in opposition to the more obvious candidacy of Walter Travers, the retiring and peaceable Hooker felt himself duty-bound to stand for the somewhat distasteful appointment.

B. HOOKER'S LIFE AND WRITINGS

Like Wyclif, Hooker passed only a small portion of his career under the restless public eye, the greater part being spent in scholarly tranquillity. Born in 1553-54, he entered Corpus Christi College, Oxford, as a clerk in 1568, was elected a Foundation Scholar of his college in 1573, and a Fellow in 1577. At Oxford he was reputed to excel in Greek, Hebrew, and logic. His seventeenth-century biographer, Izaak Walton, anticipating Hooker's future literary labors, described his studies thus: "still enriching his quiet and capacious soul with the precious learning of the philosophers, casuists, and schoolmen; and with them, the foundation and reason of all laws . . . . as he was diligent in these, so he seemed restless in searching the scope and intention of God's Spirit revealed to mankind in the sacred scripture. . . ."[1] Among his students, Hooker formed intimate and lasting friendships with two of distinguished families: George Cranmer, great-nephew of Archbishop Cranmer, and Edwin Sandys, son of his patron, both of whom proved invaluable sources of biographical detail for his writings. Following temporary expulsion from his fellowship in 1579 for resisting the nomination of the Disciplinarian Dr. Barfoot to the post of College President, Hooker remained at Corpus Christi until his departure in 1584.

At this juncture Archbishop Sandys' proposal intervened to prevent him from taking up a clerical living. His elevation to the Mastership of the Temple plunged him into the bitter waters of controversy, as he played out week by week a "sad contest" with the Temple Reader Walter Travers. Every Sunday, benchers and students flocked to hear the champion of Canterbury preach in the morning and the champion of Geneva lecture in the afternoon, the general consensus being that "Travers had the advantage in oratory," while Hooker's eloquence was tied to his pen.[2] The battle ended abruptly when the dictatorial Archbishop Whitgift of Canterbury "silenced" Travers "in peremptory fashion" on the grounds that he lacked Episcopal (as opposed to Presbyterian) ordination, and with it a licence to preach.[3] Subsequent to Travers' removal to Trinity College, Dublin, Hooker himself quitted his post in 1591 for the living of Boscombe in Wiltshire. Apparently, his resignation

1. Izaak Walton, *The Life of Mr. Richard Hooker*, in Hooker, *The Works*, 1: 18-19.
2. Shirley, *Richard Hooker*, 38.
3. Ibid., 39.

was motivated by his grief at quarrelling with an esteemed colleague, his weariness with "all the bickering and partisanship," and his desire to examine at length in writing the principles of the English Church establishment. In all probability, he deputed his clerical duties and labored assiduously in London for the next four years at the home of his in-laws (having married in 1588), with the astonishing outcome that the first four books of *The Laws of Ecclesiastical Polity* were published in 1593. Obviously, they had been taking shape in his mind from the early days of his debate with Travers. Their appearance in the wake of the executions of the Separatists Penry, Barrow, and Greenwood, along with other circumstances, suggests that Hooker's undertaking had government support and commendation, if not appointment. In 1595 he transferred to the living of Bishopsbourne (a Crown presentation), where he saw the publication of his fifth book of the *Ecclesiastical Polity* in 1597 before his death on November 2, 1600. The judgment of his contemporary admirer, William Covel, that Hooker's early death was hastened by extreme fatigue, is poetically recollected in Walton's memorial phrase: "his body worn out, not with age, but study, and holy mortifications."[1]

Hooker's untimely death before the publication of the last three projected books of his *magnum opus* has left posterity with grave uncertainties about the arrangement and authenticity of these posthumously appearing volumes.[2] The long interval before their publication has fed suspicion of extensive textual adulteration, as has their contentious subject matter. Book VI examines the spiritual jurisdiction of the Anglican clergy in the areas of penitence, confession, and absolution, in response to the Puritan demand for the discipline of lay elders. Book VII defends the institution of the episcopacy, and Book VIII the civil sovereign's power of ecclesiastical dominion. Books VI and VIII appeared together in 1648, while Book VII did not show its face until 1662.

The history of Hooker's manuscripts in the intervening years is too complicated and conjectural to permit a detailed account here, but a brief sketch is necessary to explain the degree and the content of scholarly reservations.

The initial ambiguity of this history concerns the state of Hooker's last three books at his death. According to Dr. John Spencer, to whom all the deceased's manuscripts relating to the *Ecclesiastical Polity* were entrusted, "Books VI and VII were virtually ready for publication," whereas "Book VIII was in the form of notes and a rough draft."[3] Contradicting this testimony was Covel's, that Hooker had informed him of his completion of all three

---

1. Hooker, *The Works*, 1: 77.
2. The Preface and title page of the 1593 edition of *The Ecclesiastical Polity* testify to Hooker's original plan of eight books.
3. Shirley, *Richard Hooker*, 42.

books. Despite Spencer's published announcement that the remaining books would appear "in their defaced condition,"[1] they were not forthcoming, probably owing to a Calvinist-versus-Arminian dispute between Spencer's editorial associates, Edwin Sandys and Lancelot Andrewes, over "the doctrinal contents of Book VI."[2] Spencer died in 1614, bequeathing the manuscripts to John King, Bishop of London, in whose family they remained until Archbishop Abbot about 20 years later had them removed to Lambeth Palace Library. It is thought significant that Archbishop William Laud (1573-1645), who had enthusiastically borrowed from Hooker's earlier books, left the last three buried. On his fall in 1640 they "passed into the possession of Parliament," and then, by permission of Parliament, into the hands of Hugh Peters in 1643.[3]

The most perplexing feature of the historical vicissitudes of Hooker's last three books was the sudden breaking upon the English public of Book VII, "like a bolt from the blue," 14 years after the editor of 1648 had lamented its "complete disappearance."[4] Unfortunately, responsibility for its publication rested with John Gauden, Bishop of Worcester (1605-62), reputed to be a most unscrupulous careerist and obnoxious flatterer of the powers that be. Evidently, he changed his ecclesiastical allegiances as politics dictated, carefully hedging his bets and stooping to deception and even blackmail for the sake of ecclesiastical preferment. The forging and interpolating of manuscripts was well within his moral horizon, but the former, as regards Book VII, was probably not within his capacities. Moreover, internal evidence suggests that Book VII, by and large, originated with Hooker but underwent timely revision in places to align it with the "monarchial and prelatical" tone of the Restoration of King Charles II.[5] The central textual uncertainty concerns the book's assertion of a divinely instituted episcopacy belonging to the church's essence, which runs contrary to the direction of Hooker's argument in Book V, but is susceptible of theoretical reconciliation with it. It has been thought improbable that the "prelatical Laud" would have neglected such a useful defence of the "Divine Right of Bishops."[6] As to how Gauden came by the manuscript, his known acquaintance with Hugh Peters easily accounts for this.

---

1. Spencer made this announcement in his preface to the 1604 edition of Hooker's first five books. Ibid.
2. Ibid.
3. Ibid., 43.
4. Ibid., 45.
5. Ibid., 56.
6. Ibid., 50-1.

Likewise, Book VIII has been the subject of sundry speculations regarding editorial changes. The various surviving copies are, apparently, ridden with ambiguities and incompleteness, although one larger and corrected manuscript may plausibly be deemed Hooker's own completed draft. Suspicions have especially alighted on the book's developed and repeated principles of popular sovereignty, contract and consent, in its expounding of the origin and authority of government and monarchial rule. Nevertheless, their consistency with the theoretical groundwork of Book I, as has been rightly observed, weighs against "the accusation of gross interpolations."[1] Undoubtedly, false accusations against Book VIII, as against Book VII, have been bred by the very complexity and subtlety of Hooker's thought.

C. OF THE LAWS OF ECCLESIASTICAL POLITY

Elizabeth's church had fostered a succession of distinguished and influential defenders prior to Hooker: John Jewel, John Whitgift, and Richard Bancroft, all of whom boasted episcopal degree. As befitted his humility and reverence for those in authority, Hooker in the *Ecclesiastical Polity* made due use of his predecessors' arguments, especially those contained in Whitgift's voluminous refutation of Cartwright. Indeed, his predecessors deserved to be attended to, as erudite and discerning spokesmen for the interests and principles of Elizabeth's church settlement. However, from the viewpoint of our theoretical concern with developed conceptions of law and authority in the English church, their reflections may be dispensed with in favor of a fuller consideration of Hooker's thought. For Hooker's systematic exposition of these subjects provided the theoretical completeness and consistency lacking in these earlier contributions.[2]

Most germane to our concerns are Hooker's expositions of types of law, Scriptural authority, ecclesiastical law, and the powers of ecclesiastical order, jurisdiction, and dominion, contained in Books I, II, III, VII, and VIII of the *Ecclesiastical Polity*.

---

1. Ibid., 52.
2. We pass over with reluctance Jewel's celebrated *Apology of the Church of England* against the Papacy and the Council of Trent, on account of its sound theological vindication of English church unity and order in terms of universal and apostolic faith and practice. In the final analysis, its doctrinal foci may undergird a more theologicaly satisfying understanding of law and authority than Hooker offers; but this potential is not developed.

D. The Nature and Kinds of Law

Firmly set in the natural law tradition, Hooker's understanding of law is, from the outset, ontological and theological. "The being of God," he says, "is a kind of law to his working," both to his "natural, necessary, and internal [Trinitarian] operations" and to his voluntary operations *ad extra*, eternally decreed as to "when and how they should be." Only God, infinite and perfect, is the author of the law of his working; all finite beings receive the laws of their action from "some superior, unto whom they are subject."[1] Hooker denotes the unchanging law of God's voluntary operations by the term "first eternal law," and subsumes the divinely imposed laws of finite beings under the "second law eternal." The "second law eternal" is differentiated according to the diverse "kinds of things . . . subject unto it," assuming the various names of "Nature's law," "law Celestial," "law of Reason," "Divine law," and "Human law." Briefly construed, "Nature's law" is the rule of "natural" or "necessary" agents, which is obeyed unwittingly; the "law Celestial" is the rule which angelic agents "clearly behold" and unswervingly observe; the "law of Reason" is the rule of "creatures reasonable in this world," to which "by reason they may most plainly perceive themselves bound"; "Divine law" binds the same agents, but is known only "by special revelation from God"; and "Human law" is the rule which men make, "probably gathering to be expedient . . . out of the law either of reason or of God."[2]

Hooker's non-Thomistic separation between nature's law and the law of reason flows from his sharp division of natural from voluntary agents, according as God is the efficient cause or the final cause of their motion. Whereas God causes natural agents to seek their appetitive good unknowingly and necessarily, he so directs voluntary agents that they pursue knowingly and freely the objects of their desire. The good that is freely willed is not presented by the agent's appetite alone but by his reason, and the counsel of reason is not so certain or so apparent as to leave no room for the will's dissent.

Thus, the law of reason by which voluntary agents are ruled "is the sentence that Reason giveth concerning the goodness of those things which they are to do."[3] In pronouncing its sentence, the reason depends on the universal axioms or principles of natural justice that derive from man's unassisted knowledge of himself in relation to God and to other finite beings. From the knowledge of God's existence, properties, and relation to the world, man's

---

1. Hooker, *Laws*, in Hooker, *The Works*, 1: 200. All page references are to Keble's edition.
2. Ibid., 1: 205.
3. Ibid., 1: 228.

reason lays down such axioms as "that in all things we go about his aid is by prayer to be craved," and "that he cannot have sufficient honour done unto him, but the utmost of that we can do to honour him we must," which axioms Hooker identifies with "the first and great commandment": "Thou shalt love the Lord thy God with all thy heart. . . ." Likewise, from its knowledge of the equality of natural desire in all men "to receive all good" at the hands of their fellows, man's reason formulates such rules as "That because we would take no harm, we must therefore do none," and "that from all violence and wrong we are utterly to abstain," which amount to our Saviour's second commandment to men "no less to love others than themselves."[1] These "clear and manifest" rules of duty, together with less easily known principles deduced "by necessary consequence" out of them, comprise the totality of reason's law in its self-evident intelligibility. Hooker concedes to the traditional usage that the law of reason is, indeed, the law of nature: "the Law which human Nature knoweth itself in reason universally bound unto. . . ."[2] Our obedience to that law is righteousness; our transgression of it is sin. Our conscience is the ever vigilant guardian of nature's law, rejoicing in its keeping, "(as it were) in certain hope of reward," and grieving in its violation, "(as it were) in a sense of future punishment."[3]

Significantly, Hooker proceeds from the law of reason to human law, rather than to divine law (as in his original classification), suggesting the close link between the former two types, and the derivative character of the second. Notwithstanding this link, human law differs from the law of reason in significant respects: in respect of origin, authority, content, quality, and sanction. To grasp these differences is to grasp the fundamentals of Hooker's political theory, for the origin and authority of human law is inseparable from and subsequent to the origin and authority of human government. Therefore, human government rather than law is Hooker's prior theoretical concern.

About government, the first thing to notice is that its origin is distinct from that of society; for society originates in the insufficiency of individuals to procure the necessities of life befitting human nature, while government originates in the sinful depravity of individuals, and the consequent weakness of their natural faculties. On the one hand, men "are naturally induced to seek communion and fellowship with others" in order "to supply those defects and imperfections which are in [them] living single and solely by [themselves]."[4] On the other hand, they are led by their reason to seek "to

1. Ibid., 1: 231.
2. Ibid., 1: 233.
3. Ibid., 1: 238.
4. Ibid., 1: 239.

take away all such mutual grievances, injuries, and wrongs" as infect their sinful common life "by ordaining some kind of government public, and by yielding themselves subject thereunto," as a means of "growing into composition and agreement amongst themselves."[1] In their establishment of "public regiment" they are guided by certain principles (deduced, we may assume, from the laws of reason under the conditions of depravity), the most theoretically significant of which is that of consent to political authority. After the individual's right of self-defense against threatened injury, and the community's right to withstand the perpetrators of injury, Hooker enunciates the third principle that no individual may "take upon him to determine his own right," owing to his partiality, but that all should consent to be ruled "by some whom they should agree upon." He asserts lastly that "without [such] consent there were no reason that one man should take upon him to be lord or judge over another." Hooker is inflexible on the moral indispensibility of consent to properly constituted political rule. While admitting with the ancients "a kind of natural right in the noble, wise, and virtuous, to govern them which are of servile disposition," he, nonetheless, holds that political authority (that is, "complete lawful power") comes only "by consent of men, or immediate appointment of God."[2]

Human government, then, as opposed to association or fellowship, arises from the deliberation and resolve of men wherein they mutually consent to a form of rule, to an order of union. This order, whether "expressly or secretly agreed upon," Hooker calls "the Law of a Commonweal, the very soul of a politic body, the parts whereof are by law animated, held together, and set to work in such actions, as the common good requireth."[3] In its combination of voluntarist and organic aspects, Hooker's original political act recalls Fortescue's mystical "compact" underlying political society as a legal organism. (Indeed, Fortescue's formulations are repeatedly overlooked by scholarly acclamation of the precocious clarity of Hooker's "compact" theory.) This original act of consent is paramount in determining the permanent, or persisting, right of government, which does not depend on regular repetitions of popular assent. Fortescue, much more than Hooker, requires that the constitution of political rule establish structures for the ongoing expression of public consent. Although Hooker regards with approval such representative bodies as "parliaments, councils, and the like assemblies," he does not deem them necessary to the "complete lawful power" of rulers.[4] Rather, he

1. Ibid., 1: 241-2.
2. Ibid., 1: 242.
3. Ibid., 1: 239.
4. Ibid., 1: 246.

emphasizes that the public renders its consent "to be commanded" not only through the present acts of its appointed representatives but also through the past acts of its ancestral representatives "when that society hath at any time before consented, without revoking the same after by the like universal agreement." This is so because "corporations are immortal; we were then alive in our predecessors, and they in their successors do live still."[1] Obviously, Hooker construes the principle of consent in a conservative manner, with little intimation of a doctrine of constitutional rights.

However, the introduction of positive laws into a political regime is implicitly a reinforcement of consent. For laws are devised by the universal agreement of men in a commonwealth when, perceiving "that to live by one man's will [was] the cause of all men's misery," they decided for a regiment "wherein all men might see their duties beforehand, and know the penalties of transgressing them."[2] Promulgated laws, therefore, enable public obedience based upon intelligent consent—a benefit ignored by Hooker, who describes their salutary effects in terms the production of dutiful conduct. Laws overcome two obstacles to dutiful conduct: men's ignorance of duty that is difficult of discernment, and their pretending of ignorance to escape the consequences of their fault.

These effects of positive laws suggest their material identity with the law of reason. However, according to Hooker, only one type of positive law, the "mixedly human," "establish[es] some duty whereunto all men by the law of Reason did before stand bound."[3] A second type, which Hooker calls "merely human," is defined by no material relation to the law of Reason. Rather, it is constituted by those laws "which reason doth but probably teach to be fit and convenient," not requiring them "necessarily."[4] This second type is chiefly characterized by its extreme variability from commonwealth to commonwealth, merely human laws being properly subject to innumerable contingencies of time, place, and purpose. Cutting across these two types of law is yet a third, the law of nations, which pertains not to "men as men," nor to "men . . . in some form of politic society," but rather to "several bodies politic" in their "public commerce with another."[5] All three types of law, Hooker points out, are made by both "civilly united" and "spiritually joined" political societies, that is, by both commonwealths and churches. In addition, all three types prescribe duties "grounded upon sincere [as well as] upon

---

1. Ibid., 1: 246.
2. Ibid., 1: 243-44.
3. Ibid., 1: 248.
4. Ibid., 1: 249.
5. Ibid., 1: 250.

depraved nature," although the duties grounded upon depraved nature are, not surprisingly, preponderant.[1]

Finally, as regards the constraining force of human laws, Hooker derives it, not from the "quality" of the laws themselves or "of such as devise them," but from the authoritative will of the political community, upon which, likewise, the prior power of government absolutely depends.

While the best positive laws enable men to attain only a limited and incomplete form of their natural good, their natural desire is for an unlimited, complete, and perfect good. Owing to the intellectual, moral, and spiritual defects of their fallen nature, Adam's progeny are incapable of even beginning on the path to their infinite good and highest perfection. God, Himself, by an act of supernatural grace, places and maintains His people on this path. In Christ He has revealed the way of truth and salvation "prepared before all worlds"; by His own work, He opens up for men "the way of supernatural duty" which their Saviour has prescribed: the way of faith in Christ's "eternal Verity" that plumbs the depths of God's hidden Wisdom; hope in Christ's "everlasting Goodness" that "quickens the dead"; love of Christ's "incomprehensible Beauty" that draws His creatures into the bliss of "endless union" with God.[2]

As God's supernatural work in men of faith, hope, and love requires, by His own appointment, the written revelation of Scripture, Scripture is men's highest authority for knowledge of the divine will. Its "principal intent . . . is to deliver the laws of duties supernatural."[3] That Scripture is not men's only and exclusive authority for knowledge of truth and goodness arises primarily, as we shall see, from the dependence of supernatural law on the law of reason.

Hooker's delineation of types of law in Book I comprises the foundation of all his subsequent arguments concerning authority in civil and ecclesiastical polity. On the strength of his discrimination of "Nature's law," "the law Celestial," "the law of Reason," "Divine law," and "Human law," he proceeds in Book II to dispute the Puritans' fundamental epistemological principle, "that Scripture ought to be the only rule of all our actions." He argues for the necessity of extra-scriptural authorities for human conduct, specifically, nature's law and human law conforming to it. Then in Book III he endeavors to refute the Puritans' central ecclesiological axiom derived from their epistemological principle: "that in Scripture there must of necessity be found some particular form of Polity Ecclesiastical, the Laws whereof admit not any

1. Ibid., 1: 251.
2. Ibid., 1: 261.
3. Ibid., 1: 267.

kind of alteration."¹ Instead, Hooker maintains that the church's external government does not, for the most part, accord with unchanging divine law, but rather with changeable human law "not repugnant" to the dictates of natural reason or supernatural revelation.

This groundwork of law and authority having been laid, Hooker occupies himself with answering the Puritans' particular grievances respecting the established form of English church polity. First, in Book IV, he replies to their general accusation that Elizabeth's church is corrupted "with manifold popish rites and ceremonies, which certain reformed churches have banished from amongst them."² He repudiates their contention that the affinity or identity of an Anglican custom with a Roman one is a sufficient, even valid, reason for condemning it. Next, in Book V, he answers their objections to the details of established worship (its preaching, formal prayers, sung segments and music, creeds, and celebration of the Sacraments), together with their criticisms of the ministerial order (the selection, appointment, consecration, and remuneration of clergy). Then, passing over from "the power of order" to "the power of jurisdiction," Hooker examines in Book VI the Anglican penitential rites of confession and absolution, contrasting them with their Roman counterparts, and (only implicitly) with the Puritan discipline of lay elders; he turns in Book VII to a consideration of episcopal jurisdiction: its origin, nature, right, and honors. Finally, in Book VIII, he inspects a third ecclesiastical power, distinct from those of order and jurisdiction, namely, the "power of Ecclesiastical Dominion," defending against the Puritans the view that such power is "communicable unto persons not ecclesiastical, and most fit to be restrained unto the Prince or Sovereign commander over the whole body politic."³

Let us turn now to Hooker's attack on the epistemological sufficiency of Scripture in Book II.

E. THE BOUNDS OF SCRIPTURAL AUTHORITY

It is not incidental that Hooker expounds the relationship between reason's law and divine law within the context of circumscribing Scripture's authority, for the burden of his exposition is to demonstrate the pervasive dependence of the latter on the former. The course of his argument is manifest in his opening exegesis of Scripture's claim to contain "all things that are

---

1. Ibid., 1: 172.
2. Ibid.
3. Ibid., 1: 173.

necessary unto salvation." The meaning of this claim, he confidently assures us,

> cannot be simply of all things which are necessary, but all things that are necessary in some certain kind or form; as all things which are necessary, and either could not at all or could not easily be known by the light of natural discourse; all things which are necessary to be known that we may be saved, but known with presupposal of knowledge concerning certain principles whereof it receiveth us already persuaded, and then instructeth us in all the residue that are necessary."[1]

The necessary, saving knowledge disclosed by Scripture Hooker restricts to a category of epistemological objects, namely, such as "could not at all or could not easily be known by the light of natural discourse." These objects include God's laws of supernatural duty and as well the more obscure deductions and applications of the law of reason. While the dependence of the latter objects for their intelligibility on the prior discoveries of unassisted reason is fairly obvious, the dependence of the former objects on reason's judgments, though more subtle, is for Hooker equally unassailable. God's supernatural law is bound to reason's autonomous operation in manifold and diverse ways.

Firstly, its initial credibility depends on reason's natural assessment of the authority of the Church's testimony concerning it. Scripture's own witness to God's work and will is not, for Hooker, self-authenticating, in the sense of bestowing on the inexperienced reader a certain conviction of its divine origin and truth. Rather, it is the authority of Christian teachers, past and present, that first persuades men's reason to assent to the claim of the written Word. Says Hooker:

> For whatsoever we believe concerning salvation by Christ, although the Scripture be therein the ground of our belief; yet the authority of man is, if we mark it, the key which openeth the door of entrance into the knowledge of the Scripture. The Scripture could not teach us the things that are of God, unless we did credit men who have taught us that the words of Scripture do signify those things.[2]

Knowing that "the whole Church of God hath that opinion of the Scripture," men "bred and brought up in the Church" naturally "judge it even at the first an impudent thing . . . to be of a contrary mind without cause." Of course, Hooker hastens to add that "the more we bestow our labour in reading or hearing the mysteries thereof, the more we find that the thing itself

---

1. Ibid., 1: 268.
2. Ibid., 1: 321; see also ibid., 1: 267, 1: 295, 1: 375-77.

doth answer our received opinion concerning it." Nevertheless, although the Scripture has the power to confirm men's rational conviction of its truth, it definitely lacks the power to create such persuasion. With "infidels or atheists" who repudiate the Church's authority, alternative arguments from universally apparent principles must be produced to prove the divinity of Scripture's teaching.[1] Such is the external or formal dependence of God's supernatural law on the natural law of Reason.

Secondly, God's supernatural law of duty is intrinsically or materially dependent on reason's natural law of duty as a subsequent law that "supplies the defect" of a preceding one. The subsequent law clarifies or redirects the preceding demand, which it presupposes. For example, Hooker explains:

> The law of reason doth somewhat direct men how to honour God as their Creator; but how to glorify God in such sort as is required, to the end he may be an everlasting Saviour, this we are taught by divine law, which law both ascertaineth the truth and supplieth unto us the want of that other law.[2]

Knowledge of our supernatural duty, while judging and perfecting our natural moral knowledge, presupposes it as a foundational framework. It is our natural moral knowledge that carries this worldly, ontological weight for Hooker, whose tendency is to regard God's supernatural commands, in a Marsilian fashion, as narrowly bound up with our happiness in the afterlife.

In this connection, his tireless insistence that all God's supernatural laws are "positive" is significant; for positive laws (as opposed to nature's and reason's laws) "do make that now good or evil by being commanded or forbidden, which otherwise of itself were not simply the one or the other." The permanent validity of even God's positive laws cannot be assumed, but must be gathered from their "nature and quality": moreover, "The nature of every law must be judged of by the end for which it was made, and by the aptness of things therein prescribed unto the same end."[3] Only those divinely instituted laws are permanently binding, the ends of which are everlasting and the prescribed means of continuously unsurpassed fitness to their ends. Granted that the intended purpose of divine legislation is not always scrutable to human reason, still it is incumbent upon reason to sift through the corpus of revealed positive law, making such discriminations as it plausibly can. The generally respected theological division of divine legislation into the moral, ceremonial, and judicial laws, varying in the permanence attributable to each,

---

1. Ibid., 1: 376-7.
2. Ibid., 1: 281.
3. Ibid., 1: 384.

speaks well for reason's competence in its task. In this, as in all other areas of theological judgment and arbitration, the natural powers of reason exercise supreme authority. They wrest "from the books of Scripture . . . the sense and meaning thereof," manifesting "the difference between true and false construction,"[1] deducing "by collection" theological doctrines out of the words of Scripture, and distinguishing "necessary" from "probable" collection, invincible conclusion from mere conjecture.[2] The authority of Scriptural revelation is everywhere bounded by reason's own assured authority; reason disposes of divinely revealed truth according to its invariable principles and operations, without itself apparently being at the disposal of faith's immediate and certain knowledge, without itself being demonstrably directed and empowered in its work by the Holy Spirit.

As Hooker's expository classification of law was intended to overcome the denigration of human law resulting from the Puritans' polarization of God's law and man's law, so his exposition of epistemological authority was intended to overcome the devaluation of human authority resulting from the Puritans' polarization of God's Word in the Scripture and man's word spoken by reason and tradition. He formulated the dependence of divinely revealed law on the law of reason as a refutation of the Puritan axiom "that Scripture is the only rule of all things which in this life may be done by men."[3] His arguments were designed to prove that unassisted reason authorises many human actions that are approved by God even though not explicitly commanded by His Word of Scripture; and that these include reason's determinations in matters indifferent—neither prescribed nor proscribed by God's revealed ordinance. In breaking down the Puritan opposition of God's eternally valid decrees to the blind and transient dictates of man's depraved rationality, Hooker retained a separation of reason and revelation that works to the advantage of reason's autonomy and jurisdiction. This exaggerated advantage of reason in its cooperation with faith is an aspect of Hooker's enduring bequest to the English theological tradition.

F. THE TWOFOLD FOUNDATION OF ECCLESIASTICAL LAW AND AUTHORITY

In respect of their external order, political societies are, according to Hooker, a product of rational deliberation and consent. The church, being a "spiritually joined" political society, is no exception. As with every society (that is, every community of mutual fellowship), the church needs a public

1. Ibid., 1: 378.
2. Ibid., 1: 269, 1: 329.
3. Ibid., 1: 286.

regiment—in its case, to govern and order its "public spiritual affairs."[1] And as with all public regiments or polities, the church's polity is constituted by a body of human law indebted, in the first place, to the law of reason and, in the second, to the law of God revealed in the Scripture.[2]

Moreover, in respect of its territorial scope and personal membership, the church or ecclesiastical society is identical with the commonwealth or civil society. At the highest level, even the public regiments of the two societies are personally identical. To disprove the Puritan thesis that church and commonwealth are separately subsisting "corporations," Hooker principally appeals to Aristotle's understanding in the *Politics* of the religious duty of every political society, namely, that provision to individuals of the means of "living well" involves provision of the spiritual requisites of their souls, the chiefest of which is religion.[3] Hence he proposes a political definition of the church: "the care of religion being common unto all societies politic, such societies as do embrace the true religion have the name of the Church. . . ." and "the Church of Jesus Christ is every such political society of men, as doth in religion hold that truth which is proper to Christianity."[4] It follows that "the selfsame multitude" of a Christian nation comprises both church and commonwealth, such that exclusion of members is normally from both: the executed or banished criminal is cast out "quite and clean" from the national church as well as the commonwealth, just as the excommunicated offender is "cut off" from the commonwealth in its religious communion.[5] What distinguishes church and commonwealth then is their constitutive law, whether it is "secular law" or the "spiritual law of Jesus Christ." In either case, the primacy of reason holds, as concerns outward order.

The unity of the visible church, says Hooker, consists in the "outward profession of those things, which supernaturally appertain to the very essence of Christianity, and are necessarily required in every particular Christian man." These supernatural essentials are the elements of faith in Christ's Lordship, which include baptism into His salvation.[6] External profession of

---

1. Ibid., 1: 352.
2. Ibid., 1: 381-382.
3. Hooker, *Laws*, in Hooker, *The Works*, 3: 332; Aristotle, *Politics*, bk. 6. 1322b 19.
4. Ibid., 3: 329.
5. Ibid., 3: 338-39. Exclusion is normally, but not always and necessarily, from both church and commonwealth. Hooker admits the asymmetrical case where: "A man which hath both been excommunicated by the Church, and deprived of civil dignity in the commonwealth, is upon his repentance necessarily readunited into the one, but not of necessity into the other" (Ibid., 3: 339). The possibility of asymmetrical membership, hovever, favors the Puritan assertion of two separately subsisting societies.
6. Hooker, *Laws*, 1: 339.

these essentials may, in Hooker's view, be coupled in any individual, with moral turpitude, impious idolatry, and notorious heresy, without vitiating the church's outward oneness, or cutting off the offender from it. While "retaining the law of God and the holy seal of his covenant," the idolator, the heretic, the "excommunicable" and "excommunicated" all continue "the sheep of his visible flock . . . even in the depth of their disobedience and rebellion."[1] Reformed Christians and churches are bound to "hold fellowship" with Rome and her followers, despite her "sundry . . . gross and grievous abominations," for the sake of "those main parts of Christian truth wherein they constantly still persist," and are thereby entitled to be acknowledged as "of the family of Jesus Christ."[2]

In relation to the church's unifying profession of faith, the laws of a church's polity regulate "the public religious duties" entailed by it, such as "the administration of the word and sacraments, prayers, spiritual censures, and the like."[3] A church's political laws "appoint in what manner these duties shall be performed," along with the status and requirements of the officials that perform them. In touching the manner and not the substance of supernatural duties, these laws are "accessory" rather than "necessary" to man's salvation, and, as such, they resemble other human laws in their variability among communities of faith.[4] Hooker denies that there is any theological compunction for one form of church polity to be divinely prescribed in the Scripture. Albeit God's revealed Word supplies the churches with manifold directives in matters of government, discipline and ceremonies, both general principles to follow and particular models to emulate, laws of nature and divine imperatives; still, man's natural reason is permitted a broad latitude in the interpretation, application, and combination of divinely revealed laws and examples. Moreover, in its liturgical, disciplinary, and administrative judgments, a church is most often led by the natural principles of reason, which may or may not be explicitly contained in the Scriptures.

It is a paradox of the Puritan position, Hooker shrewdly contends, that their arguments regarding ceremonial forms, clerical vestments, and ministerial offices constantly appeal to the natural laws of reason under the guise of explicit Scriptural warrant. Their conviction that "all things in the Church

---

1. Ibid., 1: 343. With regard to such repentant sinners, Hooker says that their wickedness separates them from "the visible sound Church of Christ," without severing them from the "visible Church." As regards "the act of excommunication, it neither shutteth out from the mystical, nor clean from the visible, but only from fellowship with the visible in holy duties" (Ibid., 3: 350).
2. Ibid., 1: 347.
3. Ibid., 1: 413.
4. Ibid., 1: 356.

[must] be appointed not only *not against,* but *by* and *according to* the word of God" leads them to attribute authority to such general principles as "Nothing scandalous or offensive . . . unto the Church of God," "All things in order and with seemliness," "All unto edification," "All to the glory of God" *only* as apostolic injunctions.[1] Thus, they argue that "unless the Apostle by writing had delivered those rules to the Church, we should by observing them have sinned, as now by not observing them."[2] "The truth is," however, that "they are rules and canons of that law which is written in all men's hearts; the Church had for ever no less than now stood bound to observe them, whether the Apostles had mentioned them or no."[3] In matters of ecclesiastical polity, as in other theological spheres, the edifice of divine revelation rests firmly on the foundation of human reason. Or, alternatively expressed, the supernatural foundation of the church rests firmly on the natural foundation.

The twofold foundation of ecclesiastical polity is nowhere more masterfully expounded by Hooker than in his defense of Anglican ministerial orders. Here we see the relationship between divine law and the law of reason at its most subtle and complex. In his defense, Hooker is primarily concerned with the bases and elements of clerical and episcopal authority.

He inaugurates his defense in the concluding paragraphs of Book III by setting down two Scripturally-revealed axiomatic ecclesiological principles: (1) that "God's clergy" are a permanently necessary "state" in His church to which "the rest of God's people must be [spiritually] subject"; and (2) that the clerical state has "ever been and ever ought to be" marked by the distinction of degree between bishops and "other ministers of the word and sacraments."[4]

In Book V Hooker elaborates the distinctiveness of the clergy by asserting that "the ministry of things divine" is a "function" instituted by God, and that God's ministers derive their authority from Him "and not from men." They are "Christ's ambassadors and his labourers," bearing his commission to preach, baptize, remember his passion, care for the souls of his flock, declare God's judgment on and pardon of men's sins.[5] For the fulfilment of their apostolic commission Christ imparts to them by the Holy Spirit an "indelible" spiritual "mark," "power," and "authority" that carries the promise of the Spirit's continual assistance and support in the discharge of their vocational

---

1. I Cor. 10:32, 14:26, 40; Rom. 14:6,7 (and 1 Cor. 10:31).
2. Hooker, *Laws,* in Hooker, *The Works,* 1: 361.
3. Ibid., 1: 362.
4. Ibid., 1: 413.
5. Hooker, *Laws,* in Hooker, *The Works,* 2: 455-456.

duties.¹ This "gracious donation" of Christ to his apostles and their successors is given in conjuction with episcopal ordination and consecration and is independent of the bestowal of ministerial "title" or "charge." Against the Puritan conflation of the two in consistoral ordination, Hooker maintains that the "election" or "admission" of ministers into a charge concerns only their "placing" and not their "making," so not "to infringe any way their ordination."² Matters of placement, supervision, and maintenance of clergy in their ministries are practical and political in nature, subject to regulation by variable human laws.

In these matters a church is not bound by inflexible laws, but can alter them or exempt from them as the occasion requires. To obtain a learned clergy, it can with "justice and equity" dispense individuals from the laws of residence and plurality, or grant special privileges in recognition of merit and service, rank and authority.³ These exemptions and honors are not, however, to imply that clerical authority resides in any talent, achievement, or distinction (including "the sound preaching of the word of God"), but in "canonical ordination in the Church of Christ."⁴

Similarly, there is no divinely ordained, permanently binding right of "the people" to elect their clergy prior to episcopal ordination. However popular was the election of clergy in the apostolic church (and the Puritans exaggerate the Scriptural evidence), every church is at liberty to restrict or enlarge the degree of public involvement in the placement of clergy as circumstances render appropriate. It is equally just that one or many should elect the clergy as long as the elector(s) has the lawful authority to do so. For, in line with Hooker's fundamental political principle, the actions of lawful authorities have the consent of those whom they govern. Thus, the lay or ecclesiastical patron elects to a charge on behalf of the whole Christian community whose "ancient and original interest" he represents.⁵

An identical intermeshing of divine and human law is operative in the constitution of specifically episcopal authority as of all clerical authority. Episcopal authority is comprised of the same elements as clerical authority to a superior degree; that is, it entails a "power of order" and a "power of jurisdiction." In the realm of order, to the clerical power of administering the Word and Sacraments is added the power to ordain ecclesiastical persons; in the realm of jurisdiction, to the clerical power of spiritually governing the

1. Ibid., 2: 456, 2: 462.
2. Ibid., 2: 504.
3. Ibid., 2: 517-520.
4. Ibid., 2: 526-527.
5. Hooker, *Laws*, in Hooker, *The Works*, 3: 224.

laity is added the like power to govern the clergy. The juridical superiority of the episcopate, most hotly disputed by the Puritans, is their "power mandatory, judicial, and coercive over other ministers."[1]

In opposition to the Puritans, Hooker holds that episcopal authority is divine and apostolic in origin. It was first granted by Christ to his apostles as part of their spiritual equipment for establishing the Church.[2] To the Puritan argument that the apostolic office is unique and without succession, Hooker replies by distinguishing its transmissable from its nontransmissable aspects. Whereas the apostles' commission "as special chosen eyewitnesses of Jesus Christ" and "first founders of an house of God" is unique and nontransmissable, their power of order they bequeathed to "every presbyter" and their "episcopal function" to succeeding bishops.[3] Significantly, their decision to instate episcopal successors was a practical political one.[4] Hooker concurs with Cartwright and Travers that the first form of regiment instituted by the apostles was the urban "college of presbyters" (except that he includes deacons). But he argues that they became persuaded that episcopal regiment was the only "sufficient remedy" for the "emulations, strifes, and contentions" that beset collegial government.[5] Thus, the apostles' instatement of bishops was a rationally devised political measure; but one, argues Hooker, which, "being established by them on whom the Holy Ghost was poured in so abundant measure for the ordering of Christ's Church, . . . had either divine appointment beforehand, or divine approbation afterwards," and so is "to be acknowledged the ordinance of God."[6] In defending both the divine and the human origins of episcopacy, Hooker accomplishes the adroit feat of synthesizing the conflicting views of his Anglican mentors and colleagues.

Equally adroit is his defense of the legislative sovereignty of the human political community in the face of divine ordination. Accounting the apostolic institution of bishops as a mutable divine positive law, Hooker proposes that the "whole body of the Church hath power to alter [it], with general consent and upon necessary occasions," if "it manifestly appears to her, that change of times have clearly taken away the very reasons of God's first institution. . . ."[7]

---

1. Ibid., 3: 149.
2. Ibid., 3: 151. Hooker supports his claim with the Scriptural testimony that Matthias was elected to "an episcopal office." See Acts 1:20: ". . . and his bishopric let another take." (Authorised King James Version)
3. Ibid., 3: 154.
4. Examples of such successors are furnished by Irenaeus and Ignatius: Linus in Rome, Polycarp in Smyrna, Evodius in Antioch.
5. Hooker, *Laws*, in Hooker, *The Works*, 3: 155-156.
6. Ibid., 3: 157.
7. Ibid., 3: 164.

For, although the episcopacy originates in divine and apostolic ordination, it remains in force, "rather by the custom of the Church, choosing to continue it, than by the necessary constraint of any commandment from the word, requiring perpetual continuance thereof." The church, therefore, is entitled to abrogate the episcopacy "upon urgent cause," as, for instance, might be presented by "the proud, tyrannical, and unreformable dealings of her bishops."[1] But it is only the entire visible church, deliberating through the proceedings of a general council, that exercises the prerogative of altering what God has ordained and time has made venerable, and not particular ecclesiastical groups, acting out of their conceited inspiration and narrow deliberations.

G. The Unity of English Civil and Ecclesiastical Polity

In that the English church and commonwealth are distinct regiments of *one* society, they are subject to various forms of unity. They are unified not only by identity of personal membership but also by identical participation in the fundamental societal division into estates, of which the clergy are the "chiefest." In addition, they are unified by the subordination of ecclesiastical to civil regiment in the legislative realm and by the lawful sovereignty of the monarch. Finally, they are unified by constitutional and incidental conjunctions of civil and ecclesiastical offices in particular individuals.

Firstly, by the legislative superiority of civil over ecclesiastical regiment is meant the competence of the civil law-making body—the King in Parliament—to "define" legally the external form of the church. Hooker is a child of English Reformation Erastianism in his abandonment of the medieval conception of Convocation and Parliament as autonomous and complementary legislative bodies within the realm, despite its serviceability to the royal supremacy. From his principle of sovereignty applied to ecclesiastical polity, namely, that "the true original subject of power also to make church laws is the whole entire body of that church for which they are made," he concludes that the English Parliament, as embodying "the general consent" of the English political community, has the preeminent right to legislate for the church.[2] Hooker stands with his Puritan adversaries in opposing the Roman view that the prelacy hold the power of ecclesiastical jurisdiction directly from Christ, arguing rather that Christ, confirming the law of reason, invests this power in the spiritual community, which delegates it. He joins battle with

1. Ibid., 3: 165.
2. Ibid., 3: 396, 3: 410.

the Puritans at the point of their assertion that church and commonwealth are perpetually separate and independent societies,[1] repudiating their theological disjunction between civil authority as "from God" and ecclesiastical authority as mediated "through Christ."[2] The oneness of Christ's dominion over human society is reflected in the oneness of the human legislating power. This is not to deny the superior authority of clerical wisdom in the "devising" and "discussing" of ecclesiastical legislation but only to deny that wisdom's authority issues in binding laws. The latter issue exclusively from "the general consent of all."[3]

It is only a short step from Hooker's principle of consent to his defense of the royal supremacy, that includes the monarch's "power of ecclesiastical dominion" within his realm. This is his lawful "supremacy of power" over the church "to order and dispose of spiritual affairs, as the highest uncommanded commander in them,"[4] "which neither any foreign state, nor yet any part of that politic body at home . . . can lawfully overrule."[5] For, in once establishing the headship of one man over itself, the political community has perpetually delegated sovereign rule to the kingly office; and sovereign rule, however hedged by the terms of the original contract and by subsequent custom and legislation, entails supreme legal jurisdiction in the commonwealth. This supremacy, although bestowed "at men's discretion," is held "by divine right"—with divine ordination and approbation (analogous to episcopal power).[6] Indeed, God may so dispose that kings receive their dominion by right of conquest or special divine appointment rather than by human election. In any case, their lawful rule has God's approval: they are His "lieutenants" and their power is His.[7] Moreover, according to "all law, equity, and reason," "in kingdoms hereditary birth giveth right unto sovereign dominion."[8]

Kingship does not entail unrestrained power in ecclesiastical affairs: it never entails the powers of order and jurisdiction imparted by divine appointment to the clergy alone. Furthermore, in "the best established

---

1. Ibid., 3: 328-29.
2. Ibid., 3: 379.
3. Ibid., 3: 411.
4. Ibid., 3: 340-341.
5. Ibid., 3: 343.
6. Ibid., 3: 345.
7. Ibid., 3: 344.
8. Hereditary right to kingship is lawful, just and rational on account of the "first original conveyance" of power from "the whole into one," whereby power was "to pass from him unto them, whom out of him nature by lawful birth should produce, and no natural or legal inability make uncapable." Ibid., 3: 349.

dominion . . . where the law doth most rule the king," his authority is restrained by "the received laws and liberties of the Church" and by universal Christian traditions in matters not divinely decreed. Most importantly, Hooker affirms with the Puritans that the monarch's duties toward the church are Scripturally revealed by example and precept in the history of Israel, namely, that he is required by God "to see that the laws . . . touching his worship, and touching all matters and orders of the Church, be executed and duly observed; to see that every ecclesiastical person do that office whereunto he is appointed; to punish those that fail in their office."[1]

The issue between Hooker and the Puritans concerns the extent of the royal jurisdiction over the church, in the principal matters of making laws, investing clerical authorities and judging spiritual causes. In these matters, Hooker derives the king's prerogative from the "first original conveyance" of political power and its subsequent elaboration in legal statute and custom. Thus, the king's power of ecclesiastical dominion rests finally for Hooker, not on divine but on human law: on the law of reason articulated in the construction and maintenance of political society.

To Hooker's mind, there is no law of reason or of God that proscribes the combining of civil and ecclesiastical offices in a single individual; indeed, rational deliberation and Biblical example equally commend it. What better candidate for combining both offices, Hooker reflects, than the sovereign monarch. As he reflects he casts an admiring and desirous glance at the Prince-Bishops of Mentz, Colen, and Trevers, and even in the direction of the pope reigning over his own territories.

And so Hooker's Erastian conservatism is a die cast for the future of the English church. Despite the persisting voices of Catholic and Reformed ecclesiology in its ranks, the dominant mainstream has continuously been thrown in Hooker's mold. Even today, it is characterized by theological confidence in a combination of nature known independently of revelation, the powers of unassisted rationality, and the structural and liturgical peculiarities of the still-established national church.

---

1. Ibid., 3: 417.

Conclusion

It should be apparent from this study that English theological thought about law and authority in the course of the reformation of the English church was not a seamless garment, but a many panelled one, composed of various intellectual fabrics: late medieval Thomism and Augustinianism, Renaissance humanism and conciliarism, deeply rooted constitutional doctrines, religious nationalism, continental theologies of reform—Lutheran, Zwinglian, Bucerian, Vermiglian, and Calvinist. In its distinct phases different fabrics dominated, and in different alignments. Nevertheless, there are unbroken connecting threads that render it an identifiable garment to scholarly appraisal. The strongest and most pervasive of these is the positive theoretical centrality of the concept of law and the derivation of authority from it.

From first to last, the guiding minds of the English Reformation conceded primacy to the concept of law in manifold theoretical domains: theological, ontological, epistemological, soteriological, and political. The majority regarded law as belonging to and emanating from God's being and perfection; all saw it as the form of His action *ad extra*. God articulates His eternal will as law in the creation, preservation, redemption, and sanctification of the world. In creation He establishes the lawful operation of each being, after its kind; in preservation He sustains lawful order amidst the disorder of fallen nature, containing evil and subjecting it to created good; in redemption He makes available to sinful and lost mankind the law of His salvation in the work and the words of Jesus Christ; in sanctification He empowers redeemed mankind to fulfil the law of the perfecting of human nature.

Consequently, knowledge of the natural and supernatural order and truth is knowledge of the law in its various domains. Tudor theologians may have disagreed over the sources of this knowledge, but they never disagreed over the centrality of law to their sources: thus, Scripture is pre-eminently the written revelation of God's eternal law of salvation; reason is pre-eminently the revelation in man of the natural and moral laws. Whether the power of unaided rationality is emphasized, or the sufficiency of Scripture, the substance of the claims is the same: it is knowledge of God's law. Even the most Lutheran of English reformers was never tempted to divorce God's grace from His law, displacing law as the universal form of God's will. For William Tyndale, man's consent to God's revealed law, embodied in acts of pure obedience, is the outward form of the inward work of the Holy Spirit. Obedient knowledge of God's law is, then, for Tudor Christianity the "one thing . . . needful."

Another unifying thread in the thought of the English reformers and their forerunners is the primary Scriptural locus of conceptions of law and authority. Even advocates of the law of reason, such as Fortescue and Hooker, look to Scripture for the clearest and most certain statement of law in its specific manifoldness. So Fortescue argues the right of royal succession in sovereign kingdoms from the Scriptural disclosure of natural and divine law concerning the subjection of woman to man, and Hooker argues for the fitness of many "secondary" (that is, inessential and optional) features of Anglican policy and practice from Old and New Testament models and maxims that direct and illuminate reason's public deliberations. There is no general issue of secular and ecclesiastical law and authority that the Henrician and Elizabethan reformers do not refer in the first place to Scriptural resolution.

In the civil realm Scripture manifests to them the acceptable forms of rule: the theocratic and aristocratic governments of Moses, Joshua, and the judges; the Israelite monarchy and post-exilic priestly rule; the Roman imperium recognized by Christ (Matt. 17:24-27, 22:17-21; John 19:11), by St. Paul (Acts 25:10-11; Rom. 13:1-7), and by St. Peter (I Pet. 2:18); and the best form of rule: the Israelite judges' rule by God's laws alone, for the common good, with the people's consent. It shows forth the character and duties of the godly king (the examples of David, Solomon, Josiah, Hezekiah, and Jehoshaphat from the historical books and the royal psalms). It testifies to the superiority of the secular sovereign's dignity over the priestly dignity (the superior authority of Moses over Aaron, the primacy of Melchizedek's royal office over his priestly office, and of God's kingship over Christ's priesthood). It attests to the universal obligation of subjects to submit to the ruler's will, however tyrannous and unjust (Isa. 3:4ff.; Rom. 12:17-13:7; I Pet. 2:18), unless commanded to violate God's law, in which case they are enjoined "to obey God rather than men" (Acts 5:29), after Daniel's example (Dan. 6). Moreover, in addition to the duty of righteous disobedience, Scripture authorizes and commands God's elect to admonish their wicked, unjust, and sacrilegious overlords with courage and zeal (the examples of Moses before Pharaoh, the prophets before the kings of Israel and Judah, Christ before the Pharisees), and even authorizes in exceptional instances the punishment of godless tyrants by individuals (Moses and Jehu). Finally, Scripture declares God's rule of natural equity (Matt. 7:12) from which descend the principles of just political order (such as consent of the governed, equality before the law, and the proportionate punishment of wrongdoing) and all human laws in accordance with right reason, and which establishes and regulates every just form of government.

In the ecclesiastical realm, Scripture reveals to them the ground and essence of order (inward and outward, spiritual and practical) to be God's law of man's salvation in Jesus Christ, incarnate, crucified, resurrected, and glorified. First, it proclaims the law of sinful man's justification before God by faith in Christ's work of atonement (Rom. 3:28, 5:1,16; Gal. 2:16, 3:11; Eph. 2:8). It draws out the implications of this fundamental law for the form, action, and authority of the church, namely, its constitution as a community of faith under the headship of Christ (Eph. 5:24; Col. 1:18,24), whose essential action in preaching and administering the sacraments is proclamatory of God's promises in Christ (Acts 1:8, 10:34-43; 13:38; Rom. 10:14-15; I Cor. 1:18, 21, 23; II Cor. 4:5-6; I Tim. 4:2; II Tim 4:2; Gal. 1:8-9), and whose authority derives from Christ's commissioning and empowering of his disciples (Matt. 28:19; Mark 16:15, 20; Luke 24:49; Acts 1:8, 3:13). Against the usurped juridical powers of the papacy, Scripture witnesses the spiritual and non-coercive nature of the priestly authority bestowed by Christ on his apostles, after his own example of refusing worldly rule (John 18:36), contentious judgment (Luke 12:13-14), and coercive force (John 6:15, 18:11); and with the express command that their ministry be one of humble service rather than lordly self-aggrandizement (Matt. 20:25-28; Luke 22:24-27).

In accordance with the spiritual and self-effacing vocation of Christ's clergy, Scripture discloses their equality of divine office, as inheritors of dignities bestowed by Christ equally on all his apostles: the dignity of eucharistic administration (Luke 22:19) and the dignity of remitting and retaining sins

(John 20:21-23), which is the "power of the keys," misconstrued by papists to be invested immediately in St. Peter alone (Matt. 16:19). Likewise, to those of Franciscan persuasian it reveals the status of "supreme poverty" or "evangelical dispossession" to be incumbent upon the successors of Christ's apostles, in view of their master's explicit injunctions (Matt. 5:3, 6:25-26, 31-32, 34, 10:9-10, 19:21-24, 29; Mark 10:21; Luke 3:11, 6:20, 14:33, 18:22-27), his earthly example (Matt. 8:20, 17:24; Luke 9:58), the apostles' subsequent deportment and the discipline of the congregations under their charge (Acts 4:34-35; I Cor. 6:7; II Cor. 8 and 9). Oppositely, to Puritans of every stripe, Scripture lays down the standard of a property-owning clergy, enabled by the generous maintenance of their congregations to devote themselves entirely to their ministerial tasks (I Cor. 9:1-14; I Tim. 5:17-18), without neglecting to provide for their households (I Tim. 5:8).

In the matter of ecclesiastical offices, Puritan dissenters held Scripture to support a twofold order of deacons and presbyters (I Tim. 3; Phil. 1:1; Rom. 12:6-7; I Pet. 4:11), subdivided into "distributing" and "governing" deacons (Rom. 12:8), "teaching" and "pastoral" presbyters (Rom. 12:7; I Tim. 4:6). Establishment Anglicans discerned a threefold order of deacons, presbyters, and bishops—the latter being general overseers of the church, with superior powers of order and jurisdiction derived from the apostolic office (Acts 1:20, 14:23; Tit. 1:5; I Tim. 5:22). Moreover, on the Anglican view, Scripture endorses, by the example of Israelite religious institutions, the investing of the church's chief officers with outward honours, privileges, and possessions befitting their rank (the Israelite system of tithes, offerings and sacrifices; the prerogatives and wealth of the Levites).

Finally, from Scripture Presbyterians and Separatists alike drew the strict separation of civil and ecclesiastical offices, according to the examples and exhortations of Christ, His apostles and evangelists (Matt. 20:16; Mark 10:40-45; Luke 12:13-15; John 6:15, 18:36; Acts 6:1-4; Rom. 12:16; I Cor. 9:11, 13-14, 19; II Tim. 2:4), and the self-government of Christ's gathered people under His direct lordship (Acts 15:7, 13-23, 28, 16:4; Eph. 1:20-23; Col. 1:18; Heb. 5:1, 12:22-24; II Chron. 19:5). Presbyterians further emphasized the subjection of the civil magistrate to the discipline of the saints (Matt. 18:15; I Cor. 3:22-23, 5:12-13; Col. 1:16; Deut. 17:15). Alternatively, Anglican Erastians extracted the lawfulness and salutariness of combining civil and ecclesiastical functions: the secular powers of the Israelite priesthood (as in Jer. 29:26) and the superior competence of the saints to judge in worldly affairs (affirmed by St. Paul in I Cor. 6:1-7); the legislative identity of church and realm in a Christian commonwealth (after the model of Israelite theocracy); and the ruling monarch's supreme dominion over civil and ecclesiastical affairs, entailing exemption from censure or punishment by his inferiors (after the sovereignty under God of the Israelite kings). On all these issues Tudor reformers appealed to the arbitration of Scripture as final, whatever the recognized scope of reason's authority.

The appeal of the Tudor reformers was everywhere marked by a common hermeneutical approach to the Biblical material, which supplies a third continuous strand to English reformation theology. In this approach, they assimilated the Gospel covenant established by God with man in Jesus Christ in form and substance to the Mosaic or Deuteronomic convenant, legalistically interpreted. They regarded Christ's law of salvation and righteousness as susceptible of community legislation and enforcement, whether by church or by commonwealth. Divine law could be adequately articulated in human law: in the church's *credenda*, order, and discipline; in the natural equity of English common law; in the decrees of the divinely appointed monarch, and the statutes enacted by Parliament. The English reformers retained all the medieval confidence in the power of human institutions to mediate Christ's justice and His saving and sanctifying grace. The English Lutheran founding fathers of Henry's and Edward's reigns—Tyndale, Cranmer, Latimer, and Ridley—espoused the priesthood of all believers and the imperative of universal Biblical literacy, but they also upheld the necessity of church law, of official authorization and outward conformity to prescribed forms (within limits), and of the coercion and punishment of serious offenders (at least Papists and Anabaptists) with the assistance of the secular arm. Cranmer at his most Erastian does not stop short of identifying the King's law with God's truth for the public realm.

The English Protestant turn to Calvinism after 1550 meant, if anything, increased passion for a divinely legislated polity in the church if not in the commonwealth. Human implementation of God's law received new scope (comparable to the old scope of the papal legal system), with the extension of divine command to cover practical particulars. The Presbyterians sought Biblical legal injunctions for every detail of the church's organization and comportment—in worship, teaching, and discipline, including its judicial handling of offences. The admonition and reporting of offenders was seen as the divinely apportioned task of lay elders, while their prosecution and punishment, by suspension or excommunication, were invested by God in the consistory or synod. Although the church's punishment was considered exclusively spiritual, Cartwright and Travers propounded as ardently as Wyclif the conviction that Christ's law is not wanting in corporal and material sanctions, and so is a fit instrument for overcoming the recalcitrance of the flesh. They resolutely endorsed the unchanging equity of those Mosaic "judicials" that require the putting to death of stubborn idolaters, blasphemers, murderers, incestuous persons and adulterers, arguing that, precisely because the God of Jesus Christ "withdraws His Hand" (of judgment) for His Son's sake, the civil magistrate should wield his so much the harder for the suppression of sin. Thus, they exceeded their English Lutheran predecessors in their assimilation of the Law of Christ to the Law of Moses in substance as well as form.

The Anglican opposition to Puritan Biblical hermeneutics, while loud in its protest against legalistic literalism, did not effectively counteract the pervasive fusion of the Old and New Testament covenants. Even Hooker's astute criticisms of Presbyterian legalism did not challenge the fundamental orientation to Israelite models of law and authority as permanently binding. Hooker's concern was to show the enduring authority of Old Testament legal and political forms (where they were authoritative) to be grounded in the law of reason, and not to show the divinely limited historical character of their authority. No more than his adversaries did Hooker appreciate the full institutional implications of the supersession of the Mosaic by the gospel law, the effect of this supersession on the authority and content of communal legislation, whether civil or ecclesiastical. For, while he emancipated the confessional essence of the church's outward unity—its confession of the lordship of Jesus Christ, crucified and resurrected—from servitude to the inessential features of this unity absolutized by the Presbyterians, he subjected it to another servitude, namely, to the universal claims of political rationality. The law of the commonwealth for the church holds the same inviolable place in Hooker's argument that literal Biblical injunction held in Presbyterian argument. In both cases a rival, limiting authority and law to that of Jesus Christ has been erected.

It is the theocratic aspiration, fed by Old Testament sources denuded of their prophetic dimension, that gives overall theological coloration to English civil and ecclesiastical polity in the sixteenth century. This aspiration simultaneously binds the English Reformation to the political past and the political future of the West, to medieval Christendom and to the secular unitary state, the latter being the inverse of the former. For Hildebrandine Catholicism and Hobbesian statism have in common with Tudor Erastianism the denial of any systemic tension or conflict between God's law and man's law, the righteousness of Christ and the righteousness of the human community. They all hold out an integration of faith and polity that does not admit of prophetic and eschatological criticism. Neither Henrician nor Elizabethan public policy seriously recognized incongruity between the evangelical unity of the church and the regal- constitutional unity of the commonwealth, between the

Christological form of the communion of saints and the external form of the earthly church, between the Scriptural Word of God read and preached and the word of duly established secular and spiritual authorities, or finally between the judgment of the individual Christian and the order of the Christian public. The theological tensions in which the reforming spirit had come to birth had suffered dissipation in the grinding machinery of practical reform. By the established churches of the Tudor monarchs, Wyclif's polarities of evangelical and civil possession, righteous and worldly authority, Christian humility and prelatical pride, the truth of Scripture and the error of human tradition, were either repudiated or conveniently interpreted. By the Presbyterian dissidents the latter three polarities were invoked in a onesided and unself-critical manner, to place the Genevan discipline beyond questioning.

Having said this, it is crucial to add that the dissipation of these theological tensions was never complete in the course of English church reform. It was not as if the English "permitted . . . [religious renewal] . . . to pass away as in a dream," to use Hooker's haunting phrase. With the awakened insight into the authority of God's law in Scripture, into the corrupt waywardness of much of the Roman church's teaching, worship, and discipline, into the responsiveness of the individual's faith to the saving truth of Christ and the equality of the faithful, into the evangelical freedom of Christ's gathered disciples and their power of self-government under the gospel law, the English Reformation irreversibly happened. After the transformations of theological perspective in the sixteenth century, neither the English church nor the English commonwealth could escape the turbulent dynamism of emancipated faith.

If the theological constructions of certain guiding lights of English reform, from Wyclif to Hooker, had drawn impetus from earlier accomplishments in political thought, they undoubtedly also gave impetus to subsequent political reflection and conduct. In the seventeenth century, Reformation ideas respecting Biblical authority and revelation, individual faith and conscience, and democratic church polity were refracted in the democratic and republican sentiments and developments connected with the Long Parliament, the Civil Wars and the Interregnum, the egalitarianism of Cromwell's army and the Independent sectaries, and the emergence of rudimentary religious toleration in Cromwell's Commonwealth. Likewise, the English natural-law, constitutional tradition, invigorated by the battle against papal law and authority, contributed to the rise of the Commons as a more representative institution under James I and Charles I, and the consolidation of its power in the Glorious Revolution of the 1680s. On the other side, however, the monarchist and socially conservative elements of Reformation theology fed the "divine right" theories of the Stewart kings and the Restoration bishops.

In the light of rigorous scrutiny, it may be apparent that no seventeenth-century theological stance—neither Presbyterian nor Independent nor Anglican—expresses the truest insights of the English Reformation as adequately as their original framers. These subsequent postures may strike us as theologically imbalanced exaggerations of sixteenth-century positions. This perhaps suggests the historical inevitability of theology becoming increasingly rigid ideology when in the public-political realm.

Nevertheless, we are not on this account entitled to dismiss the political accomplishments of the seventeenth century as inauthentic public expressions of Christian truths. The principles and institutions upheld by the Presbyterians and Independents—political consent and representation, and ecclesiastical self-government by the Presbyterians; social equality, public religious freedom and legal toleration of religious difference by the Independents; and the universal civil responsibility to defend God's laws by both—all were valid. All were historically significant societal embodiments of Scripturally witnessed truths concerning God's law for created and sinful mankind, for His government of the nations, for man's salvation in Christ, and for the nature of Christ's gathered people. We may legitimately judge them to be superior embodiments of these truths as compared with the prevailing Tudor-Anglican conceptions of the divinely elected sovereign king, the national church under royal headship, and the paramount duty of subjects to obey their rulers, without denying the theological truths served by the earlier Reformation conceptions. Yet, in their undialectical formulation, these seventeenth-century positions were also theologically ambiguous and deficient, alike to their Anglican rivals, equally implicated in the corporate waywardness of the sinful human community.

It is, in conclusion, salutary for our theological reflection on law and authority from within the modern liberal majoritarian situation to attend first to the challenging substance of the English Reformers' theopolitical understandings, and only then to the ambiguities with which they were beset.

BIBLIOGRAPHY

A. PRIMARY SOURCES

"An admonition to the Parliament" [of 1572], in W.H. Frere and C.E. Douglas, eds., *Puritan Manifestoes, A Study of the Origin of the Puritan Revolt* (London, 1954), pp. 1-55.

Aquinas, St. Thomas, *On Kingship, To the King of Cyprus*, trans. Gerald B. Phelan, intro. I. Th. Eschmann, O.P. (Toronto, 1949).

Id., *Summa Theologiae*, Vol. 28: *Law and Political Theory*, ed. Thomas Gilby, O.P. (London, 1963).

Aristotle, *The Politics*, trans. and intro. T.A. Sinclair (Harmondsworth, Middlesex, 1962).

Augustine, Saint, *Concerning the City of God against the Pagans*, trans. Henry Bettenson, intro. David Knowles (Harmondsworth, Middlesex, 1972).

Aylmer, John, *A Harbor for Faithful and True Subjects (against the First Blast)* (1559).

Bancroft, Richard, *Dangerous Positions* (1593), largely reprinted in R.G. Usher, ed., *The Presbyterian Movement in the Reign of Queen Elizabeth* (London, 1905).

Beza, Theodore, *The Right of Magistrates over their Subjects*, in Julian H. Franklin, *Constitutionalism and Resistance in the Sixteenth Century* (New York, 1969), pp. 101-35.

Browne, Robert, *A Treatise of Reformation without Tarrying for Any* (1582, reprinted, London, 1903).

Calvin, Jean, *Institutes of the Christian Religion*, 2 vols., trans. Henry Beveridge (London, 1962).

Cartwright, Thomas, *A reply to an answer made of M. Doctor Whitgift* (1574).

Id., *The second reply of Thomas Cartwright* (1575).

Id., *The rest of the second reply* (1577).

Cranmer, Thomas, *Miscellaneous Writings and Letters of Thomas Cranmer*, ed. John Edmund Cox, for the Parker Society (Cambridge, 1846).

Fortescue, Sir John, *The Works of Sir John Fortescue*, collected and arranged by Thomas (Fortescue) Lord Clermont (London, 1869).

Gerson, Jean, *De Potestate Ecclesiastica*, in *Oeuvres Complètes*, vol. 6: *L'Oeuvre ecclésiologique*, ed. P. Glorieux (Paris, 1965), pp. 210-50.

Goodman, Christopher, *How Superior Powers ought to be Obeyed of their Subjects* (1558).

Hooker, Richard, *Of the Laws of Ecclesiastical Polity*, in *The Works of Richard Hooker*, ed. John Keble, 7th edition, 3 vols. (reprinted, New York, 1970).

Humphrey, Laurence, *De religionis conservatione et reformatione vera* (London, 1559).

Id., *Optimates* (London, 1559).

Jewel, John, *An Apology of the Church of England*, ed. J.E. Booty (Charlottesville, VA, 1963).

Knox, John, *The Political Writings of John Knox*, ed. and intro. Marvin A. Breslow (Washington, 1985).

Marsilius of Padua, *Defensor Pacis*, in Alan Gewirth, *Marsilius of Padua, the Defender of Peace* (Toronto, 1980).

Ockham, William of, *An Princeps Pro Suo Succursu*, in *Guillelmi de Ockham Opera Politica*, 3 vols., Vol. I., ed. J.G. Sikes (Manchester, 1940), pp. 230-71.

Id., *Breviloquium de Potestate Papae*, ed. L. Baudry (Paris, 1937).

Id., *Dialogus I*, *Opera Plurima*, Vol. I (Republished, London, 1962).

Id., *Octo Quaestiones de Potestate Papae*, in *Opera Politica*, Vol. I, pp. 13-221.

Id., *Opus Nonaginta Dierum*, Chapters I to VI, in *Opera Politica*, Vol. I, pp. 293-374; Chapters 7 to 124, in *Opera Politica*, Vol. II (Manchester, 1963).

Ponet, John, *A Short Treatise of Politic Power*, in Winthrop S. Hudson, ed., *John Ponet (1516?-1556), Advocate of Limited Monarchy* (Chicago, 1942).

St. Germain, Christopher, *Doctor and Student*, 15th edition (1751).

Starkey, Thomas, *A Dialogue between Pole and Lupset*, ed. Kathleen M. Burton (London, 1948); ed. T. F. Mayer (London, 1989).

Tanner, J.R., ed., *Tudor Constitutional Documents, A.D. 1485-1603* (Cambridge, 1951).

The First and Second Prayer Books of King Edward VI, intro. Douglas Harrison (London, 1968).

The Forty Two Articles (1553) and The Thirty Nine Articles (1571), reproduced in Oliver O'Donovan, *On the Thirty Nine Articles, A Conversation with Tudor Christianity* (Exeter, 1986).

Travers, Walter, *A full and plain declaration of ecclesiastical discipline* (1574).

Tyndale, William, *Doctrinal Treatises and Introductions to Different Portions of the Holy Scriptures*, ed. Henry Walter, for the Parker Society (Cambridge, 1848)

Whitgift, John, *Works of Archbishop Whitgift*, 3 vols., ed. J. Ayre, for the Parker Society (Cambridge, 1851-3).

Wyclif, John, *Tractatus De Civili Dominio*, 4 vols. ed. J. Loserth, for the Wyclif Society (London, 1885, 1900, 1903, 1904).

Id., *Tractatus De Ecclesia*, ed. J. Loserth, for the Wyclif Society (London, 1886).

Id., *Tractatus De Officio Regis*, ed. A.W. Pollard and C. Sayle, for the Wyclif Society (London, 1887).

Id., *Tractatus De Veritate Sacrae Scripturae*, 3 vols., ed. Rudolf Buddensieg, for the Wyclif Society (London, 1905, 1906, 1907).

B. SECONDARY SOURCES

Allen, J.W., *A History of Political Thought in the Sixteenth Century* (London, 1928).

Baumer, Franklin Le van, *The Early Tudor Theory of Kingship* (New Haven, Conn., 1940).

Black, J.B., *The Reign of Elizabeth 1558-1603*, Vol. VIII of *The Oxford History of England*, ed. G.N. Clark (Oxford, 1936).

Brachlow, Stephen, *The Communion of Saints, Radical Puritan and Separatist Ecclesiology 1570-1625* (Oxford, 1988).

Burns, J.H., "New Light on John Major", *The Innes Review* 5 (1954), pp. 83-100.

Carlyle, R.W. and Carlyle, A.J., *A History of Mediaeval Political Theory in the West*, 6 vols. (Edinburgh and London; 1903-1936).

Chrimes, S.B., *English Constitutional Ideas in the Fifteenth Century* (Cambridge, 1936).

Daly, L.J., *The Political Theory of John Wycliff* (Chicago, 1962).

Davies, Godfrey, *The Early Stuarts 1603-1660*, Vol. IX of *The Oxford History of England*, ed. G.N. Clark (Oxford, 1937).

Dickens, A.G, *The English Reformation* (London, 1964).

Elton, G.R., *Reform and Renewal, Thomas Cromwell and the Commonweal* (Cambridge, 1973).

Id., *The Tudor Constitution, Documents and Commentary* (Cambridge, 1960).

Farr, William, *John Wycliff as Legal Reformer* (Studies in the History of Christian Thought, Vol. 10) (Leiden, 1974).

Faulkner, Robert K., *Richard Hooker and the Politics of A Christian England* (Berkeley, 1981).

Figgis, J.N., *Political Thought from Gerson to Grotius 1414-1625*, intro. Garrett Mattingly (New York, 1960).

Franklin, Julian H., *Constitutionalism and Resistance in the Sixteenth Century* (New York, 1969).

Id., *Jean Bodin and the Rise of Absolutist Theory* (Cambridge, 1973).

Gierke, Otto von, *Natural Law and the Theory of Society 1500-1800*, 2 vols., trans. Ernest Barker (Cambridge, 1934).

Gray, John R., "The Political Theory of John Knox", *Church History* 8 (1939), pp. 132-47.

Haigh, Christopher, ed., *The Reign of Elizabeth I* (London, 1984).

Hudson, Winthrop S., *John Ponet (1516?-1556), Advocate of Limited Monarchy* (Chicago, 1942).

Hughes, Philip E., *The Theology of the English Reformers* (London, 1965).

Jacob, E.F., *The Fifteenth Century 1399-1485*, Vol VI of *The Oxford History of England*, ed. G.N. Clark (Oxford, 1961).

Jones, Norman L., *Faith by Statute, Parliament and the Settlement of Religion 1559* (Royal Historical Society Studies in History Series, No. 32) (London, 1982).

Kenny, Anthony, *Wyclif* (Oxford, 1985).

Knappen, M.M., *Tudor Puritanism, A Chapter in the History of Idealism* (Chicago, 1939).

McConica, James K., *English Humanists and Reformation Politics under Henry VIII and Edward VI* (Oxford, 1965).

McFarlane, K.B., *Wycliffe and English Non-Conformity* (Harmondsworth, Middlesex, 1972).

McGrade, A.S., *The Political Thought of William of Ockham* (Cambridge, 1974).

Mackie, J.D., *The Earlier Tudors 1485-1558*, Vol. VII of *The Oxford History of England*, ed. G.N. Clark (Oxford, 1952).

Morris, Christopher, *Political Thought in England, Tyndale to Hooker* (London, 1953).

Oakley, Francis, "On the Road from Constance to 1688: the Political Thought of John Major and George Buchanan", *The Journal of British Studies* 2 (1962), pp. 1-31.

Id., "Almain and Major: Conciliar Theory on the Eve of the Reformation", *The American Historical Review* 70 (1964-5), pp. 673-90.

O'Donovan, Oliver, *On the Thirty Nine Articles, A Conversation with Tudor Christianity* (Exeter, 1986).

Pearson, A.F. Scott, *Church and State, Political Aspects of Sixteenth Century Puritanism* (Cambridge, 1928).

Id., *Thomas Cartwright and Elizabethan Puritanism* (London, 1925).

Ridley, Jasper, *John Knox* (Oxford, 1968).

Id., *Thomas Cranmer* (Oxford, 1962).

Ryan, John J., *The Nature, Structure and Function of the Church in William of Ockham* (Studies in Religion, No. 16) (American Acadamy of Religion, 1979).

Shirley, F.J., *Richard Hooker and Contemporary Political Ideas* (London, 1949).

Skinner, Quentin, *The Foundations of Modern Political Thought*, 2 vols. (Cambridge, 1978).

Stout, Harry S., "Marsilius of Padua and the Henrician Reformation", *Church History* 43 (1974), pp. 308-18.

Tierney, Brian, "Ockham, the conciliar theory and the Canonists", *The Journal of the History of Ideas* 15 (1954), pp. 40-70.

Usher, R.G., ed., *The Presbyterian Movement in the Reign of Queen Elizabeth* (London, 1905).

Walzer, Michael, *The Revolution of the Saints, A Study in the Origins of Radical Politics* (London, 1966).

www.ingramcontent.com/pod-product-compliance
Lightning Source LLC
Chambersburg PA
CBHW021810220426
43662CB00006B/261